*Outcomes in Community
Care Practice*

NUMBER SEVEN

OUTCOMES IN SOCIAL CARE PRACTICE

Edited by Hazel Qureshi

SOCIAL POLICY RESEARCH UNIT

THE UNIVERSITY *of York*

CONTENTS

Acknowledgements

This work was undertaken by the Social Policy Research Unit which receives support from the Department of Health; the views expressed in this report are those of the authors and not necessarily those of the Department of Health. The authors would like to acknowledge a number of other important contributors to this work. Evaluative interviews with a range of participants were undertaken by Jane Carlisle, Jennifer Harris, Jan Heaton, and Suzanne Mukherjee. Sally Baldwin and Jennifer Harris read though and made useful comments on the full text. Editing for consistency and preparation of camera ready copy were undertaken by Claire Arnott, Dianne McLaren and Sarah Starkey. Lastly, although there are too many to name, we would like to acknowledge the invaluable contributions of the staff, older people, disabled people and carers who were involved in the research and development projects in the two authorities.

About the contributors

Hazel Qureshi is Professor of Social Care at the Social Policy Research Unit, University of York, and head of the SPRU Outcomes Team. She led the overall programme of work which generated the projects described in this publication.

Charles Patmore is Research Fellow at the Social Policy Research Unit, University of York. As part of the SPRU Outcomes Team, he led its work with older people.

Elinor Nicholas is Research Fellow at the Social Policy Research Unit, University of York. As part of the SPRU Outcomes Team, she led its work with family carers.

Claire Bamford is currently Senior Research Associate, Centre for Health Services Research and Institute for Ageing and Health, University of Newcastle. Previously she was a Research Fellow with the SPRU Outcomes Team and led its work with younger people with disabilities.

About copying material from this publication

In the case of this particular publication, SPRU is happy for organisations, which purchase or provide care, to freely copy the questionnaires, instruments and other practical documents, which are included as appendices to chapters. While SPRU retains the copyright, a prime purpose for including these documents is to enable them to be widely used free of charge.

An exception is certain appendices to Chapter Four, because SPRU does not hold copyright on these and reproduces them only through kind permission of the copyright holders. These appendices are clearly marked with the names of the copyright holders, whose permission is needed for any further reproduction.

While SPRU welcomes reproduction of its own documents in the appendices, please note that the normal rules of copyright apply to the main text of this publication.

The appendices are presented as evidence of the products of our collaborative work with authorities, not as unalterable templates for practice or recording. These documents reflect adaptations of ideas about outcomes for use in specific local circumstances. In a number of cases they were to be subject to revision after being further tried out in practice. They may or may not be applicable in other contexts: this is for prospective users to decide. In our view it is the underlying ideas, and the process of working out how to apply them in practice which produces real change, not the use of new forms per se.

Please note that you can obtain shorter, comprehensive descriptions of each project covered by Chapters Two, Three, Four, Five and Six via five issues of SPRU's *Research Works* series on the SPRU website: *http://www.york.ac.uk/spru* . Click on *Publications,* then click on *Research Works.* Look under *Research Works* published in 2000 for a set listed as Outcomes Programme productions. The latter includes a sixth issue of Research Works on the general introduction of an outcome focus. These descriptions may be useful to circulate to colleagues for discussion or training purposes.

CHAPTER ONE
INTRODUCTION

By Hazel Qureshi

The aim of the Social Policy Research Unit's outcomes programme was to develop and test practical ways in which agencies which provide, or purchase, social care could collect and use information about the outcomes of services for users and carers. The programme focused on older people, carers and disabled adults of working age with physical or sensory impairments. User and carer involvement has been a strong theme at all stages. In commissioning a five year programme of research and development on this topic, the Department of Health recognised that medium-term work was required to address the methodological, practical and conceptual questions involved. The first stage of the programme consisted of research with a range of stakeholders to clarify outcome concepts suitable for social care practice, and to identify realistic opportunities in the current social care context to use these outcome ideas in practice. The second stage, reported here, involved researched development work over two years aiming to introduce a greater outcome focus both into care management and the collection of feedback from service users and carers. A range of questionnaires, practice tools and guidance were developed and implemented on a trial basis in partnership with two authorities. This report of the five development projects gives attention to both the outputs and the development process in each case, and concludes by drawing out common issues and lessons for future work.

Policy and practice background
The policy emphasis in social care 1995/6, when the SPRU outcomes programme was commissioned, was on the introduction of market principles into social care, and the implementation of the purchaser/provider split. The evaluative thrust was on the successful adoption of new procedures and systems, for example care management, and the primary outcome focus, particularly in services for older people, was on destination: whether the service user remained at home or not. In this context, when the development projects were initially planned, we found it necessary to emphasise local development and 'ownership' of outcome-related changes as essential pre-conditions for success in implementation, given the absence of any external policy pressure on authorities to implement such changes.

In the new policy context since 1997 the emphasis has shifted, and the importance of a more sophisticated conception of final outcomes has increased. The market has been de-emphasised as a basis for policy but the importance of accountability and consistent adherence to standards and, of obtaining Best Value, keeps the question of outcomes, and using outcome information, firmly on the agenda. Service users' (or patients') and carers' experience of services is given a new prominence in frameworks for performance measurement in health and social care, although the emphasis is now on their participation and influence as citizens rather than simply as customers. The development of national standards and performance frameworks is emerging as central across the public sector, and specifically in relation to social care in the social services White Paper *Modernising Social Services*, subsequent consultation papers, guidance and legislation:

> Our third way for social care moves the focus away from who provides the care, and places it firmly on the quality of services experienced by, and the outcomes achieved for, individuals and their carers and families.
> (Modernising Social Services, 1998, Cm 4169, Para 1.7)

At the same time, substantial practice benefits are envisaged from a clearer focus on outcomes in care management:

> At the individual level care planning needs to be thorough and outcome focused.
> (Social Care Group,1998, para 3.4)

Reports from the Social Care Group on care management arrangements, case recording, and management information have all emphasised the importance of outcomes, and the limited extent to which outcomes are recorded in case records, communicated to providers, reviewed in practice, investigated by asking users, or reflected in management information. (Challis *et al.*, 1998; Goldsmith and Beaver, 1999; Social Care Group, 1998, 1999; Warburton, 1999). For example:

> Records rarely offered a complete account of work with users, often failing to capture positive and creative work and outcomes achieved.
> (Goldsmith and Beaver, 1998, para 1.11)

> SSDs often do not seek to find out how service users experience care management and service delivery, and they do not seem too interested to learn in a systematic way of the impact on users' and carers' lives.
> (Warburton, 1999, Para 1.15)

How do we obtain information about outcomes for users and carers? There are two main sources: data collected from users and carers by direct survey; and data collected during routine agency procedures. An example of the first source is the user satisfaction surveys expected of Social Services Departments (SSDs) as part of the modernisation agenda; an example of the second is individual case records. Statistical returns collected by Department of Health, CIPFA or the Audit Commission rarely focus on outcomes. A recognised shortcoming of this kind of information in relation to making judgements about performance is the lack of any information related to outcomes(Department of Health, 1999). This lack reflects the limited degree to which organisational culture and professional practice currently focus on outcomes in day-to-day activity.

The projects described in this report offer a range of practical ways to address the concerns outlined above.

The development projects in the context of the SPRU outcomes programme

The SPRU outcomes programme did not aim to construct scientific measurement tools for research purposes, but rather to investigate whether and how outcomes can be assessed as part of regular or routine practice, in ways that are practical and useful. 'Outcome' is interpreted as the impact or effect on the lives of service users or carers, and the emphasis of the programme is on non-clinical, or social care, outcomes rather than health care outcomes. 'Part of regular or routine practice' means a continuing or repeated method which is a useful part of the regular activity of any agency providing or purchasing social care. The primary agency focus is local authority social services although the approach is applicable, in principle, to any context in which social care is provided.

Early scoping studies carried out in 1995/6 gave rise to the following implications for ensuing research and development:

- The need to clarify concepts and review existing knowledge in order to make progress. Managers, practitioners and other stakeholders needed a coherent framework which would clarify issues and reflect their perception of the purposes and activities of social care.

- Research and development would benefit from being closely linked. The stage had not yet been reached where a 'hands-off' evaluative approach to methods of collecting and using outcome information might be adopted.

- In the absence of external pressure to collect and use outcome information, (as was the case in the policy context at that time), the only way to establish such systems would be to embed them in existing activities, in a way that would be 'owned' by those participating.

- To develop a framework for understanding social care outcomes that would be regarded by stakeholders as legitimate, it was important to resource the involvement of service users and carers in any development work. Not enough was known about the views of many groups of service users, particularly older people.

- Practical tools that were less demanding than research measures were required for practice. Feedback of outcome information should be a positive, constructive experience for staff. Requirements to collect data should fit in with what people were doing already.

- Information about service inputs and evaluation of process remained important. For example, aspects of process deemed important by users - such as the kind of relationships developed with staff, and the degree of control they are able to exercise over services - must be integrated with consideration of outcomes.

A framework for outcomes of social care

Through extensive consultation with stakeholders, the first stage of this programme produced a clear conceptual framework for understanding the outcomes of social care, and the ways in which they are distinct from outcomes of health care (Qureshi *et al.*, 1998; Bamford *et al.*, 1999). From our consultations with users, carers, staff and managers we identified three different kinds of outcome which social care services were aiming to achieve:

- *Maintenance* of quality of life - for example maintaining acceptable levels of personal comfort and safety, social contact, meaningful activity, control over daily life and routines.

- *Change* - for example improving confidence, or accessibility of the environment, reducing risk, or regaining self-care skills.

- *Impacts of service process* - for example whether people feel treated as an individual, valued or respected, and whether services fit well with other sources of help and with individual preferences and life choices.

The achievement (or otherwise) of maintenance outcomes can be assessed at any given point in time by checking whether the person's state (currently and retrospectively) meets a defined acceptable standard. The dimensions of quality of life we identified reflect user and staff views about important outcomes and are discussed in detail in Qureshi *et al.* (1998) and Bamford *et al.* (1999). There was considerable commonality in the dimensions identified by older and younger disabled people, and, where there were differences, these largely reflected differences in life cycle expectations, for example younger people identified access to employment and active involvement in parenting as important, whereas older disabled people did not. Carers attached importance to the quality of life of the person they cared for, to their own quality of life and to the impacts (positive or negative) of the caring role. Further consideration of defining appropriate standards for maintenance is to be found in Chapter Two.

Change outcomes, in contrast, generally reflect attempts to tackle problems or remove barriers which stand in the way of achieving desired levels of quality of life. The achievement of change outcomes has to be measured or assessed by looking at differences between two or more points in time, and by comparing achieved changes with those expected or anticipated when services were provided.

This model of outcome measurement as evaluating changes is prominent in health services, particularly in the secondary sector where the emphasis is on 'cure' rather than 'care'. The language often used in health is of baseline and post intervention measurement. In social care there may well be no 'baseline', or it will be hypothetical. For example, an older person being discharged from hospital receives a package of services designed to support their independence at home. In such an instance the purpose of services is precisely to prevent a hypothetical baseline of unmet need from arising at all. Hopefully there will be no 'time one' at which it could be measured. There is no way to 'measure' the outcome of such services except by making a judgement about what would happen in their absence.

Service process outcomes reflect impacts of the way in which services are delivered, and can thus only be assessed (at one point in time, and retrospectively) after at least some services have been delivered to the user. Again, comparison has to be with defined standards. The finding that such outcomes are of importance to users and carers reinforces the view that the impacts of process can be as important in generating user satisfaction or dissatisfaction as other outcomes. This view has often been expressed in research by, and with, service users and carers (Harding and Beresford, 1995; Turner, 2000).

This framework seemed to us meaningful for describing the bulk of social care activity because, while acknowledging that changes or improvements were being sought in some instances, it emphasised that much activity was directed towards continuous maintenance. We found a widespread view that much social care activity for older and disabled people is not directed towards improving health and social functioning of individuals. An illustrative quote from a middle manager is:

> Eighty per cent, 85 per cent of people, perhaps more than that ... the role that we have is either about trying to maintain their present levels or to support gradually deteriorating levels of independence, and the number of occasions working with older people that I can put in a care plan and some services with an expectation that they would gain from that rehabilitation, become less requiring of support or whatever, are very few indeed.
> (Principal Care Manager)

This has the implication that, if social care activity for individuals were to be judged solely against criteria reflecting improvements in individual functioning, then widespread success would be unlikely to be demonstrated. In the current state of knowledge, we would argue that we simply do not know what the current balance is between activity aimed at improvements and activity aimed at maintenance, let alone what the right balance might be. It should perhaps be emphasised that aiming for maintenance over time does **not** imply an unchanged level of service input - indeed in circumstances where a person's health or environment is deteriorating, considerable changes in service levels may be required in order to maintain quality of life.

5

Identifying development opportunities

In the first stage of the programme, as well as identifying stakeholder perspectives on outcomes, we also sought to identify potential opportunities both to directly collect outcome-related data, and to introduce a greater outcome focus in routine or regular practice. The intention was to select a range of available opportunities and work in partnership with the relevant authority to attempt to implement them. The expectation was that such exercises would generate both potentially useful methods and greater understanding of the factors which enhanced or inhibited their implementation. What constituted an opportunity? Given that, as a research organisation, we had no powers to impose experimental innovations on authorities, 'adoptability' had to be a key criterion. Drawing on Rogers' work on the diffusion of innovations (Rogers, 1995), Smale (1996) identifies five attributes affecting adoptability:

- Relative advantage: the degree to which an innovation is perceived by potential adopters as better than the idea it supercedes

- Compatibility: the degree to which an innovation is perceived as consistent with existing values, past experiences and needs of potential adopters

- Complexity: the degree to which an innovation is perceived as relatively difficult to understand and use

- Trialability: the degree to which an innovation may be experimented with on a limited basis

- Observability: the degree to which the results of an innovation are visible to others.

Further, the rapid diffusion of innovations is assisted by: the presence of enthusiasts or product champions; consonance with existing policies or established bodies of opinion; local appeal to those with power to promote change; the capacity to meet locally perceived needs of users or staff; adaptability to local circumstances; simplicity and low resource requirements.

On the basis of these ideas we sought to construct innovations which might solve problems recognised as such by those who would have to implement the solutions, which would not require large investment of resources (unless there was already a recognition of the need for this), and would fit in well with existing or planned changes which were already moving in the same direction. At the same time the 'core' of the development work, from our point of view, was the explicit introduction of outcome concepts, and domains of outcome identified by users, carers and frontline staff, into agency practice (either through surveys or as an integral part of frontline practice).

Subsequent development work, the subject of this report, has sought to take forward outcome ideas into routine practice in two ways: first, as an explicit emphasis in care management practice, including: assessment of older people; separate assessment and review of carers; and provider briefing in home care; second, as an underpinning for exercises, such as surveys, to collect outcome information from service users and carers.

The intention of the work on *assessment and older people* is to provide a clearer link between assessment and care planning by being explicit about the outcomes which services (and other sources of assistance) are aiming to achieve, and by ensuring that specific user or carer preferences or priorities are made explicit and met, as far as is practicable. Once intended outcomes and preferences are established, the *briefing sheet* is intended to convey to provider managers and to provider staff the intended purpose of their interventions, as well as important user preferences, and, in the case of frontline staff, the specific activities which they should undertake to implement or act on these. The project on *carers* takes the outcome focus deeper into practice, aiming to help practitioners responsible for assessing and reviewing carers' needs, to identify, with carers, what social care services should be aiming to achieve and how far these things have been achieved. Successfully achieving an outcome focus in practice seemed to us a necessary first step before the recording of outcome data on a routine basis could be expected, although, clearly, separate surveys of users and carers could be conducted without achieving change in routine activity.

Two projects have involved separate collection of information directly from service users. One of these used a *postal survey* designed by a mixed group of stakeholders to collect evaluative information from users and carers about an integrated occupational therapy assessment, equipment and adaptations service. The other - *a programme of 'customer visits'* - involved local agency managers in directly interviewing small samples of service users, and in reviewing aggregated information from this process. These projects are described later .

In all of the projects the intention was to attempt to change, in the given locality, existing practice in the direction of a greater focus on outcomes which we knew were important to users (and were recognised as the responsibility of services). Certainly it was hoped to produce generally useful products as a result, but it was also intended that a descriptive evaluation of this process would then cast light on factors which were barriers or facilitators to improving the outcomes focus of day-to-day work in practice. This report describes the end results, and the process of development.

References

Bamford, C., Vernon, A., Nicholas, E. and Qureshi, H. (1999) *Outcomes of social care for disabled people and their carers*, Outcomes in Community Care Practice, Number Six, Social Policy Research Unit, University of York: York.

Challis, D., Darton, R., Hughes, J., Stewart, K. and Weiner, K. (1998) *Care Management Study: Report on National Data,* Social Services Inspectorate, Department of Health: London.

Department of Health (1999) *The Personal Social Services Performance Assessment Framework,* Department of Health: London.

Department of Health (1998) *Modernising social services*, Cm 4169, London: The Stationery Office

Goldsmith, L. and Beaver, R. (1999) *Recording with Care: inspection of case recording in social services departments,* Social Services Inspectorate, Department of Health: London.

Harding, T. and Beresford, P. (1995) *What Service Users and Carers value and expect from Social Services Staff,* NISW/Open Services Project, Report to Department of Health.

Qureshi, H., Patmore, C., Nicholas, E. and Bamford, C. (1998) *Overview: Outcomes of social care for older people and carers*, Outcomes in Community Care Practice, Number Five, Social Policy Research Unit, University of York: York.

Rogers, E. M. (1995) *The Diffusion of Innovations,* 4th Edition, The Free Press: New York.

Smale, G. (1996) *Mapping Change and Innovation*, HMSO: London.

Social Care Group (1998) *Care Management Study: Care Management Arrangements,* Department of Health: London.

Social Care Group (1999) *Meeting the Challenge: Improving Management Information for the effective commissioning of Social Care Services for Older People: Management Summary,* Social Care Group, Department of Health: London.

Turner, M. (2000) "*It is what you do and the way that you do it*", Report on user views on the introduction of codes of conduct and practice for social care workers by the four national care councils, commissioned from the Shaping our Lives User Group by the Office for Public Management: London.

Warburton, R. (1999) *Meeting the Challenge: Improving Management Information for the effective commissioning of Social Care Services for Older People: Handbook for Middle Managers and Operational staff*, Social Care Group, Department of Health: London.

CHAPTER TWO
SUMMARISING INTENDED OUTCOMES FOR OLDER PEOPLE AT ASSESSMENT

By Hazel Qureshi

1. INTRODUCTION

Explicit identification of intended outcomes has been identified by the Social Services Inspectorate as a key element in the recording of assessment and care planning with older people, but one which is often absent (Goldsmith and Beaver, 1999). Clarity about intended outcomes has a potentially crucial role, first, in establishing shared expectations, for all those involved in assessment, and, second, in making evident the links between identified needs and appropriate service responses. The latter is important for performance monitoring and performance management, as well as possibly improving the effectiveness of care packages. A range of barriers to being explicit about outcomes in practice has been identified both in the literature, and in our previous studies in SPRU. These barriers include genuine conceptual problems, and incompatibilities with professional and organisational culture, as well as a degree of anxiety about performance itself (cf. Qureshi, 1999). In our earlier studies, limited central government interest was also cited as a barrier (Nocon and Qureshi, 1996), but new policy emphases on clarity of objectives, performance management and delivering quality services, have encouraged the development of a greater focus within social care services on outcomes for users and carers, and have led to increased interest in ways of improving professional skills in this area.

This chapter describes the process of developing a useable and practical way to assist assessors in ensuring that intended outcomes and user and carer preferences are clearly but succinctly summarised when older people are assessed. The adoptability of outcome ideas was enhanced by working with care managers, and their managers, in meetings, workshops and a pilot implementation to integrate outcome ideas with relevant practice issues in assessment. We believe that the resulting documentation could, if combined with appropriate opportunities for staff involvement, training and development, be useful in other authorities with an interest in introducing an outcome focus in assessment. The documentation comprises: the outcome summary (a one page form, containing six headings), and a prompt list of commonly identified outcomes. We have some evidence that establishing intended outcomes in this way helps to focus the assessment, provides a link between identified needs and services, and a basis for clear information to providers about what they are expected to achieve, either in a short term or a continuing way. These documents are presented as appendices.

There is currently considerable variation in the way in which assessment is carried out in different authorities, and consequently variation in the supporting documentation (Social Care Group, 1998). The current variety is the end product of a process of development and change within local authority social services, which began with the 1993 reforms, and which throughout the 1990s included an intensive focus on assessment, to the exclusion, until recently, of other important aspects of the care management process such as review. The identification and summary of intended outcomes is *not* another method of assessment, and not intended to replace or supplant existing assessment documentation or procedures. We believe this enhances its adoptability. Rather it is an explicit recognition of an essential step between assessment and the construction and implementation of a care plan.

Our previous research has led us to take the view that achieving a realistic way of conducting outcome-focused assessment routinely in the current social care context is not simply a matter of presenting staff with 'tools' in the shape of forms to complete. The conceptual confusions and professional scepticism generated by the concept of outcomes have to be addressed, and replaced by a framework which is meaningful to those involved, both service user and assessor, and has evident practical uses. To generate genuine 'ownership' by staff, consideration of outcomes has to be embedded in a process which is seen to incorporate recognised professional good practice. Our aim in this project was to establish in one authority a process through which care managers were supported in identifying the intended outcomes for older service users and carers. In the longer term, such a process is an essential prior step before the possibility of collecting outcome data from routine care management information can be developed.

2. INITIATION OF THE DEVELOPMENT PROCESS

Our partner authority (in this, and the following three chapters) is a metropolitan district serving a population of approximately 486,000 people. 300,000 of these live in a city with a pronounced industrial past, though unemployment is now appreciably higher than the national average. The remainder live mainly in three outlying communities which preserve distinctive characters. The largest of these retains the geography and character of a separate town. The authority's proportion of people over pensionable age is slightly higher than national comparator figures. Ethnic minorities are over 20 per cent of the population. While people with Pakistani or Bangladeshi connections are 15 per cent of the overall population, their age profile and their distribution within the authority has made them less salient for this research than this figure might suggest. Conversely, older people from Polish, Ukrainian and Baltic communities are currently more salient to the Social Services Elderly Division than might be expected from the much smaller size of these communities. At the time of the research a high proportion of social care was provided by Social Services' own workforce - around 95 per cent of home care hours, for instance.

During the first phase of the research and development process in our partner authority, it was evident that there was no great desire on the part of managers, or practitioners, to change the assessment documentation in any radical way. Considerable attention had been paid over several years to establishing a consistent format for assessment with older people (which was used across the authority in community and hospital settings), and to training staff in the implementation of a needs-led approach. In comparison, implementation of regular review of those receiving longer term assistance was relatively underdeveloped. The evidence is that this, in general, reflects the situation to be found nationally (Challis, 1998; Challis *et al.*, 1998; Warburton, 1999). Both of these aspects - the desire not to radically change assessment (yet again) and the relative neglect of review - were potential barriers to implementing an outcome focus in routine practice. However, there was evidence locally that minor well-supported changes in assessment would be acceptable: for example, existing problems were recognised in relation to the identification of functional mental illness in older people - again a considerable national problem (Bannerjee and Macdonald, 1996) and so some improvements to the section of the assessment relating to mental health were being planned. Although more volatile and complex cases were reviewed as and when the necessity to make new decisions arose, the implementation of a system of regular review of all on-going cases was at that time regarded as impracticable, given resource implications, and not a high priority although some improvements in the review system were planned. A previous systematic review, by one area team, of all cases where respite care was received was thought to have produced little benefit, in the sense that it revealed few instances where changes in services were required.

From our initial consultations with staff and managers it seemed that there were a number of recognised local problems or areas of difficulty where potential benefits were envisioned from a better understanding (and communication) both of intended outcomes, and user and carer preferences. Middle managers, responsible for staff who undertook assessment, had commented that links between needs (in the assessment) and the service response (in the care plan) were not always clear, and that in home care objectives rarely went beyond the very general, such as keeping people at home. It was felt by managers that this failure to record specific objectives might omit to demonstrate good practice which was in fact occurring, or equally, might suggest that there was at times too unthinking a leap between 'needs' and services. In addition, both staff and managers observed that this lack of clarity sometimes meant that valuable information gleaned during assessment, about the purposes for which services were to be provided, was not being communicated to provider managers or, subsequently, to provider staff (cf. Patmore *et al.*, 1998).

Again, these local views reflect well-recognised areas of difficulty nationally. In the 8th Report of the Chief Inspector of Social Services it was observed:

> Assessment is a critical social work tool and fundamental to the [care management] process. Inspections often discover that workers are not clear why they are intervening in a situation and how their intervention will tackle the problems or improve the life of those with whom they are involved
> (SSI, 1999, para. 1.23)

Equally, the SSI report on case recording (Goldsmith and Beaver, 1999) drew attention to the need for a change of culture and for information from the assessment to flow to relevant providers:

> We concluded that most SSDs need to promote a culture in which ... aims, work and outcomes ... should be recorded more consistently.
> (para 1.12)

> ... in most departments providers complained about the paucity of information from commissioners and records did not demonstrate that information had been shared.
> (para 4.8)

SPRU researchers took account of local views in suggesting, as one development proposal which might be adoptable, modification to care planning documents to include statements of intended outcome, and indications of ways in which staff might direct their work to ensure these outcomes were achieved. This proposal (with others) was presented to the local advisory group in February 1998, to the divisional management group in March 1998, and subsequently planning for the implementation of the projects which had been agreed, began at the meeting of the advisory group in May 1998. The Social Services Department at this stage did not wish to change their care plan document per se, which they felt was working well, but the idea of a clearer more focused briefing for providers, and greater clarity about intended outcomes, was greeted positively. One subgroup was set up to pursue the 'Care Plan' project, the first meeting being in July. Later in the year, after several initial meetings it was decided that the task effectively fell into two separate parts and so the subgroup split into two further subgroups: one to focus on the briefing sheet for providers (Chapter Three) and one to consider summarising intended outcomes at assessment.

The reasons for this decision were as follows. Since a purchaser/provider split had not been fully introduced in home care services, single-service assessments were carried out by senior home care staff who also had a provider function. Thus it was logical for them to identify outcomes, priorities and preferences with the user and be responsible for ensuring that their staff were appropriately briefed. Changes in recording and briefing for home care were already underway, and a briefing sheet for home care fitted well into this existing work. This separation had the advantage that the briefing sheet could be implemented as part of on-going changes in the management of home care, an opportunity that would otherwise soon pass, but the disadvantage that the immediate link between assessment by care managers and the preparation of briefing sheets for providers was lost. The briefing sheet thus became a tool for provider managers in home care to inform provider staff, and one working group pursued this development task (reported in detail in Chapter Three), while another working group sought to consider how to introduce a focus on outcomes as a way of improving assessment.

14

The ensuing process of developing and testing a form for recording intended outcomes in assessment took place as follows:

1. Five meetings of a working group formed specifically to concentrate on the assessment process for older people.

2. Two workshops for 17 staff who undertook assessments, in which the outcomes frameworks and proposed tools were introduced and discussed.

3. A pilot study involving 30 assessments by 12 members of staff (care managers and home care organisers) to test the tools (format for recording intended outcomes, and prompt checklist) with older people.

Each of the above is discussed in more detail below.

3. PLANNING

The working group consisted of two members of the SPRU team, one principal care manager (with management responsibilities across the department for assessment 'paperwork'), one home care manager and two care managers. The group was formed as a subgroup of the local outcomes project advisory group which oversaw the implementation of the research and development in the authority, with the addition of two care managers. The subgroup reported back regularly to the local advisory group. The brief was to develop documentation that would support the introduction of a greater specificity about intended outcomes into the assessment process. To this end the documentation would: embody the findings of the first stage SPRU research about perceptions of outcomes; be designed to fit with existing, or planned, recording; minimise demands for additional paperwork; underpin and extend good practice in care management with older people.

No older users or carers were involved in this group. We took the view that this stage of the project largely concerned matters of relevance to the department and the improvement of its own procedures. There had been considerable user and carer involvement in initially developing the outcomes framework which we were attempting to integrate into practice. The users consulted had not expressed interest in the contents of their records, but rather in having opportunities to feedback their evaluative opinions to people with sufficient power to act on them. This aim was being pursued in other projects. Goldsmith and Beaver (1999) similarly found that older people were not very interested in what was held in their records: what mattered to them was the quality of service they received (para. 4.2).

Initial perspectives on outcomes

Care managers in the stage one research, while they recognised the legitimacy of demands for accountability, did not immediately perceive a practical use for an outcome focus in assessment. They regarded individual situations as too varied, and often too complex, to clearly specify general outcomes to be sought (Patmore *et al.*, 1998 ch 3(j)). In common with other staff, they emphasised the limited extent to which they worked in a context where improvements in health and social functioning were the likely expectation. Thus it became clear that without opportunities to discuss the concept in some depth, and to relate to a conception of outcomes which they recognised as appropriate to their situation, the introduction of a requirement to summarise intended outcomes at assessment would be likely to generate confusion and resistance.

To achieve credibility among care managers it was important to recognise that assessment is where the agency agenda and the user agenda meet and have to be reconciled. Richards (2000) observes that the idea of 'needs-based' assessment referred to two principal aims of the 1993 community care reforms: to ensure that individuals received services appropriate to their needs; and to target services on those with the greatest needs. For individual practitioners the first aim requires an understanding of the user's agenda, but the second in contrast demands an agency focus in which the user's characteristics and situation are considered in terms of agency rules about eligibility. This tension at the heart of assessment is not the only source of potential conflict, as Smale *et al.* (1994) noted:

> ... conflict often exists between the demands and needs of referrers, carers and dependent people; between different 'users' of services and between other people in the 'client's' family and wider network. Undertaking assessments and care management has to be **negotiated** within these conflicting needs, attitudes, expectations; as have definitions of the 'problem', and its 'solutions', to arrive at, and maintain a workable and good enough package of care, as defined by users. (Smale *et al.*, 1994, p3)

Baldock (1997) adds to this potent cocktail the ideas of 'product complexity' and 'consumer complexity' in social care, which relate to the way in which the actions and responses of the service user are an integral part of the production of social care, with the consequence that users' specific and individual preferences and priorities (and those of their carers) influence the likely success or failure of community care to a much greater extent than the particular nature of any service intervention. For Baldock, these factors underlie difficulties in establishing the general effectiveness of specific social care interventions, but here they are introduced to reinforce the idea that assessment can involve the negotiation of complex and difficult paths through conflicting expectations and requirements, although the underlying aim for most social workers, as expressed in our initial focus groups, was around preserving individual autonomy in adverse circumstances:

> 'to support people actually making their own decisions about what makes their... about their own life, as long as possible.'

> 'it's allowing someone to still have control of their life and make decisions for themselves and live their life as they see fit without others imposing their own [views on] what they should do.'

One of the care managers on the planning group was particularly interested in the 'exchange' model of assessment, developed by Smale *et al.* (1993), in which the user is regarded as the expert on their own situation, the worker as an expert on available services and negotiating problem solutions, and the process of assessment is regarded as an exchange of information: this last in contrast to a 'questioning' model for the interaction. Although this model was not specifically advanced or discussed in the subgroup, nor necessarily held by other practitioners who contributed their expertise, the emphasis in the outcome summary on agreeing outcomes, discussing options, eliciting user and carer priorities, and the assessor's responsibility for summarising conclusions, are evidently congruent with this approach.

4. CONTENT OF DRAFT ASSESSMENT SUMMARY

After considerable discussion, the draft summary achieved by the group integrated questions which reflected the SPRU outcomes framework, with ideas about more general good practice in assessment. The draft version of the outcome summary as agreed was two sides long, at the end of the assessment form. The sections covered the following issues, although at draft stage 'options' and 'assessor's conclusions' were in one section together, and summary of needs was entitled 'day-to-day support needs':

- Summary of needs
- Changes expected (relevant to future service delivery)
- Agreed outcomes to plan for
- How could these outcomes be achieved (specify options considered)
- Specific preferences about how these outcomes are to be achieved or how services are to be provided
  - Expressed by user
  - Expressed by carer(s)
- Assessor's conclusions

Each of these sections is now discussed in turn.

Summary of needs

This section went through a number of changes of title and function, but emerged as a much shortened version of the original summary of needs which had concluded the previous assessment documentation. From the SPRU perspective it had originally been entitled 'day-to-day support needs' and intended to summarise areas of quality of life intended for maintenance. However, workers wished to have somewhere to summarise the information which had previously comprised their concluding summary of needs, and proved able to include an indication of areas to be maintained under the 'agreed outcomes' heading. The 'summary of needs' is used for a brief pen picture of the day-to-day problems and obstacles to achieving an acceptable quality of life that the care plan will have to address. For example:

AB has poor short-term memory. Her husband is in hospital and she is currently being supported by her son. He has to return to work. She needs: supervision with meals and medication; assistance to purchase food; reassurance through the night; transport to enable her to visit her husband in hospital.

Changes expected (relevant to service delivery)

The subgroup had considerable discussion about this heading, and practitioner concern about this was reinforced in the workshops. The initial intention was to address issues relating to expectations about the long or short-term nature of needs for day-to-day support. The section signals whether it is expected that services for an individual will be likely to have to be increased or decreased in future. A decrease might occur if support was being given during natural recovery or active rehabilitation; in contrast an increase might be expected if the person was known to have a degenerative condition such as motor neurone disease or Alzheimer's disease. Factors not related to physical or social functioning, such as the impending departure of informal carers, or completion of adaptations, or a house move, can also be relevant here. The department decided to record a review date in this section, if relevant changes were anticipated, for example:

> It is expected that the husband will be discharged from hospital within two weeks and that he will be physically able to return to his caring role. It is likely, however that practical help with meals and shopping might still be required.

There had been quite a considerable number of objections raised to this question: ranging from comments that the direction of change might be unknown or uncertain (not a problem as this was a perfectly acceptable response, although in the event less common than we expected), through to concerns about sharing information about a negative prognosis with users who did not wish to know this, or who had not been given this information by medical staff responsible for their care. Some of the discussion led to the insertion of the qualification 'relevant to service delivery' which had previously been absent.

The question of information sharing does raise important practice issues, and there may sometimes be justifications for not sharing information when it is not specifically requested. Since the main purpose of the pilot was to enable staff to experience the use of the new framework, they chose whether or not to share the information with users, but future work to draw up guidelines about information sharing might well be valuable. In the pilot study this question produced useful interpretable information in every case, to the extent that it was possible to demonstrate the potential value of aggregating responses. This issue will be dealt with later in the chapter.

Agreed outcomes to plan for

Here outcomes to be maintained are recorded (in general terms), together with any changes or improvements to work for, in factors which otherwise prevent the achievement of acceptable quality of life. Examples are improvements in ability to move

18

about inside and outside the home, regaining of confidence and skills, reduction of risk, increases in benefits received, reduction in the involvement of a carer. The intention of the subgroup was that staff would receive initial training and briefing on the SPRU framework to assist them to complete this section. The findings of the initial outcomes research were to provide a general framework to assist in recording, but specific intended outcomes for a particular older person were also to be recorded.

As might be expected, some reservations about information sharing arose from the existence of conflicting views, in more complex cases, about what outcomes should be aimed for. Staff gave examples of where the change being worked for might be persuading someone to accept services, or that their carer needed a break. It was felt that it would not be useful to write this down and give it to the prospective service user. The prevailing view was that what should be recorded in this section of the summary was what had been agreed to be the outcomes to be achieved by the care plan. Hence the summary section records *agreed* outcomes to plan for.

Options considered
The purpose of this section is to ensure that consideration and discussion of alternative ways in which outcomes might be reached is made evident. If only one (service) option is available this will then be clearly recorded. It had been envisaged that there might be discussion about alternative ways of reaching the same general outcome, for example should access to social contact and company be met by opportunities to develop new relationships, or by facilitating contact with people already known: clearly the service implications are different. The SPRU team had envisaged that consideration of alternative services might be a part of such discussion, but there was some debate in the workshops over whether services could be mentioned at all, reflecting existing practice that the assessment was meant to identify needs first, separately from consideration about available services. The possibility of meaningfully making such a separation had been queried by staff in our focus groups just as it has been challenged in the literature (Smale *et al.*, 1994; Richards, 2000). Some care managers in the workshops pointed to information about services as an essential element supporting choice by users within decision-making processes prior to completing a care plan. User literature supports demands for such information. There was eventually general agreement that if agreed outcomes to plan for had been established, then it made sense to discuss possible service options along with any other ways of reaching them. After the workshops and the pilot study, this section was separated from the assessors conclusions with which it had previously been integrated.

Preferences and priorities for users and carers
From the researchers' perspective these sections were regarded as important for recording any individual preferences or priorities which related to the way in which services were to be delivered, or outcomes were to be achieved. The identification and recording of these preferences or priorities was a response to the importance of service process outcomes, as identified by users and carers in our initial stakeholder

consultation, and also, of course, identified in other literature (e.g. Harding and Beresford, 1995). The outcomes work suggested that service packages might vary in the extent to which they supported users' cultural and religious preferences, and fitted in with existing patterns of care giving and receiving within the family. Equally, the way in which services were delivered might or might not enable individuals to pursue their choices about lifestyle and activities. The potential for achievement of these outcomes should be considered at assessment.

In addition, from a practice perspective this section was the place to summarise the separate and, on occasions, conflicting priorities of the user and any carer, before indicating, in the assessor's conclusions, the way forward which was being agreed. In this way the processes of negotiation and, possibly, compromise involved in reaching the care plan would be made explicit. In addition there would be a clear communication to providers, and managers monitoring performance, about different perspectives and, in the assessor's conclusions, how they were to be reconciled or taken forward.

Assessor's conclusions

Here the assessor sums up the path which has been chosen in the light of their analysis, and negotiations with the service user and other parties with a legitimate interest. After the pilot study, participants expressed a preference for 'options considered' and 'user and carer preferences' to precede, and be separate from, the assessor's conclusions, as would be the logical flow in practice.

Having a developed a draft set of headings which was thought suitable for structuring the summary, the next step was to share this with assessors and gain their views on its relevance and ease of use.

5. THE WORKSHOPS WITH STAFF

The workshops were conducted around half-way through the subgroup's operation, by SPRU staff in collaboration with the department's training section, and were designed to:

- Outline the findings of the earlier SPRU research, with a particular focus on the outcomes identified by users and carers

- Introduce frameworks and tools emerging from the subgroups working on outcomes in assessment for older people and for carers

- Work with staff on how these frameworks and tools might apply to their practice, and obtain feedback on possible changes that would facilitate this

- Affirm and build upon current good practice in care management.

The above programme was delivered to participants through a mixture of presentations, plenary discussions, work in pairs and work in groups. The findings were generally

20

well-received, although 'maximising benefit income' was thought to be sufficiently frequently addressed, to be added to outcomes already listed as a result of the initial research. There was some feeling that the comprehensiveness of the types of outcomes identified made it more relevant to social worker/care managers rather than home care managers because the latter undertook less comprehensive assessments, usually for a specific service. However, the department was keen to have common documentation for assessment even if different staff groups used it in different ways. In the light of feedback and questions raised in these workshops, and from subsequent evaluation forms, the documentation was revised as already described and, at the request of staff, a prompt list of outcomes was prepared which could be used by them as an aide memoire. Once this process was completed, a limited pilot implementation was set up to test the use of the outcomes summary in practice. The handout for the workshops is reproduced in the appendix, together with the version of the prompt list which was used for the pilot study. The current version of the checklist (i.e. with a small number of additions suggested by the pilot) is reproduced on the following pages. The prompt list is preceded by some brief notes for staff.

The outcomes prompt list
The descriptions which follow each of the maintenance outcomes reflected an attempt by SPRU researchers to ensure consistency in use of the checklist, by expanding on the meaning of the specified outcome domains. In assessing whether or not maintenance outcomes are being achieved at any given point in time, a comparison with an implicit or explicit standard **is** being made, whether acknowledged or not. In effect, therefore, these descriptions are the researcher's inferences about the standards which it is aimed to maintain. The descriptions were not drawn from any documents or statements of objectives by the department. The standards, as stated here, are thus empirically rather than normatively determined. That is, the descriptions reflect what researchers think standards actually are, rather than reflecting a decision about what they ought to be. None of the workers or managers who saw the checklist queried or contradicted it, so the standards at least had face validity to staff.

Change outcomes, in contrast, do not relate to standards in the same way. Ultimately, of course, we may be seeking to establish a quality of life for the user which meets the desired maintenance standards, and so the planned changes aim to contribute to achieving this. Changes for the better result from tackling barriers to achieving quality of life, or reducing risks. In practice, whether the difference between the initial state and the state at subsequent review is 'good enough' will be a matter of judgement in the circumstances of the individual case. Of course, evaluative judgements may differ, depending on who makes them. Deciding, or agreeing, on the adequacy of changes may well be a process of negotiation which takes place at review.

Notes for staff on outcomes prompt list

Social Policy Research Unit

During SPRU's research, staff indicated that a great deal of the work of social services involved providing support continuously, day after day. Much work undertaken by home care is of this kind. The 'outcome' is that a person's day-to-day needs are met, and continue to be met. *Maintaining quality of life* in this way involves outcomes such as personal cleanliness and comfort; clean environment; personal safety; having social contact and company; having interesting or stimulating activity; having control over everyday life and routines. Sometimes maintenance is needed short term (perhaps during recovery or rehabilitation), but frequently no specific end-point for services is envisaged, indeed an increase in services may be anticipated if the person's condition is deteriorating.

Of course it might sometimes be necessary to improve someone's quality of life before it is possible to reach the situation where it can be maintained. In contrast to continuous maintenance, services sometimes actively work towards *changes or improvements*, which if achieved, mean that there is a possibility that fewer services will be needed, or that future services will be able focus on maintenance. Changes for the better result from tackling barriers to achieving quality of life, or reducing risks. Examples mentioned were: improving the person's functioning (ability to get about, confidence, skills, feelings, behaviour); eliminating risks, improving access to benefits; improving relationships with family members or carers.

Finally, once services are being delivered, there are *service process outcomes* which are the results or impacts of the ways in which services are delivered. One such outcome is the extent to which the user feels that assistance from services fits well with other sources of assistance, and with their own life choices or cultural or religious preferences. Other impacts of services reflect the ways in which people are treated by staff, and the extent to which people feel they have a say in services.

During the training courses some people said that a checklist of the kinds of outcomes which might be relevant would be helpful. The following is a list of common examples, it does not include every possible outcome, and the outcomes themselves are expressed in quite general ways. Sometimes people will wish to list more detailed or specific outcomes for a particular person. The list which follows is meant as a reminder of some of the more common possibilities.

'MAINTENANCE' OUTCOMES : common domains of outcome and description of a standard for each domain

(These outcomes have to be maintained in a continuing way although the level of services required to achieve this may vary over time. They may be maintained in the short term, during recovery or rehabilitation for example, or in the long term, perhaps where deterioration in the person's condition is expected.)

The older person	
Personally clean and comfortable	An older person who is not able to carry out their own personal care is personally clean and comfortable, presentable in appearance, has a nutritious and varied diet, and is in bed or up at appropriate times of day.
In a clean and comfortable environment	The immediate environment is clean enough to avoid harm to health and prevent deterioration in morale.
Safety	The older person feels as safe and secure as they wish to be AND the worker is satisfied that the risk levels are acceptable or the client prefers to continue to accept the risks involved.
Contact and company	The older person is able to access sufficient contact with significant others and opportunities for wider human contact and social participation (to avoid isolation).
Keeping active and alert	The person is able to pass their time in activities which interest and stimulate them, at home and outside the home (if wished).
Control over daily life	In so far as the person is able to express preferences, they feel that they have control over, and can plan, their daily life and routines. (Can also apply to carer)

The carer	
Maintain health and well-being (physical, mental, emotional, spiritual)	Negative impacts of caring on health and well-being minimised; able to have sufficient sleep, exercise and some fulfilment/satisfaction within their life.
Able to have a life of their own	Can enjoy free time, leisure activities or is able to keep employment, friends or social/community links, or meet other obligations.
Supported in the caring role	Feels that services offer appropriate help, emotional support, information and share responsibility for the quality of life of the older person.
Peace of mind	The carer is free from excessive or persistent anxiety about the well-being of the person they care for.

CHANGE OUTCOMES: changes which result from tackling barriers to achieving quality of life, or reducing risks

(An end-point to the intervention can be defined, at which the intended improvement can be said to have been achieved, or partly achieved, and the level of services required can be reduced, or the focus of continuing services becomes maintenance.)

Recovery or Rehabilitation outcomes

Regaining skills and capacities (for independent living)	Only an outcome of services if social care staff are explicitly working on specific activities which are designed to help people to re-acquire skills and capacities.
Improving confidence and morale (older people and carers)	Regaining the confidence to deal positively with changed life circumstances, and/or personal and societal attitudes towards ill health and disability.
Improving ability to get about	Become more able to get around freely within the home or outside. (Many possible methods: equipment, adaptations, therapy, mobility training)
Reducing symptoms (for example of depression or anxiety)	(May be a joint outcome of health and social care services.) Experiencing fewer symptoms, feeling less depressed or anxious, sleeping better, relating better to others.

Other examples

Reducing or eliminating risk of harm	Modifying the environment, averting homelessness, dealing with possible physical abuse or injury (if risks are being reduced and kept at lower levels by continuing service input then maintaining personal safety is perhaps more appropriate than this category).
Maximising benefit income	Could be a one-off aim, but if managing finances on a continuing basis were involved this would become a maintenance outcome.

Family and carer related

Improving significant/close relationships	Enabling people to see each other's point of view, reducing tensions within relationships; mediating between conflicting interests.
Enhancing motivation or capacity to give care	Reducing distress or improving satisfaction in caring for carers, leading to caring being experienced as more manageable or rewarding.
Improving confidence and sense of expertise in care giving	Helping carers to make informed choices and feel confident and equipped to provide care; increasing knowledge and skills.
Reducing carer involvement	Enabling carer to draw boundaries about what they will do, or to give up altogether.

PROCESS OUTCOMES: the results or impacts of the way in which the package of services is provided

Services 'fit' with (or support) other sources of assistance and life choices	
'Good fit' with cultural and religious preferences	The person feels that services take account of preferences about relevant issues, such as the way in which domestic tasks are performed, expectations of family members, staff characteristics, language skills and the nature of appropriate food and activities.
'Good fit' with family and other assistance	The person feels that services are delivered in ways that fit in well with their ideas about appropriate roles for family members, and support choices about care giving and receiving.

Influence over services, and impact of interactions with staff	
Having a say over personal and domestic assistance	The user or carer can, if they wish, influence tasks performed, timing or personnel involved, in order to achieve their desired outcomes
Feeling valued and treated with respect	The person feels accepted despite symptoms or difficulties; treated as someone with legitimate right to services; treated as a fellow human being (with some warmth and friendliness); treated as someone different from others, with individual needs; their privacy and confidentiality are respected

Note: The above list of process outcomes did not form part of the prompt checklist used in the pilot implementation. Service process outcomes were discussed in the workshop and generated some interest. In retrospect we feel it is valuable to include them, as they do have relevance to the way in which the individual package is structured and delivered, and so need to be considered during care planning, even though they cannot be measured until after services have been received, and generally measurement is 'after only' rather than 'before and after'.

6. THE PILOT IMPLEMENTATION

The pilot implementation involved 12 staff: seven social worker/care managers, two senior practitioners, and three home care organisers. Half of those involved worked in hospital settings, half in the community, with at least one worker from each of these settings within each category of staff. A minority of the staff had attended the workshops described above. Staff were recruited and briefed during May 1999 by the two care managers who had been on the planning group. The original target was that each assessor would complete four assessment summaries and give structured feedback, via a self-completion form, on the experience of doing so. The assessments, in anonymised form, were to be made available to SPRU, whose task was to analyse the completed summaries, and the assessors' diary sheets, and feedback preliminary results of analysis as part of a workshop to exchange information with participants, planned for September. In the event, not all participants reached the target numbers, but a total of 30 assessments were completed, which was judged sufficient to draw some conclusions about the experience of using the tools.

Although it had been anticipated that one assessor's diary sheet would be filled in for each assessment, some people felt that one set of comments covered all the points they wished to make about several assessments, whereas others had varying points to make in relation to different older users, and so used more than one sheet. A total of 17 sheets (from 11 participants) and 30 assessment summaries were thus available for analysis.

Staff were invited to identify positive/helpful features and difficult/unhelpful features of the assessment summary. More comments were placed under the positive than the negative heading (9/7), but of more importance is that the type of comments were qualitatively different. The most frequently mentioned difficulty was the time required (four comments), although in all of these cases it was not the length of the summary required which posed the difficulty but the complexity (and unfamiliarity) of the thinking required:

> 'More time consuming due to need to separate threads of what was needed and why.'

> 'Trying to separate issues and put them into the right sections was difficult. Took a lot of thinking and time.'

In one comment on difficulties there was a suggestion that the thinking became easier with practice:

> 'Initially I tended to jumble up outcomes with services but this became easier as subsequent forms were completed.'

In contrast to these difficulties, the majority of positive comments reflected more general perspectives on the effects of a focus on outcomes on the assessment process as a whole, and indicated that the intentions of the summary were being realised:

'Good - it made clear the rationale for the service being provided.'

'Clearer indication of the aims of support.'

'This was a **very** clear cut case so there was no ambiguity about intended outcomes. However, having to state outcome so precisely helped to put any risks into context.'

'(User) has a complex family situation and conflicting views between family members. I thought this form helped to highlight why a particular path had been chosen and offer important info to nursing home on family situation and views held therein.'

One worker commented on a possible benefit to users of a summary of intended outcomes instead of 'needs':

'An easier way of sharing the assessment with users without the negative aspects of their abilities being highlighted.'

This last comment is reinforced by literature from the user movement and by disabled people (Turner, 2000; Morris, 1997) who have argued for a greater focus in assessment on what is to be achieved (as well as how), and have indicated that an exclusive focus on 'needs' runs the risk of seeming to concentrate on inabilities and deficiencies on the part of the user.

The diary sheet also directly asked workers whether the assessment summary and checklist had made any difference to: the assessment process; the care plan or planning process; the way the package was implemented or delivered; the way the package was reviewed. Again the total responses were 17, and occasionally no answer was possible, for example where review had not yet taken place. However the answer 'yes' was given in relation to assessment (seven times); care plan (eight times); package delivery (nine times); review (seven times). One illustrative comment about review was:

'Yes, because an important indicator became whether (user) had experienced discomfort or not, and not merely whether nursing needs were being met.'

A comment on the care plan was:

'Yes, care plan geared towards rehab goals.'

Analysis of the completed assessment summaries revealed some variation in the extent to which outcomes had been clearly identified. As a rule of thumb, the researchers asked 'could the achievement of this outcome be checked in six months time?'. This did not mean that measurable outcomes had to be specified, but rather that the intended outcome could be the basis for discussion at review of the kind 'To what extent has this happened?' or 'Is this occurring as it should', depending on whether the

27

outcomes related to changes or continuous maintenance. If outcomes were unclear, then the remainder of the assessment form was checked to ascertain whether, in the opinion of the researcher, there was sufficient information to specify intended outcomes more clearly. Of the twelve workers it was felt that four had clearly identified outcomes to be worked for and separated them from consideration of suitable services, five more had specified at least some outcomes but not all of them unambiguously and not always with a clear separation from services, and three had either specified services alone or not stated outcomes in a clear way. In most cases where outcomes were lacking or ambiguous there did seem to be sufficient information in the rest of the assessment form to make it possible specify outcomes more clearly. An example of clear identification in an assessment by a hospital-based social worker was:

'1) For (user) to return home. 2) For help to be clean and comfortable and to have a varied diet at suitable times of the day. 3) For (user) to feel safe in the home. 4) For there to be sufficient human contact through day and night. 5) For user to have, as far as possible, choices in relation to who provides support. 6) For risks in relation to pressure areas to be minimised. 7) For user to be transferred in a way that reduces the risk of physical harm to herself and others. 8) For (user's) confidence and morale to be improved.'

Another example, reflecting mental health concerns and intended changes for a carer, was:

'Reduction in level of depression - improved mental health. Improved coping skills and confidence. Independence with self-care - regain skills and capacities. Reduce carer involvement.'

In the subsequent de-briefing meeting (in September 1999) between participants and researchers the issues raised were discussed at greater length and views exchanged on possible improvements and changes. SPRU analysis of the data from the pilot was presented and small group discussion was focused on a number of questions which had arisen in the course of analysis of the material from the pilot. The issues about whether or not the summary was suitable for home care staff assessors remained salient, and these staff asked for more space to record 'day-to-day support' in the summary. An important issue for future implementation was that training was regarded as useful. It was agreed that people needed to know what was meant by outcome and to have the opportunity to debate and discuss this. People who had attended the workshop had definitely found it of value, and analysis of their completed summaries did reveal them to be among those most capable of clear identification of outcomes. However there were workers who managed to do this without the benefit of the workshop. In general, though not universally, the checklist had been found to be helpful. Some who had not used it felt in retrospect that it would have helped.

In the light of the pilot, and the discussion at the de-briefing meeting, a number of changes were made to the layout and wording of questions on the form, and a specific separate final section for 'assessor's conclusions' was introduced. Comments received on the other new elements in the assessment (a page of screening questions on mental health and a risk assessment summary) were also fed back to the implementation advisory group so that the department could act on them also.

7. DISCUSSION OF THE DEVELOPMENT PROCESS

Our approach had something in common with social work in partnership (Marsh and Fisher, 1992) in that we were attempting to find ways to embody a set of principles (derived from previous work with users, carers and staff) into practice, by working with managers and care managers in the organisation. Marsh and Fisher found their progress hindered by what they labelled as the DATA response from workers (we Do All This Already) but they were able to facilitate critical reflection on their practice by workers which enabled them to understand ways in which their existing practice fell short of partnership principles. In contrast, in the current study there were few workers initially who believed that they currently summarised outcomes clearly. Instead, we initially met reservations about the possibility of doing so meaningfully, given the nature of the care management task with older people, and wariness about the uses for which outcome information might be required (cf Nocon and Qureshi, 1996; Patmore *et al.*, 1998 ch 3(j)). Thus, when we presented findings about the intended outcomes which had been identified by older service users, carers and staff in the first stage of the programme, there was some relief that 'outcome' which had seemed to some an unnecessarily mystifying piece of jargon, could be interpreted within a framework which they recognised, and which had added credibility because of the extensive user consultations which had been conducted locally. While we are confident that some staff can summarise outcomes without extensive training or opportunities for discussion, there are many others who benefit from, and enjoy, the chance to hear and discuss research findings and improve their confidence about the concept of outcomes and its fit with their work. Our future intention is to build on our existing materials to develop and test training resources to assist departments with such a process.

SPRU's agenda in the development work was to find a way of ensuring that intended outcomes were recorded, clearly distinguishing between maintenance and improvement, as well as considering the user or carer preferences which might affect the achievement of process outcomes. In addition, SPRU researchers believed that it would be important to record anticipated changes that were likely to influence the duration or kind of services needed, if that were possible. The care managers in the planning group were positive about outcome ideas, and believed that the 'needs summary' as it stood was not an adequate conclusion for the assessment. However their primary concern in developing new documentation was that it should more accurately reflect (especially in complex situations) the good practice which they believed was being undertaken. A second concern was that the assessment forms themselves should reflect their actual flow of information collection and decision-making and thus be easier to fill in. The manager wanted to coordinate all the proposed changes in assessment, deriving from management concerns across the department (outcome summary, mental health screening questions, risk assessment recording, links to carer assessment, changes in logic) in order to ensure that changes were introduced simultaneously in a planned way, so as to make sure that the proposed changes fitted coherently with each other, and to minimise the number of times that staff would have to become familiar with changes in assessment.

In many ways these concerns were mutually reinforcing, and in our view led to a new summary (with supporting documentation) which was well linked to our outcome concerns, clearly relevant to practice issues in assessment, and likely to be adopted because of its links into other departmental changes. The only downside from the research point of view was that the multiple changes happening together made it more difficult to conduct a distinct evaluation of the use of outcome summary per se. Although our evaluation forms asked specifically for comment on the summary (and we did get appropriate responses, which have been described in the chapter), frequently workers responded with comments about the other changes, and their impact (or problems). It was usually, but not always, possible to distinguish the subject of comments, but this multiplicity, while probably practically useful to the department, did mean less direct comments on the outcome summary than we might have hoped for. However the workshop with participants after the pilot did concentrate on outcomes and was helpful in illuminating, and expanding on, the written comments. This experience suggests there may be some tension between 'adoptablity' and 'researchability' in undertaking researched development. Seeking to link a specific development to other compatible changes makes for difficulties in subsequent attribution. Packwood *et al.* (1998), studying business process re-engineering in a hospital, observed that after the change intervention was completed, different stakeholders held quite different views on what had actually brought about observed changes in practice and procedures, with some attributing them almost entirely to the change intervention, and others taking the view that this had been largely irrelevant.

8. LOOKING TO THE FUTURE - MEASUREMENT AND AGGREGATION
Measuring outcomes
Can these outcomes be assessed or measured? The simple answer is yes. For practical purposes a simple judgement about whether needs are being met, or expectations of change achieved, or the right balances being struck, may be adequate. Professionals are making these judgements all the time, as a basis for deciding on action, and so are users and carers. The possibility that a systematic programme of reviews will be implemented is much increased since the inclusion of this requirement in the modernisation agenda. As long as some form of review takes place, the potential exists for obtaining professional and user judgements about the achievement of these outcomes (both at the particular point in time, and retrospectively). In making judgements, the standards of comparison, or expectations, of older people, their carers and staff who work with them, may differ of course. This makes it important for a department to be clear about the standards it aspires to, and the limits that overall resources and fairness in distribution may dictate.

A request for a simple rating of the extent to which a person's needs are being met, in relation to a particular area of quality of life, leaves the rater to make the decision about the appropriate target level. Possible differences in opinion between raters are recognised in instruments such as the Camberwell Assessment of Need which allows independent ratings by user, staff and carer (Phelan *et al.*, 1995). Attempts by researchers to ensure consistency of response to such questions by describing what is meant by 'met need' are, in effect as we have said, effectively specifying standards. The descriptions included in the SoCQoL, which is designed to measure social care outcomes for older people (and actually concentrates on maintenance outcomes) appear to be observed standards (Netten and Smith, 1998), as are the standards listed in the prompt checklist in this report. It is important to recognise that setting standards is not primarily a technical issue, to be solved by researchers, but a political decision.

With regard to change outcomes, given the consumer complexity and product complexity in social care identified by Baldock (1997), it is unlikely that there will be a body of suitable normative data to appeal to for comparison, except perhaps in relation to very specific kinds of health-related changes such as symptom relief, or clinical rehabilitation. Generally, a judgement, or a set of judgements, about what changes are good enough in the circumstances will be made, and can form the basis for discussion, and decisions about future action.

Taken together, the standards set for maintenance of quality of life could constitute eligibility criteria. That is, a person is eligible for services if, as a consequence of ill health or disability, their quality of life falls below the defined standards, or is at risk of doing so. In the work currently being described, the authority did not define eligibility in this way, nor is it common to do so. However there is an example of an authority in which these principles do underpin eligibility and assessment. Northumberland Social Services and Northumberland Health have an agreed set of outcome-focused eligibility criteria which underpin assessment. The relationship between equitable distribution of available resources and the standards which can generally be reached is recognised here through the specification of minimum, target and desirable levels of outcome in a range of domains: minimum standards are guaranteed, target standards are what will generally be possible within current resources, and desirable standards can only be reached when all have achieved the target standards. This system has considerable intellectual coherence, and seems to be well understood by users and carers. Since the standards are published they are open to argument and public debate. We have proposed future work to evaluate this approach, which we regard as potentially a considerable step forward in the application of outcome ideas.

Aggregation for management information
Even very simple information is potentially useful if aggregated. Future proposals include further work to determine whether the practice-based responses to the requirement to list intended outcomes will have sufficient commonality to form a basis for aggregation. If so it will be possible to build a coding frame from the 'bottom up' which fits with what is actually being done at the front line. As an illustrative example, SPRU had anticipated that aggregated information from the 'anticipated changes' question, in conjunction with other information, would be of importance to managers.

During initial research, managers had informally estimated that the proportion of work undertaken in contexts where improvements in a person's health or functioning could reasonably be expected, might be as low as 15 per cent (Qureshi *et al.*, 1998). Indeed, one concern about assessing outcomes was that any model of outcome assessment should not depend on expectations of being able to detect improvements in health or social functioning, and had to be appropriate for reflecting the achievements of work in many situations where only deterioration in health and social functioning could reasonably be expected. However, in trying to explore the current prevalence of work directed towards different kinds of outcomes, we were unable to find any data nationally or locally that would indicate the proportion of cases in which the future scenario involved expected improvements, let alone any information that would indicate the 'right' balance. As an illustration of the possible format of aggregate information, which could be derived from the outcome summary, the answers to the change question in the 30 pilot assessments were coded and aggregated. The results were summarised as follows:

Expected, possible or probable *deterioration*	13
Expected or possible *improvement*	9
Stable	2
Continuing *fluctuation*	2
Don't know yet (awaiting medical assessment)	2
Specified change not related to individual functioning	2

If these proportions were to be repeated when larger numbers become available, then there would be clear implications that situations where improvement is expected are in a minority, and that a relatively substantial proportion of work is with people whose condition is expected to deteriorate. While there is no reason to suppose that the particular group of assessments was biased, no claim is being made that these figures would be repeated should larger numbers of assessments be available. However, the potential usefulness of this aggregated information, in beginning to understand the nature and prevalence of the kinds of work being undertaken, is evident from this exercise.

9. CONCLUSION

After receiving a report on the pilot, the advisory group decided that the assessment summary should in principle be introduced throughout the authority. However, first the integration with the products of the project on carer assessment had to be finalised. The carer assessment had been developed in a separate project, and the assessment of the older person therefore had to include some trigger questions to enable consistent decisions to be taken about the depth and complexity of work to be undertaken with the carer, should there be one. Following agreement on the format of this integration a further pilot is to be undertaken which will include the new assessment summary, and the new carer-related documentation. Once assured that the package as a whole works and can be used by staff, a plan for rolling out the new documentation and procedures across the authority, together with necessary training and support, will be implemented. The role of SPRU in continued development is limited to providing advice, although there is agreement that further joint work which investigates the wider use of the outcome summary, and the integration of this kind of information into review systems, and into the developing computerised information system, would all provide valuable further data if such work is funded.

In our work with staff and managers, we were not, and are not, making claims that identifying outcomes more explicitly constitutes necessarily an improvement in practice to the extent that demonstrably better outcomes for users or carers will result . Given the reported issues that this project was intended to tackle, for example, the need to make ends/means connections more explicit, our main concern was that intended outcomes should be better demonstrated in recording, because this was important in itself from the point of view of performance management, provider information and structuring of subsequent reviews. From this point of view, simply to replace the existing open-ended summary of needs which previously concluded the assessment, with a more structured summary which included identification of intended outcomes, was sufficient for success. The reports back from the pilot suggested that there might also be improvements in practice in terms of focusing the assessment process, providing summaries which were more positive and forward-looking from a user perspective, and ensuring that the process of negotiation and information-giving, which led to the assessors' decisions about how to deploy agency resources, was clearly evident. However, the process would have to be subject to considerable further testing, to establish whether such benefits were widespread, and whether they extended to improving actual outcomes.

SUMMARY OF CHAPTER TWO

The aim of this development project was to incorporate outcome ideas into assessment, by assisting care managers to construct a written summary of intended outcomes for older people, and their carers (if any), to underpin care planning.

More explicit recording of intended outcomes has been called for in many Social Care Group reports and policy documents. Local managers considered that greater specificity about outcomes would potentially:

- make differences between good and less good practice more evident
- clarify the basis for care planning decisions; improve skills of care managers working with older people: help to focus service effort; provide a basis for future reviews
- feed usefully into computerised client information systems under development in the authority.

Some possible barriers to implementation included: a reluctance to change documentation and procedures for assessment; wariness about the concept of outcomes at the front line and about its applicability to social care practice; parallel time-consuming developments and changes in response to other local and national agendas; workload and existing demands for recording.

A working group was established which included SPRU researchers, care managers and middle managers with relevant responsibilities. In consultation with the overall local Advisory group, the working group developed draft documentation to record a brief summary of assessment, to include both a summary of outcomes based on the framework derived from SPRU research, and ideas about good practice in assessment. The documentation and framework were discussed in two workshops/training sessions with staff to explore their views on its potential usefulness in practice. In response, some changes were made to the summary document, and a checklist of outcomes was prepared for staff to use as a prompt list when recording an assessment summary. A pilot implementation was conducted which involved 30 assessments. Staff completed the assessment summary and evaluative feedback forms.

Positive comments suggested that the summary: helped to focus the assessment; was experienced as a more positive document to share with users (in contrast to a summary of 'needs'); made the aims of support clearer; emphasised or reinforced user aims and preferences; and helped to produce a succinct statement of the path which an assessor might have to steer in balancing risks, or addressing conflicting views. Negative comments centred on the layout of the form and the structure of some of the questions and prompts; its doubtful applicability to simple single-service assessments; and the amount of thinking time needed to disentangle outcomes from services and needs. This last was thought to reduce with experience and practice. The form was revised in the light of comments, and the importance of prior training and briefing of staff was noted for future implementation.

SUMMARISING INTENDED OUTCOMES FOR OLDER PEOPLE AT ASSESSMENT

The department decided to implement the assessment summary throughout its services to older people. Integration with the results of the project on outcomes for carers had first to be achieved. Trigger questions to determine the level of work to be undertaken with carers were devised for inclusion in assessment documentation. A further pilot of integrated assessment documentation was then undertaken, prior to full implementation.

The outputs which may be generalisable are outcome summary documentation (two sides of A4) and a prompt list of outcomes for older people and carers. A basis has been established for developing a training resource to assist departments wishing to introduce a greater outcome focus into assessment. Time and resources for training, briefing and discussion with staff will be essential for future implementation in other areas. There is scope in future to use this work to support the development of systematic reviews, and use of some data for aggregation for management information.

References

Baldock, J. (1997) Social Care in Old Age: More Than a Funding Problem, *Social Policy and Administration* 31 (1), 73-89.

Banerjee, S. and Macdonald A. (1996) 'Mental Disorder in an Elderly Home Care Population: Association with Health and Social Service Use', *British Journal of Psychiatry* 168, 750 - 756.

Challis, D. (1998) *Care Management,* Briefing Paper prepared for Department of Health seminar: London.

Challis, D., Darton, R., Hughes, J., Stewart, K. and Weiner, K. (1998) *Care Management Study: Report on National Data,* Social Services Inspectorate, Department of Health: London.

Goldsmith, L. and Beaver, R. (1999) *Recording with Care: inspection of case recording in social services departments,* Social Services Inspectorate, Department of Health: London.

Harding, T. and Beresford, P. (1995) *What Service Users and Carers value and expect from Social Services Staff,* NISW/Open Services Project, Report to Department of Health

Marsh, P. and Fisher, M. (1992) *Good Intentions: developing partnership in social services,* 'Community Care' and Joseph Rowntree Foundation: York.

Morris, J. (1997) *Community Care: working in partnership with service users*, Venture Press: Birmingham.

Netten, A. and Smith, P. (1998) *Developing a measure of social care outcome for older people: interim report*, Discussion paper 1487, PSSRU, University of Kent: Canterbury.

Nocon, A. and Qureshi, H. (1996) *A Social Services Perspective*, Outcomes in Community Care Practice Number Three, Social Policy Research Unit (report for Department of Health).

Packwood, T., Pollitt, C. and Roberts, S. (1998) GOOD MEDICINE? A case study of business process re-engineering in a hospital, *Policy and Politics* 26 (4), 401- 415.

Patmore, C., Qureshi, H., Nicholas, E. and Bamford, C. (1998) *Outcomes project: Stage 1 Report to Social Services*, Working Paper Number 1537, Social Policy Research Unit, University of York: York.

Phelan, M., Slade, M., Thornicroft, G., Dunn, G., Holloway, F., Wykes, T., Strathdee, G., Loftus, L., McCrone, P. and Hayward, P. (1995) 'The Camberwell Assessment of Need: The Validity and Reliability of an Instrument to Assess the Needs of People with Severe Mental Illness', *British Journal of Psychiatry* 167, 589-595.

Qureshi, H. (1999) Outcomes of Social Care for Adults: attitudes towards collecting outcome information in practice, *Health and Social Care in the Community* 7 (4), 257-265.

Qureshi, H., Patmore, C., Nicholas, E. and Bamford, C. (1998) *Overview: Outcomes of social care for older people and carers*, Outcomes in Community Care Practice, Number Five, Social Policy Research Unit, University of York: York.

Richards, S. (2000) Bridging the Divide: Elders and the Assessment Process, *British Journal of Social Work* 30 (1), 37-49.

Smale, G., Tuson, G., Ahmad, B., Darvill, G., Domoney, L. and Sainsbury, E. (1994) *Negotiating Care in the Community*, HMSO: London.

Smale, G., Tuson, G., Biehal, N. and Marsh, P. (1993) *Empowerment, Assessment, Care Management and the Skilled Worker*, HMSO: London.

Social Care Group (1998) *Care Management Study: Care Management Arrangements*, Department of Health: London.

SSI (1999) *Modern Social Services - A Commitment to Improve,* 8th Report of the Chief Inspector of Social Services, The Stationery Office: London.

Turner, M. (2000) '*It is what you do and the way that you do it*', Report on user views on the introduction of codes of conduct and practice for social care workers by the four national care councils, commissioned from the Shaping our Lives User Group by the Office for Public Management: London.

Warburton, R. (1999) *Meeting the challenge: Improving management information for the effective commissioning of social care services for older people: Handbook for middle managers and operational staff*, Social Care Group, Department of Health: London.

APPENDICES TO CHAPTER TWO

The following are supplied as appendices

- **Handout** summarising outcomes for older people identified in the consultation phase of the programme. This was prepared for workshops with staff.

- **Assessment Summary:** first version developed by the working group.

- **Assessment Summary:** second version revised after workshops with staff.

- **Assessment Summary:** third version with tick boxes added by the authority after the pilot study.

- **Outcomes prompt list:** aide-memoire prepared at staff request to remind people of common outcomes and preferences which might be entered in the relevant sections of the summary.

Handout for training course
17 March 1999

Outcomes for Older People

Hazel Qureshi
Social Policy Research Unit, University of York

"QUALITY OF LIFE" OUTCOMES
(Achievements have to be compared with target levels, accepting individual subjective differences e,g. in needs for company)

- *Personally clean and comfortable* (to be personally clean, presentable in appearance, physically comfortable, and enjoy a normal pattern of eating)
- *In a clean and comfortable environment* (a disputed area: for older people this reflected maintenance of their own standards, and public demonstration of continuing to manage, in contrast services focused more on health and safety issues)
- *Safe and secure* (regular contact to reassure, and access to help in emergency)
- *Able to avoid social isolation* (able to access social contact and company, perhaps with existing friends and relatives, perhaps with new contacts)
- *Able to keep active and alert* (having something to do, and somewhere to go)
- *Able to maintain control over day to day life* (able to plan and organise life, and to enjoy a normal pattern of life)

"CHANGE" OUTCOMES
(Achievements can be observed by comparing states before and after assistance is given, and deciding whether changes meet expectations)

- *Reducing risk* (risks might include homelessness, self neglect or self harm, harm from others, dangers in the physical environment)

Recovery or rehabilitation outcomes (may need joint health/social care input)
- *Regaining skills and capacities* (for independent living)
- *Improving confidence and morale* (older people and carers)
- *Improving ability to get about* (equipment, adaptations or therapy)
- *Reducing symptoms* (for example of depression or anxiety)

"PROCESS" OUTCOMES
(Achievements can be assessed through feedback from older people or carers, or observation)
- *Valued and treated with respect* (as someone with legitimate needs for services, who is valued despite their symptoms or difficulties, whose privacy is respected)
- *Treated as a person* (as a fellow human being, deserving of warmth, but also as an individual different from others)
- *Having a say in services* (able to influence the timing, pace and content of tasks performed, according to your own perception of your needs)
- *A "good fit" with existing care giving and receiving within the family* (enhancing choices about giving and receiving care, supporting those who give care)
- *A "good fit" with cultural and religious preferences and requirements* (domestic tasks performed in appropriate ways, proper understandings about expected roles of family, staff with appropriate language skills and respect for culture or religion)
- *Value for money* (proper influence over tasks and quality, given the charges paid)
- *The right balance of dependence/independence* (not taking over, but not leaving too much for the person or their family to do)

Figure 3.3.1: OUTCOMES FOR OLDER PEOPLE WHO ARE DISABLED OR ILL

General aims

Overall desired outcomes

Service inputs

What is done

Service process outcomes

How it is done

Desired impacts of service delivery

Specific quality of life outcomes

Desired impacts, or end results

- Maintain quality of life
- Retain or regain maximum control and independence

↓ ↓

e.g. Care management

Home care

Day care

Resource centres

Breaks

Equipment and adaptations

Rehabilitation

'PROCESS' OUTCOMES

- Valued and treated with respect
- Treated as a person
- Having a say in services
- A 'good fit' with existing care giving and receiving within the family
- A 'good fit' with cultural and religious preferences and requirements
- Value for money
- The right balance of dependence/independence

'QUALITY OF LIFE' OUTCOMES

- Personally clean and comfortable
- In a clean and comfortable environment
- Safe and secure
- Able to avoid social isolation
- Able to keep active and alert
- Able to maintain control over day-to-day life

'CHANGE' OUTCOMES

- Reducing risk
- Regaining skills and capacities
- Improving confidence and morale
- Improving ability to get about
- Reducing symptoms

ASSESSMENT SUMMARY TOOL
Explanatory Note

The three versions of the Assessment Summary Tool which follow show the development of the tool which resulted from discussion with practitioners and managers within the partner authority. The preceding chapter explains this process in more detail.

Version 1

This was the version prepared by the planning group and presented to practitioners at a preparatory workshop before testing it in practice.

Version 2

This revised version incorporated changes suggested by practitioners at the preparatory workshop and was the version used in the first phase of piloting.

Version 3

Additional changes were made by the authority subsequently in the light of experience from the pilot, resulting in a third version. Following further piloting, this version is to be introduced into routine practice within adult services across the whole authority.

ASSESSMENT SUMMARY

SUMMARY OF DAY-TO-DAY SUPPORT NEEDS
(Resources should not be identified)

- *User's Needs, i.e. personal care, physical and mental health, social and other associated needs.*
- *Carer's needs, e.g. practical help, relieve stress, reduce anxiety, employment, sleep, break from caring, developing caring skills.*
- *Highlight RISK factors/mobility, wandering, memory, vulnerability - gas, electric, etc.*

ANTICIPATED CHANGES IN NEEDS
Are user's or carer's needs likely to increase, decrease, remain stable or fluctuate in the next year, and why is this expected?

AGREED OUTCOMES TO PLAN FOR
e.g   changes in confidence, control over life, independence with self-care, mobility, mental health, physical health, finances, important relationships, etc.
changes in risk level, e.g risk of falling, wandering, risky behaviour, medical emergency

ASSESSOR'S VIEWS ON HOW THESE OUTCOMES COULD BE ACHIEVED

SPECIFIC PREFERENCES ABOUT HOW THESE OUTCOMES ARE TO BE ACHIEVED, OR HOW SERVICES ARE TO BE PROVIDED

1.   Expressed by user

2.   Expressed by Carer(s)

Is the person happy for the information in the document to be shared with the people involved in their care?

 Yes [ ]   No [ ]

Signed		Date of completion	
Designation		Office	

Version 2 - revised after preparatory work-shop with practitioners

ASSESSMENT SUMMARY

SUMMARY OF DAY-TO-DAY SUPPORT NEEDS
(Resources should not be identified)

- *User's Needs, i.e. personal care, physical and mental health, social and other associated needs.*
- *Carer's Needs, e.g. practical help, relieve stress, reduce anxiety, employment, sleep, break from caring, developing caring skills.*
- *Highlight RISK factors/mobility, wandering, memory, vulnerability - gas, electric, carer's physical and/or mental health, etc.*

ANTICIPATED CHANGES IN NEEDS RELEVANT TO FUTURE SERVICE DELIVERY
Are user's or carer's needs likely to increase, decrease, remain stable or fluctuate in the next year, and why is this expected?

AGREED OUTCOMES TO PLAN FOR
e.g   *changes in confidence, control over life, independence with self-care, mobility, mental health, physical health, finances, important relationships, etc.*
changes in risk level, e.g risk of falling, wandering, risky behaviour, medical emergency

HOW COULD THESE OUTCOMES BE ACHIEVED
Specify all available options

SPECIFIC PREFERENCES ABOUT HOW THESE OUTCOMES ARE TO BE ACHIEVED, OR HOW SERVICES ARE TO BE PROVIDED

1.   Expressed by user

2.   Expressed by Carer(s)

ASSESSOR'S CONCLUSIONS

Is the person happy for the information in the document to be shared with the people involved in their care?

Yes		No	

Signed		Date of completion	

Designation		Office	

ASSESSMENT SUMMARY

SUMMARY OF USER'S AND CARER(S)' NEEDS

THINKING AHEAD

Are user's or carer's needs likely to increase, decrease, remain stable or fluctuate in the foreseeable future and why is this expected?

Will these changes require a planned review?   Yes ☐   No ☐   Suggested date for review ....

AGREED OUTCOMES TO PLAN FOR

Checklist User:	Increased physical abilities	☐	Increased confidence or skills	☐	Improved mental health	☐
	Higher morale	☐	More social opportunities	☐	Have finances in order	☐
	Essential physical needs met	☐	Quality of life maintained	☐	Cleaner environment	☐
	Safer environment	☐	Changes in behaviour	☐	Risk(s) reduced/removed	☐

Checklist for Carer(s):	Improved physical health	☐	More time for self	☐	More social/leisure time	☐
	Greater peace of mind	☐	More confidence in caring role	☐	Improve skills for caring role	☐
	Find caring more satisfying	☐	Feel more in control	☐	Reduced level of carer input	☐
	Increased income	☐	Improved personal relationships	☐		☐

Additional information:

HOW COULD THESE OUTCOMES BE ACHIEVED?

SPECIFIC PREFERENCES ABOUT HOW THESE OUTCOMES ARE TO BE ACHIEVED, OR HOW SERVICES ARE TO BE PROVIDED

1.   Expressed by user

2.   Expressed by Carer(s)

ASSESSOR'S RECOMMENDATIONS

Is the person happy for the information in the document to be shared with the people involved in their care?

Yes		No	

Signed		Date of completion	

Designation		Office	

OUTCOMES PROMPT LIST

Social Policy Research Unit
University of York

Guidance notes for staff

The Outcomes Prompt List has emerged from research and development work undertaken by SPRU in partnership with social services staff within the Outcomes Programme. During SPRU's research, staff indicated that a great deal of the work of social services involved providing support continuously, day after day. Much work undertaken by home care is of this kind. The 'outcome' is that a person's day-to-day needs are met, and continue to be met. *Maintaining quality of life* in this way involves outcomes such as personal cleanliness and comfort; clean environment; personal safety; having social contact and company; having interesting or stimulating activity; having control over everyday life and routines. Sometimes maintenance is needed short term (perhaps during recovery or rehabilitation), but frequently no specific end-point for services is envisaged, indeed an increase in services may be anticipated if the person's condition is deteriorating.

Of course it might sometimes be necessary to improve someone's quality of life before it is possible to reach the situation where it can be maintained. In contrast to continuous maintenance, services sometimes actively work towards *changes or improvements*, which if achieved, mean that there is a possibility that fewer services will be needed, or that future services will be able focus on maintenance. Changes for the better result from tackling barriers to achieving quality of life, or reducing risks. Examples mentioned were: improving the person's functioning (ability to get about, confidence, skills, feelings, behaviour); eliminating risks, improving access to benefits; improving relationships with family members or carers.

Finally, once services are being delivered, there are *service process outcomes* which are the results or impacts of the ways in which services are delivered. One such outcome is the extent to which the user feels that assistance from services fits well with other sources of assistance, and with their own life choices or cultural or religious preferences. Other impacts of services reflect the ways in which people are treated by staff, and the extent to which people feel they have a say in services.

During the training courses some people said that a checklist of the kinds of outcomes which might be relevant would be helpful. The following is a list of common examples, it does not include every possible outcome, and the outcomes themselves are expressed in quite general ways. Sometimes people will wish to list more detailed or specific outcomes for a particular person. The list which follows is meant as a reminder of some of the more common possibilities.

'MAINTENANCE' OUTCOMES : common domains of outcome and description of a standard for each domain

(These outcomes have to be maintained in a continuing way although the level of services required to achieve this may vary over time. They may be maintained in the short term, during recovery or rehabilitation for example, or in the long term, perhaps where deterioration in the person's condition is expected.)

The older person	
Personally clean and comfortable	An older person who is not able to carry out their own personal care is personally clean and comfortable, presentable in appearance, has a nutritious and varied diet, and is in bed or up at appropriate times of day.
In a clean and comfortable environment	The immediate environment is clean enough to avoid harm to health and prevent deterioration in morale.
Safety	The older person feels as safe and secure as they wish to be AND the worker is satisfied that the risk levels are acceptable or the client prefers to continue to accept the risks involved.
Contact and company	The older person is able to access sufficient contact with significant others and opportunities for wider human contact and social participation (to avoid isolation).
Keeping active and alert	The person is able to pass their time in activities which interest and stimulate them, at home and outside the home (if wished).
Control over daily life	In so far as the person is able to express preferences, they feel that they have control over, and can plan, their daily life and routines (can also apply to carer).

The carer	
Maintain health and well-being (physical, mental, emotional, spiritual)	Negative impacts of caring on health and well-being minimised; able to have sufficient sleep, exercise and some fulfilment/satisfaction within their life.
Able to have a life of their own	Can enjoy free time, leisure activities or is able to keep employment, friends or social/community links, or meet other obligations.
Supported in the caring role	Feels that services offer appropriate help, emotional support, information and share responsibility for the quality of life of the older person.
Peace of mind	The carer is free from excessive or persistent anxiety about the well-being of the person they care for.

CHANGE OUTCOMES: changes which result from tackling barriers to achieving quality of life, or reducing risks

(An end-point to the intervention can be defined, at which the intended improvement can be said to have been achieved, or partly achieved, and the level of services required can be reduced, or the focus of continuing services becomes maintenance.)

Recovery or Rehabilitation outcomes	
Regaining skills and capacities (for independent living)	Only an outcome of services if social care staff are explicitly working on specific activities which are designed to help people to re-acquire skills and capacities.
Improving confidence and morale (older people and carers)	Regaining the confidence to deal positively with changed life circumstances, and/or personal and societal attitudes towards ill health and disability.
Improving ability to get about	Become more able to get around freely within the home or outside. (Many possible methods: equipment, adaptations, therapy, mobility training)
Reducing symptoms (for example of depression or anxiety)	(May be a joint outcome of health and social care services.) Experiencing fewer symptoms, feeling less depressed or anxious, sleeping better, relating better to others.

Other examples	
Reducing or eliminating risk of harm	Modifying the environment, averting homelessness, dealing with possible physical abuse or injury (if risks are being reduced and kept at lower levels by continuing service input then maintaining personal safety is perhaps more appropriate than this category).
Maximising benefit income	Could be a one-off aim, but if managing finances on a continuing basis were involved this would become a maintenance outcome.

Family and carer related	
Improving significant /close relationships	Enabling people to see each other's point of view, reducing tensions within relationships; mediating between conflicting interests.
Enhancing motivation or capacity to give care	Reducing distress or improving satisfaction in caring for carers, leading to caring being experienced as more manageable or rewarding.
Improving confidence and sense of expertise in care giving	Helping carers to make informed choices and feel confident and equipped to provide care; increasing knowledge and skills.
Reducing carer involvement	Enabling carer to draw boundaries about what they will do, or to give up altogether.

PROCESS OUTCOMES: the results or impacts of the way in which the package of services is provided

Services 'fit' with (or support) other sources of assistance and life choices	
'Good fit' with cultural and religious preferences	The person feels that services take account of preferences about relevant issues, such as the way in which domestic tasks are performed, expectations of family members, staff characteristics, language skills and the nature of appropriate food and activities.
'Good fit' with family and other assistance	The person feels that services are delivered in ways that fit in well with their ideas about appropriate roles for family members, and support choices about care giving and receiving.

Influence over services, and impact of interactions with staff	
Having a say over personal and domestic assistance	The user or carer can, if they wish, influence tasks performed, timing or personnel involved, in order to achieve their desired outcomes
Feeling valued and treated with respect	The person feels accepted despite symptoms or difficulties; treated as someone with legitimate right to services; treated as a fellow human being (with some warmth and friendliness); treated as someone different from others, with individual needs; their privacy and confidentiality are respected

Note: Within the Outcomes Programme, the above list of *process outcomes* did not form part of the prompt checklist used in the pilot implementation. Service process outcomes were discussed in the workshop and generated some interest. In retrospect we feel it is valuable to include them, as they do have relevance to the way in which the individual package is structured and delivered, and so need to be considered during care planning, even though they cannot be measured until after services have been received, and generally measurement is 'after only' rather than 'before and after'.

CHAPTER THREE
BRIEFING SHEET FOR HOME CARE STAFF: A METHOD FOR FOCUSING SERVICE AROUND EACH INDIVIDUAL USER

By Charles Patmore

1. INTRODUCTION

Improving quality is a central objective of the Government's modernisation agenda. Most conceptions of quality in social care include some reference to the importance of responsiveness and flexibility in relation to differing individual needs and circumstances (for example Henwood *et al.*, 1998). The recent Social Care Group study of case recording indicated that providers complain of paucity of information from assessors, and that important data about individuals can get 'lost' in the system and may not be communicated to the appropriate people (Goldsmith and Beaver, 1999, paras 4.8, 8.12). To enhance quality it is important that key information about the intended purposes of services for an individual and the actions required to achieve these are effectively communicated. This chapter describes the development of a practical way to ensure that individual preferences and priorities of older people, and agreed outcomes sought, are recorded and communicated as part of instructions to staff who are going to work with those older people on a day-to-day basis.

The 'briefing sheet' for home care staff is a short document which can communicate to staff, before every service contact, key facts about why a client is receiving service, particular results sought, any issues for which staff should be alert concerning this particular client, and any key preferences expressed by the client about how the service is provided. It is intended for services where quite often staff need to serve clients whose needs are not known to them by heart.

The briefing sheet grew out of a recommendation in the 1998 Stage One Report to Social Services (Patmore *et al.*, 1998). Development began in partnership between SPRU and Social Services in autumn 1998. In May 1999 a prototype briefing sheet was tested as part of some new documentation to be kept in home care clients' homes. In September 1999 the briefing sheet was evaluated positively and, with post-trial modifications, it was incorporated by the Social Services in a new home care record book, produced in February 2000. Introduction of the home care record book into the home of every home care service client in the authority was in progress during 2000. The modified briefing sheet is shown as an appendix to this chapter.

This project was undertaken with the same partner authority whose population is described at the beginning of the second section of chapter two.

2. ORIGINS OF THE BRIEFING SHEET

During stage one research, Social Services staff commented that a problem in investigating service outcomes was that new work patterns meant that staff were quite often serving people whom they did not know well, so that they sometimes did not really know what outcomes they should be pursuing (Patmore *et al.* 1998). Some staff argued that a necessary first step towards a greater focus on outcomes was a system for briefing staff on the aims of service for each client. For instance, one area manager believed that on every client contact staff should have available a very simply written document to 'remind them why they are there in each case'. Introducing such a document was widely supported among all staff interviewees - indeed it was the only type of additional routine paperwork which had widespread support. While such documents were seen as desirable for all social care services, home care was particularly often named as the service where it was now necessary. In this authority, home care meant the home care service provided by Social Services since only three per cent of home care clients were served by independent sector providers at the time.

The home care service had been changing its clientele to focus on people who were more dependent, often people who might otherwise require residential care - a trend found widely in the UK (Wistow and Hardy, 1999; Department of Health, 1998a). Such clients needed multiple daily visits. There was pressure to supply many visits around certain peak times - getting up, mealtimes and going to bed. To enable such visits, clients were now receiving their service from larger numbers of different home care assistants. Since this service uses the same small teams to provide daytime home care on seven days a week, the need to rotate service-givers was also driven by the need to provide time-off-in-lieu for weekend working. Additionally, during stage one research, staff were anticipating the creation of some much larger home care teams to enable more flexible response at times of high demand. This would further increase the number of different staff who served some clients - and, likewise, the number of clients whose circumstances each home care assistant needed to understand. In early 1998 some home care patch teams were amalgamated to create larger teams - for instance ten home care assistants serving 70 clients. It became common for clients to receive service from between six to ten different home care assistants. This is the context in which staff wished better means for briefing home care staff, something which had been done mainly verbally.

What sort of information should the briefing document provide?

According to staff in the stage one research, there was a need for the most basic facts about the client and the particular purposes for which home care was being given. Also, home care organisers and senior home care assistants worried that the trend towards service by many different home care assistants was reducing ability to recognise changes in clients' well-being. There was thus a case both for written information on an individual's health vulnerabilities for monitoring purposes - and also for some means for recording observed changes in health and abilities. There was also a concern that a rushed and less personal style of working was leading staff to overlook a minority of clients who needed some temporary rehabilitative help from home care: for instance encouragement to gradually resume household tasks following return from hospital or prompting to carry out rehabilitative exercises prescribed by a physiotherapist. Home care staff needed something to remind them to carry out such roles. They also needed prompting to monitor any resulting improved functioning, which might mean that help from home care could be reduced. The stage one report commented how certain staff believed that inattention to opportunities for rehabilitation and moderate service reduction was costing significant quantities of home care hours on a long-term basis. Since the stage one research, such attention to rehabilitation and the general promotion of independence has been highlighted by government (Department of Health, 1998b; Fiedler, 1999).

Care managers and family carers supplied another function for the briefing sheet. During stage one they raised a need to somehow inform home care assistants about certain clients from whom instructions to terminate home care service should not be taken at face value. For instance, there were people with moderate dementia who might have required lengthy persuasion from family members or care managers before they would accept home care because they could not recognise how much they needed such help. In certain cases, it was argued, home care staff needed standing instructions to refer any cancellation instructions to superiors or care managers. Also, it was suggested, home care needed prompting about ways to deliver service which would make it more attractive to these occasional reluctant clients and thus keep them engaged with the service.

Yet another function for the briefing sheet was suggested by interviews with home care clients in stage one. Some commented how distressing they had found occasional comments from home care assistants, who did not know their circumstances, which conveyed uncertainty as to whether they really needed so much help, or implied that they might be exaggerating their difficulties. These clients were very aware that it would not be obvious to new home care assistants what history of, say, broken bones or angina was the reason for their receiving home care. They wished all staff who visited them to understand their difficulties. This function, too, was envisaged for the briefing sheet.

A sample of 100 most recent care plans for older home care clients was studied to see how much information of the type being sought was already supplied there. Only in a few cases were there even brief messages which fitted these purposes. Much of the information in care plans simply described tasks. Thus the case was made for a new briefing document for home care staff which should communicate reasons for service being given to a client, particular results to be sought, and any personal vulnerabilities or changes in the client's health, abilities or social circumstances for which staff should watch out. As the area manager had put it, this document should 'remind them why they are there in each case'.

This briefing document was envisaged as usefully linked to a local document, known as a 'Green Book', which was kept in the homes of selected, especially vulnerable home care clients in two of the authority's five area office catchments. This Green Book resulted from initiatives by local home care organisers. The Green Book supplied space for home care assistants to record observations on matters of concern during each visit, so that changes could be monitored by subsequent visitors. It was envisaged that the briefing sheet could sometimes highlight to home care assistants issues which they should monitor via the Green Book. For instance the briefing sheet might carry an instruction to prompt a client daily to carry out rehabilitative exercises prescribed by a physiotherapist. Staff could then record daily in the Green Book whether the client actually did the exercises and note any consequent improvements.

Communicating service users' preferences and personal priorities

There was one further function envisaged for the briefing sheet: to remind home care staff about any important personal priorities or preferences expressed by a client. During individual interviews with clients in stage one, it became apparent that home care clients differed appreciably as to what they viewed as important quality features or service process outcomes. Henwood, Lewis and Waddington (1998) and Bell (1998) have presented lists of common service users' values and preferences rather as guidelines for improving quality for users of home care services in general. They cite, for instance, staff reliability, service through a few familiar workers, punctuality, staff flexibility to provide small extra services. The group interviews with home care clients in SPRU's stage one research yielded a broadly similar picture. However, individual interviews conveyed that different individuals had markedly different values or preferences. Often it would be only particular items from such lists which mattered to an individual, while others were of no concern. Rather than a set of service standards to be followed for all clients, there seemed a need for a means for briefing staff on the values, priorities or preferences specific to each individual. After the stage one research, additional individual interviews were conducted with some home care clients from the stage one group interviews. These showed how, given an individual interview, the same people also showed markedly differing individual priorities concerning home care. Three examples can be given of contrasting personal priorities or preferences concerning home care.

Mr A was 70 years old and suffered severe mobility difficulties which entailed 18 hours home care per week. But he led a very active lifestyle. He had engagements outside his home on seven days a week - largely attending meetings connected with his substantial church and voluntary sector roles. He named only one priority concerning home care, a truly major priority, which was that he be helped to get up and get ready at 8.00 am punctually every day, so that he would be in time to be collected for his various meetings. No other issues mattered to him. He was fully content with receiving service from 10 different home care assistants. He had no interest in home care flexibility concerning small extra tasks - thanks to the large social network which his community work sustained he could, he said, phone people who would help him any time he needed it. Likewise, although he lived alone, his lifestyle meant he did not need home care as a source of company. He was very satisfied with home care because the service went out of its way to supply him with the early first visit on which his lifestyle depended.

Mr B was 83 years old, lived alone and suffered from angina and repeated fractures. In consequence he went out quite rarely. Home care staff could make a valued contribution to his social life - he much enjoyed conversation with certain staff and was a careful, thoughtful listener as well as a talker. Mr B's top preference was that he should be always served through the same three home care assistants, rather than the six who currently visited him. He did not wish to receive all his service from a single home care assistant because he had experienced that and found it too painful when she eventually changed her job. He strongly wished that he should know in advance who would give him his next visit; currently he was much troubled by repeated last minute changes in service rotas. Also, if he did not feel like lunch, he wished home care assistants to be allowed to spend their allotted time talking with him instead of cooking. But staff punctuality was not important to him, as long as he could be sure they would eventually turn up.

Mr & Mrs C were both blind, which influenced their priorities concerning home care. They named two items as equal top priorities. They wanted the bathroom to be very well cleaned. Also they wanted their meals to be served at set times, so that they could plan their day round these times. In a small flat with one table, even home-based activities required timing so that they did not conflict with meals being brought in. They found the unpredictability of their meal-times compelled them to waste time in long, frustrating waits. They would be happy to leave it to home care to set meal times, as long as home care gave advance notice and adhered to this. They also named another slightly lower priority. This was to be served through fewer home care assistants, so that the latter could learn the extra tasks required on account of this couple's blindness. Some home care assistants seemed not properly briefed on this and Mr and Mrs C found it hard to prompt them. Also, fewer home care assistants should mean they got to know where things were kept in their home, which was likewise difficult for these clients to show staff.

These three examples convey how individuals' priorities concerning home care can vary and how these logically reflect differing individual circumstances. Tailoring a service to precisely what matters to each individual should produce a service which clients would experience as high quality. Uniform standards, devised around commonly named areas like punctuality or continuity among care staff, may fail to satisfy service users in the precise areas that really matter to them, while costing home care great effort to standardise its performance in areas which are unimportant to many individuals. An individualised approach to service quality supports the ideal of a service 'centred on users' which is promoted in *Modernising Social Services* (Department of Health, 1998b).

Thus an additional and important role for the briefing sheet was as a channel for informing home care staff about each client's priorities and preferences. It was hoped that the differences between individuals' priorities might make them easier for staff to accommodate. For instance Mr A and Mr B expressed priorities so different that they do not compete with each other. As will be described, older home care clients' priorities and preferences turned out to cover a much wider variety of issues than so far mentioned. While home care staff quite often informally discover and follow some clients' preferences, formal systematic investigation of these is relatively new. However, examples exist within home support services in Britain (Colhoun, 1998) and the United States (Kane *et al.*, 1999).

3. THE DEVELOPMENT PHASE - PRIOR TO TESTING

Development work on the briefing sheet began properly in October 1998. Initially it was conducted through a working group comprising three SPRU staff and three Social Services staff. This group addressed the briefing sheet in conjunction with revision of assessment and review documents. A prototype briefing sheet was designed and refined. This was then presented for comment to the home care organisers and senior home care assistants within one area office. (In this authority home care organisers typically managed four senior home care assistants. Each senior home care assistant would manage a team of between six and ten home care assistants, which served between 35 and 70 clients.)

This consultation meeting discussed where the briefing sheet should be held. Everyone agreed that the briefing sheet should not be carried by home care assistants on their visits. Senior home care assistants wished two copies of the briefing sheet per client. One copy, they thought, should be held in the client's home. A second copy, which might sometimes carry additional sensitive information, should be held at the home care team's office base, where they could use it in the planning of work or during staff supervision or weekly team meetings.

Soon afterwards the briefing sheet project was transferred to a different Social Services working group. This was one which had been charged to produce a new, standardised set of documents for placing in the homes of home care clients throughout the authority. It seemed evident that, unless the briefing sheet were somehow involved with this initiative, it could not be considered for inclusion within the new home care document pack in clients' homes. Accordingly, the briefing sheet project was transferred to become part of the home-based documents project instead.

While linkage to the home-based document project proved a great advantage, it did compel an emphasis on use of the briefing sheet within clients' homes, rather than use by staff at the home care team base, which the first consultation with home care staff had also wished to see explored. While the latter was also attempted during the pilot exercise, eventual implementation inevitably focused on the home-based copy of the briefing sheet, since the core purpose of the second project group concerned home-based documents.

Nevertheless it seems likely that a staff-based briefing sheet will eventually be developed once the briefing sheet is in clients' homes. Senior home care assistants will need some sort of copy of the briefing sheet simply to keep track of the instructions on briefing sheets in clients' homes and to know when these should be changed. These copies could then also be used in client reviews, at team meetings or in staff supervision. Indeed during SPRU's test of the briefing sheet there was some such spontaneous, though small-scale, use of the copies of the briefing sheet held at each team's base.

4. TESTING THE BRIEFING SHEET

For its trial, the prototype briefing sheet was incorporated within a proposed new home care record book. This was to be kept in clients' homes and on every visit staff would record arrival and departure times plus any important observations on a client's welfare or messages to the next staff who visited. While using the record book, staff were expected to read the briefing sheet. The trial was organised by home care management, though SPRU contributed substantially to its design. Selected for participation were five Social Services home care teams managed by two different home care organisers. Team staffing and caseloads were in the ranges already mentioned. These particular teams were selected because they had long experience in use of the Green Book, mentioned earlier, to which the new home care record book was an extension. They were thus not representative of the authority's home care teams, most of which had never used any such documents. The reason for choosing these teams was that the briefing sheet had greatest chance of being used to its potential immediately, since these teams were accustomed to reading information left in clients' homes and valued this method. The usefulness of the briefing sheet could thus be investigated under optimal conditions during a two-month period - without doubts as to whether a longer period for staff familiarisation might have produced better results. Of course a disadvantage from using these teams was they would not show how much management might be needed to introduce the practice among the many teams who had never used documents in clients' homes. At this stage, however, the prime question was whether the briefing sheet was worth introducing at all.

Home care staff were briefed via meetings and detailed guidance notes. The aim was to complete briefing sheets for around eight clients in each of the five home care teams during an eight-week period, then assess results. Home care organisers would complete the briefing sheet for all new clients during the eight-week period, while senior home care assistants would do this for selected established clients. For each client, there would be two copies of the briefing sheet. One would be kept in the client's home. The other would be held by the senior home care assistant at the team's base. The senior home care assistant's copy could provide information when planning service rotas - noting the examples of clients' personal priorities which were given earlier. Also there was the possibility of using the briefing sheet as a prompt during supervision sessions, team meetings or reviews.

The evaluation of the briefing sheet was intended to answer the following questions.
- How useful did staff find the briefing sheet? Would they wish it to become part of routine practice?

- Could any clear benefits for clients be demonstrated?

- How were different sections of the briefing sheet used? Which proved most useful?

- Could staff fulfil the roles expected of them in the operation of the briefing sheet?

- Did home care assistants feel they understood the messages which the briefing sheet carried from their managers?

- How burdensome was the briefing sheet to fill in and then to use?

- Were there notable differences between new clients and established clients in terms of the briefing sheet's usefulness? (There might be grounds for introducing the briefing sheet for new clients only, since it seemed less likely that it would benefit clients who had been receiving service for years.)

- Were there notable differences in usefulness of the briefing sheet for clients receiving intensive home care compared to, say, clients receiving simply weekly shopping deliveries? (There might prove to be little which needed saying about the latter.)

Staff were instructed in a procedure for assigning the briefing sheet to a random selection of their established clients. This was intended to produce a stratified sample comprising both people receiving intensive home care and people who received a weekly visit only. It had been expected that the briefing sheet would be completed for around 40 clients in total. In the event only 27 took part, 23 of whom were established clients.

After eight weeks, the briefing sheet was evaluated using the following sources:
- Analysis of the contents of the various sections on the sheets
- Written questionnaires to home care assistants about their experience of the briefing sheet
- Written questionnaires to senior home care assistants and home care organisers
- A tape-recorded discussion with five senior home care assistants and one home care organiser at the close of the trial
- 'Results Summary' forms. Senior home care assistants visited each briefing sheet client and completed a 'Results Summary' form. This assessed any actual consequence arising from the briefing sheet during the study period and collected any feedback from client or family.

5. RESULTS FROM THE TEST OF THE BRIEFING SHEET

The actual content of the briefing sheets

Essential to understanding the project's usefulness is the nature of the instructions which the briefing sheets communicated to home care assistants. These can be categorised as follows:

Alerting staff to a client's problems or needs

- For seven clients, the briefing sheet drew staff's attention to problems in standing or walking, or a history of falls or related problems connected with arthritis or hip replacements.

- For three clients, the briefing sheet drew attention to Alzheimer's disease or other cognitive impairments.

- For two clients, that extra time and patience must be used in giving the service - in one case owing to risk of falls, in the other owing to deafness.

- For other single clients there was information as follows: that a client was 95 per cent blind; that a client was in constant pain; that a client needed prompting about health care appointments; that a client was socially isolated; that a client's husband had mobility problems; that a client had been found wandering; that a client had just left hospital; that a client was actually 95 years old, though this was not apparent.

Instructions to monitor particular issues

For eight clients there were instructions that particular issues should be monitored:
- Ear infections leading to balance problems, which had caused serious falls
- Depression and tiredness, which signal that an injection is due
- A characteristic sign that a particular client is falling ill
- Signs that a client, who is 95 per cent blind, may have lost further sight
- Whether important help from a neighbour is continuing
- Lack of appetite and decline of mobility

- Any improvement in mobility, hence possible reduction to service
- Bed sores and swollen legs.

Instructions to follow directions given by particular clients
- There were three clients for whom staff were instructed to follow any directions given by the client. There were specific reasons why these clients were singled out. For a fourth client, staff were instructed to follow any request she made concerning shopping.

Encourage acceptance of services
- Concerning two clients, staff were briefed to promote acceptance of particular extra services - in one case encourage the client to permit cleaning, in the other encourage a family carer to use relevant relief services.

- In a third case, where managers were concerned to maintain the client's acceptance of help, staff were to prioritise good communication with the client.

Instructions to assist rehabilitation
- For two clients, staff were instructed to support the physiotherapist by prompting rehabilitative exercises and encouraging daily living activities.

Other briefings
These concerned:
- In three households, prompting medication
- In two households, door key arrangements - for instance where to place the key of a client with poor eyesight
- Instruction to offer to make telephone calls for a client with hearing problems.

Clients' personal priorities or requests
These were listed - sometimes alongside management instructions on how to respond to them. Some requests had long been recognised and observed. Others were discovered during this exercise and to varying degrees efforts were made to observe them. Among the categories of request listed below, it was requests for greater consistency of worker which these particular home care teams found hardest to fulfil.
- Four requests concerned the timing of the first home care visit of the day. Two people wanted early visits, while for a third the family sought a late start. A fourth person wished more predictable timing for their breakfast visit. There was a fifth person who sought a later lunch service.

- Four people sought to be served by the same home care assistant as much as possible - for instance the same home care assistant for a week at a time or a month at a time.

- Three people named as their preference that staff should be able to spend more time with them during a visit. One sought that home care assistants should not be under such time-pressure that they arrived at her home rushed and stressed.

- Two people sought that their shopping or pension collection be done on different days.

Other priorities, named only by single clients, were as follows:
- Wishes Social Services to arrange honestly priced gardening, electrical and plumbing services
- Wishes one extra visit from home care on five days each week
- Wishes additional amount of care for a little while, since she has just left hospital
- Wishes more help during periods when family are on holiday (for a client who lives alone)
- Would like home care to collect and deliver medication
- Would like home care to always wipe cooker after use.

There were some people who did not wish to register any personal priority or preference.

It can be seen how some idiosyncratic individual priorities have been identified through the individual questioning of clients by home care staff. As will be described shortly, this questioning did result in some of these preferences being met. This would not have occurred if quality had been addressed only through a uniform set of standards based on commonly mentioned concerns.

Comparison was made between the usefulness of the briefing sheet for intensive home care clients and for clients who received only single weekly visits, for instance for weekly pension collection or shopping deliveries. There had been doubts as to whether it was worth applying the briefing sheet to the latter. A count was made of the number of items of specific useful information on each briefing sheet. Recipients of intensive home care had on average twice as many such items per sheet as did recipients of once weekly visits. Nevertheless it was striking how much useful information did appear on the latter group's briefing sheets and how, indeed, some changes were made to their services as a result. The conclusion was reached that the briefing sheet was worth using with all home care clients.

Demonstrable effects of the briefing sheet on home care clients' services

The Results Summary forms showed that constructive changes had occurred to five clients' services as a result of the briefing sheet exercise.
- One client agreed at last to allow household cleaning for hygiene purposes, which previously she had resisted. The briefing sheet had instructed staff to prompt her concerning the case for this. Success occurred within a period of only four weeks for which she was on the briefing sheet.

51

- One client, recovering from a broken arm, was prompted by home care staff to undertake rehabilitative exercises recommended by the physiotherapist. Previously she was not doing them.

- One client's personal preference was that she should receive extra help from home care during the holidays of family members, who normally gave her much help though they do not live with her. Such extra help was subsequently arranged.

- One client began to get his medication ordered and collected for him - as his personal preference.

- One client began getting her breakfast at an earlier time of her preference - usually on five days out of seven.

All these clients, whose services were affected, were established clients rather than new. Thus it was evident that the briefing sheet could benefit clients who were already long known to the service. Three of the five had already been receiving monitoring via the Green Book. This showed that the briefing sheet was able to add something to this existing documentation.

No other clients were known to be directly affected by the briefing sheet. One, however, expressed liking for the briefing sheet as helpful to self and staff. Three others commented that it was acceptable. No other comments were recorded.

On the one hand it is noteworthy that the briefing sheet could produce changes during this short period for five established clients. On the other, too much emphasis should not be placed on clearly identifiable changes as a measure of the briefing sheet's value. Review of the content of briefing sheet entries, listed earlier, shows much important information which would rarely, if ever, lead to a distinct change to a client's services - and hardly within the extremely short trial period. Many briefing sheet messages, for instance, are prompts to staff for preventing problems. They would not necessarily result in change to service.

Home care assistants' views on the usefulness of the briefing sheet

Eighteen home care assistants returned completed questionnaires. In response to direct questions, fourteen of them affirmed that the briefing sheet should be used in some shape or form in the future. Nine wished it to become used eventually for all home care clients. The other five either wished modifications to the procedure or for it to be limited to sub-groups, like clients with memory problems or intensive care clients. The four remaining home care assistants declined to pass judgement on the briefing sheet, which seemed to reflect preference for existing information systems. No-one chose the option that the briefing sheet be abandoned as not useful. Table 1 gives some additional feedback on perceived usefulness.

Table 3.1. Home care assistants' responses

How useful was the briefing sheet?	*Number of home care assistants replying*
Very useful	5
Quite useful	11
Hard to say	2
Rarely useful	none
Not useful	none

A common sentiment among home care assistants was that the briefing sheet was useful when a team began service to a new client, or when an home care assistant was assigned to work temporarily with another team, or came back from holiday or sick leave to work with clients about whom they did not remember much. It could also be useful when casual staff or agency staff were used.

Some illustrative comments from the questionnaires were as follows:
Knowing beforehand from reading the briefing sheet, you seem to give a more friendly approach, as if you are very familiar with this particular client and can talk about their problems etc.

All home care clients need the briefing sheet, as every client's circumstances change at some time, e.g. needing more help or not as much.

All clients should have one as then a new home care assistant would not have any excuse for not making sure that the client is getting the best care we can give. The more information, I think, the better.

Issues in using the briefing sheet
Home care assistants were unanimous in finding the entries on the briefing sheet short enough yet full enough to be understood in the short time available for reading. Half found reading the briefing sheet moderately time-consuming while half rated it as hardly making a difference. It seemed quite easy to remember about the briefing sheet, though many staff did not read it on every visit once they felt they had learned its contents. Ten out of 18 home care assistants said that there were at least some clients for whom they found it very helpful. Only three home care assistants said usually it had told them nothing that they did not know already. Considering that 23 out of 27 clients in the study were established users of the service, the feedback suggests that the structured questions on the briefing sheet were certainly adding to existing briefing methods.

Views of senior home care assistants and home care organisers

The senior home care assistants were much less positive about the briefing sheet than the home care assistants. Only one senior home care assistant wished the briefing sheet to be used after the trial had finished - she sought it for new clients. The others stated that they could not pass judgement. Judging from their comments in questionnaires and at the group discussion, two sentiments seemed to lie behind this disenchantment. Senior home care assistants felt their existing systems, notably the Green Book, were already fully adequate. Also the process of filling in the briefing sheet had proved very burdensome. Because of the short length of the trial, they had needed to pay each briefing sheet client extra visits rather than complete the briefing sheet in the course of a visit they were doing anyway, for instance for a routine review. Three senior home care assistants assessed the initial filling-in of the briefing sheet as 'very time-consuming'. One described the experience as 'quite harrowing'. SPRU construed the unexpectedly heavy burden on senior home care assistants as the major reason for the decline in their enthusiasm during the trial. Home care organisers, in contrast, had filled in the briefing sheet for new clients at the same time as they had done their routine assessment and this had not proved taxing.

Despite the burden, senior home care assistants did acknowledge some benefits. They had noticed the favourable responses of home care assistants. The briefing sheet could sometimes thrust information under one's nose somewhat better than the Green Book, according to one senior home care assistant. But it was the section on client preferences which they saw as the main gain. However there were also senior home care assistants who feared that such recording of clients' preferences could bring heavy additional demands on home care.

Another issue was raised by a home care organiser. How could important but sensitive information be communicated on the home-based briefing sheet? An example from the briefing sheet trial was the need to warn that a new client was suffering from dementia but she did not recognise this and that staff should watch carefully for household problems which suggested further mental decline. How could this be communicated so that staff understood but the client was not distressed? The home care organiser felt that much important information is too sensitive for documents in clients' homes, which cannot substitute for verbal briefing. In practice this home care organiser showed how sensitive topics could be approached through skilfully worded messages on the briefing sheet, if home care assistants would read carefully between the lines.

Following the evaluation, home care management decided to implement the briefing sheet city-wide. This decision appeared influenced by the favourable response of the home care assistants. It was the home care assistants' estimates of usefulness which mattered most, a home care manager commented, since they were the people whose actions the briefing sheet was intended to influence.

Conclusions from the trial of the briefing sheet
The briefing sheet was able to collect substantial amounts of the sort of information for which it was designed. It clearly proved possible for this information sometimes to be utilised, as shown by changes which occurred to some clients' services even within this short period. In particular, the question about clients' preferences showed potential for producing change in service. The briefing sheet appeared useful for both new clients and established ones, for both recipients of intensive service and people receiving one shopping call a week. The home-based copy of the briefing sheet seemed usable by home care assistants, even user-friendly perhaps. Home care assistants said they understood its messages and that it was not impossibly time-consuming. It was widely rated as useful when workers met clients whom they knew poorly or not at all. Generally home care assistants wanted to see the briefing sheet used routinely in some form or other. All staff groups - home care assistants, senior home care assistants and home care organisers - were able to undertake the roles envisaged for them in the routine operation of the briefing sheet. Concerning the few new clients, coordination between home care organiser and senior home care assistants seemed to have gone as intended.

The schedule for introducing the briefing sheet seriously underestimated the work involved for the senior home care assistants in initially filling it in. The trial showed that the briefing sheet should be filled in only as part of other tasks, which home care organisers and senior home care assistants would be doing anyway. The briefing sheet could be introduced for new clients alongside assessment, as was done in this exercise, and for established clients during any individual client review which is being conducted anyway. Senior home care assistants should not have to quickly fill in new briefing sheets for numbers of established clients as part of mass introduction of the method, in addition to their ordinary work. If the briefing sheet is to be filled in productively, time is needed to discuss certain sections with clients, family carers and team members. Such discussions proved productive during this exercise. It should be stressed, though, that burden on staff appears a problem only around initial mass introduction for established caselists. Nothing from this experiment suggested much of a burden from routine management of briefing sheets or their completion when new clients started.

Modifications to the briefing sheet
Analysis of entries on the briefing sheet produced a recommendation that sections on reasons for service and results sought from service should be combined into a single question, in view of how they had been used. Social Services wished a section about hard-to-engage clients to be deleted on space grounds; on any reckoning it would be relevant in only a few cases and the briefing sheet's box for miscellaneous issues could be used for these cases. Social Services also sought that, in respect of clients' personal priorities and preferences, the home-based briefing sheet should carry only management instructions relevant to home care assistants. Thus it would contain

mention only of those client requests which management were instructing home care assistants to follow. So five sections from the prototype briefing sheet were selected for incorporation into the new authority-wide home care record book and this revised version is supplied as an appendix.

One implication of the modified recording about clients' priorities and requests is that additional record systems are needed to carry other information about these - about requests which are the concern of senior home care assistants only, like preferences about visit times, which senior home care assistants need to know when devising the service rota, and preferences which management at present cannot fulfil. This is a reminder of the need to develop a team-based counterpart document, like the copies of the briefing sheet which were available at the five team bases in the test exercise. These team-based copies did not have great impact as working documents during this trial, though in three teams they were used in discussions at team meetings and in one team also during some client reviews and in another also in staff supervision. An issue appeared to be that each senior home care assistant already had a private record system of their own devising, which they did not wish to partly duplicate. But team-based counterparts to the briefing sheet inevitably will be needed. Team leaders will need such documents to know when they should alter entries on the home-based document. They will need such documents for planning their team's rota of visits. Also they might find them useful for information which is too sensitive for home-based documents.

6. THE BRIEFING SHEET: AN APPRAISAL

Social Services introduced the revised briefing sheet in two forms across the whole authority. For those home care clients with lower priority needs, largely those receiving weekly shopping services, the briefing sheet is placed in clients' homes on its own. For all other home care clients, the majority, the briefing sheet is part of a home care record book which also includes signed and timed entries for every call by home care staff, together with a 'daily record' space for recording observations from each visit, as in the original Green Book. This combination of documents seems to have much potential. For instance, the briefing sheet may carry instructions for prompting a client towards greater self-care, while the 'daily record' records the making of such prompts and their outcomes. Likewise, a supervisor could investigate the fulfilment of certain client preferences mentioned on the briefing sheet by examining the 'daily record' to see the timing or length of visits or the numbers of different staff involved. During the trial of the briefing sheet, a senior home care assistant used the documents together to check how often a client received breakfast at the time which she had requested on the briefing sheet.

As in the trial, for new clients the briefing sheet will be filled in by the home care organiser as part of the initial assessment. It will thereafter be maintained and updated by the senior home care assistant who should revise entries on a client's briefing sheet as a client's circumstances change - one or two changes each year might be expected.

Challenges to anticipate

Finding an appropriate pace for the introductory stage is probably the major challenge in utilising the briefing sheet. This is the only part of the briefing sheet's use which makes serious demands on staff time but, as the trial showed, there could be serious problems if the pace for introduction is excessive. The value of the briefing sheet is probably proportional to the time invested in discussion with a client, family carers and home care staff before filling it in. A promising approach might be to gather the information during visits which are scheduled anyway for purposes of routine review. Another challenge is instructing staff in writing informative entries. During the trial some staff proved much better at this than others. Following the trial, examples of constructive entries were supplied for future guidance notes. The trial showed a particular need to illustrate how to enter reasons for giving service, since some staff tended to enter standard, uninformative phrases. The revised Guidance Notes, in the appendix, supply positive examples. It will also be necessary to monitor how well different team leaders are proceeding with the task. Those more senior staff who undertake this monitoring would need themselves to be well briefed on how to fill in the form effectively.

SPRU anticipates that the documents will generate some controversies which the home care service will need to work through in the course of time. One will be the issue, already raised during the trial, about what sensitive information can be placed on briefing sheets in clients' homes. Home care managers and home care organisers seem more likely to emphasise the risks from such entries while senior home care assistants emphasise the gains. Likewise, arguments for entries about prompting clients to take medication will probably be regularly raised by senior home care assistants, as occurred during this trial, while more senior home care staff will probably highlight the hazards of such entries, as also occurred. Home care assistants can play an important but ill-defined role in prompting or monitoring clients' use of medication. Junior home care staff may feel that they should not stand idly by when there is a risk that important medication may be forgotten or misused. They may wish the briefing sheet to inform them what a client should be taking. More senior staff may reflect how rapidly doctors may change medication and on the presence of discontinued medication in clients' homes. They may fear the consequences of outdated or inaccurate instructions on the briefing sheet. There will be some variations in how different teams approach clients' personal preferences and possibly some controversy about these. Teams may vary in the range of possible preferences which their clients voice. Variation can be expected too, in different parts of the service, concerning which preferences staff are told to fulfil, reflecting different managers' outlooks and different circumstances. Different solutions to common dilemmas will be explored and some debate will ensue. In the course of time, though, some approaches will probably triumph over others in the opinion of service givers. The briefing sheet will probably become used in a more uniform fashion.

Range of application

The briefing sheet is applicable to many home care services, whether local authority or independent sector. Sinclair *et al.* (2000) interviewed home care staff in a variety of teams from four different local authority services and eight independent sector agencies. They found the same problem about staff knowledge of clients' circumstances which originally prompted the briefing sheet. They write:

> The number of clients seen, and in particular the number who are not regular clients, has a bearing on the worker's familiarity with what the client needs. The greater the number of clients seen, the less likely were the workers to say they always knew what their tasks were, who else was involved, what the care plan was or the salient facts about the client's condition (all associations significant beyond 0.0001 on chi-square test).
> (Sinclair *et al.*, 2000)

The briefing sheet is most useful for services where staff are required to work with large numbers of people whom they do not know well and, especially, for clients who live alone, have many areas of frailty or vulnerability and have cognitive or communication problems which prevent them briefing staff themselves. It seems plain that in many home care services the briefing sheet will be very relevant. Even if a service can successfully organise teamwork so as to use a few consistent workers for every client, there will always be staff turnover and some temporary assignment of unfamiliar workers as part of covering for staff holidays, illnesses or client emergencies.

The shift of many home care services towards clients with greater frailties, as home care increasingly substitutes for residential care, means ever more information concerning clients' vulnerabilities which needs to be communicated to staff. Reliance on verbal briefings seems particularly hard to support. The case for the briefing sheet is also strong where a client receives service from more than one home care provider - for instance from combinations of local authority and independent sector providers - since the problems of verbal briefings are particularly plain here. Service reorganisations are another situation where the need for the briefing sheet can stand out sharply. As mentioned earlier, in the authority where this work was conducted some home care teams were amalgamated to create larger, more flexible teams. Traditional reliance on verbal briefings meant difficulties during this period when many staff needed to learn key facts about many unfamiliar clients.

Short accounts of the briefing sheet have been written, which may be useful for raising the idea among the many home care services which might benefit (Patmore, 2000; Patmore, 2001a).

Possible future development

Future developments for the briefing sheet include its use as a structure for client reviews. This seems likely within the authority studied. Entries for 'Changes to work towards', 'Changes to watch for' or 'Client's special needs/requests' offer helpful focal points for a review - whether this is conducted by the leader of the client's home care team or a specialist reviewing officer. Additionally there would appear potential for aggregating results from review of some sections of the briefing sheet for audit purposes. For instance, it should be possible to compare the performances of different home care teams in terms of the proportion and types of clients' preferences which they fulfil. Likewise it should be possible to compare home care teams on the proportion of their briefing sheets which carry messages about change-oriented work. However, interpreting such comparisons would require sensitive reflection on the complex factors involved (Patmore 2001b).

Another development of the briefing sheet would be explicit collaboration with health staff. During the trial, as shown, there were briefing sheet entries which referred to health care, where home care staff play a significant though ill-defined role. During earlier use of the Green Book, from which the 'daily record' derives, community nurses and GPs had sometimes made entries in the Social Services document when visiting home care clients' homes. A case might be made for a section on the briefing sheet which is reserved for health staff to make entries, just as they seem likely to use the 'daily record'.

There is also the possibility of briefing documents being developed for other social care services. For instance, certain of the authority's day centres for older people were identified as needing some such document on account of their large client lists. A small pilot study in 1999 clarified some important features required for a briefing document in the day centre situation.

To conclude, the briefing sheet for home care is a tool for enabling desired outcomes to be pursued more consistently and for enhancing service quality. It most obviously prompts staff to pursue particular outcomes through reminding staff about rehabilitation aims and other specific changes which are sought. This function is timely in view of recent government emphasis on using opportunities for enhancing or supporting older people's remaining abilities (Department of Health, 1998b; Fiedler, 1999). However, it seems likely to benefit a rather larger proportion of home care clients through conveying various instructions about monitoring clients' health or social vulnerabilities or areas of risk. The recent study by Sinclair *et al.* (2000) notes how important in home care functions is continuous monitoring for difficulties in clients' practical affairs and physical and emotional states. The test of the briefing sheet found it was often used to prompt staff to monitor particular vulnerabilities - sometimes through explaining a client's problems and sometimes, as illustrated earlier, through naming developments to watch for. Through highlighting clients' individual preferences the briefing sheet is a means for individualising quality assurance and a means for clients to specify additional service outcomes which matter to them. Thus on a number of fronts and from a number of viewpoints, the briefing sheet enables service to be better centred round users.

SUMMARY OF CHAPTER THREE

The 'briefing sheet' for home care staff is a very short document which can communicate to staff, before every service contact, key facts about why a client is receiving service, particular results sought, any issues for which staff should be alert concerning this particular client, and any key preferences expressed by the client about how the service is provided. The latter point reflects earlier research, which found that older home care clients sometimes held strong but very individual desires concerning the help they wanted. The other points reflect that often home care staff need to monitor particular health vulnerabilities and take account of these when providing service. The briefing sheet is intended for services where quite often staff need to serve clients whose needs and circumstances they do not know by heart.

In May 1999 the briefing sheet was tested along with other documents in a prototype home care record book, to be kept in home care clients' homes for reading by staff when they visit. It was tested in the homes of 27 clients for two months and, in September 1999, was evaluated positively. After post-trial modifications, it was incorporated by Social Services within a new home care record book and introduced into all clients' homes (as shown in the appendices). For new clients, this section of the home care record book will be completed as part of the home care assessment process. Subsequently the leader of each home care team will update and manage the document; updating is expected quite frequently.

The test of the document showed important information being communicated about clients' health vulnerabilities and about problems which staff needed to monitor. It appeared able to supply useful information about both long-established clients and new ones, about both recipients of intensive home care and people who received weekly visits only. Home Care Assistants generally found it useful – particularly for work involving new staff, temporary staff, new clients or clients with communication difficulties.

During the two-month test period the document proved able to benefit some clients through communicating their preferences and also through communicating messages from management to remind staff to undertake rehabilitation roles or to persuade particular clients to accept extra services.

Routine usage of the document did not appear to be time-consuming. However, great care is needed not to over-burden staff during any mass-introduction of the document.

There is potential for using the document in client reviews and staff supervision. Potential can be seen too for how audit of the document could supply useful information. Likewise the record of actions on its instructions, elsewhere in the home care record book, could be included in audit.

References

Colhoun, A. (1998) *Improving the quality of purchasing in home care*, Report to Kensington and Chelsea Social Services Department, London.

Bell, L. (1998) *Caring for Quality: an audit of the views of users of home care*, Joint Initiative for Community Care.

Department of Health (1998a) *Community care statistics: 1997 day and domiciliary personal social services for adults,* England.

Department of Health (1998b) *Modernising Social Services*, Social Care White Paper, Cm4169.

Fiedler, B. (1999) *Promoting independence: preventative strategies and support for older people: report of the SSI study,* London: Department of Health.

Goldsmith, L. and Beaver, B. (1999) *Recording with care: inspection of case recording in social services departments* London: Social Services Inspectorate, Department of Health

Henwood, M., Lewis, H. and Waddington, E. (1998) *Listening to Users of Domiciliary Care Services*, Leeds: University of Leeds, Nuffield Institute for Health, Community Care Division.

Kane, R. H., Degenholz and Kane, R. (1999) 'An experiment in systematic attention to values and preferences of community long-term care clients' *Journal of Gerontology: Social Sciences* 54b (2), 109-119.

Patmore, C., Qureshi, H., Nicholas, E. & Bamford, C. (1998) *Outcomes for older people and their family carers: stage 1*, Report to Department of Health DH 1537, York: University of York, Social Policy Research Unit.

Patmore, C. (2000) *Briefing home care staff about older people's individual needs.* Research Works Series, University of York, Social Policy Research Unit.

Patmore, C. (2001a) On the record, *Community Care,* 22-28 March, 22-23.

Patmore, C. (2001b) 'Improving home care quality: an individual-centred approach', *Quality in Ageing* 2 (3), 15-24.

Sinclair, I., Gibbs, I. & Hicks, L. (2000) *The Management and Effectiveness of the Home Care Service,* Report to Department of Health, University of York, Social Work Research and Development Unit.

Wistow, G. and Hardy, B. (1999) 'The development of domiciliary care: mission accomplished?', *Policy and Politics* 27 (2).

APPENDICES TO CHAPTER THREE

The following are supplied as appendices:

- **The five section briefing sheet, adapted from the prototype briefing sheet, which was adopted for routine use for all home care clients following the evaluation described in chapter three.**

- **Guidance notes for using these sections, adapted from the original guidance notes.**

BRIEFING SHEET FOR PROVIDER STAFF

CLIENT'S NAME..

ADDRESS...

1. Main reasons for service / results sought from the service

2. Any changes to work towards

3. Any changes to watch for

4. Client requests or special needs

5. Additional or practical information
(Anything else important to remember when working with this person or their family carers?)

GUIDANCE NOTES FOR FILLING IN THE BRIEFING SHEET

These guidance notes have been adapted from those used in the test of the original document, to reflect modifications found necessary.

Section 1 "Main reasons for service / results sought from the service"
This should give Home Care staff some background for understanding the client's needs. It could include explanation for why a person is receiving Home Care and the nature of their difficulties. It could include information like that a client began Home Care following a bereavement or an accident, or that Home Care is a client's only regular social contact. This section should contain sufficient detail to add to staff understanding of a client's situation. It should **not** be merely filled in with standard phrases like "to support client in her own home" or "to help preserve client's independence" - because these do not tell staff much.

Here are two examples of informative entries.
> "Mrs A recently had a fall, resulting in lost confidence in her mobility. Arthritis has flared up, making walking even more difficult. Unable to carry food from kitchen. Walks with a zimmer. Is a little unsafe at present in kitchen due to being unsteady in a small area, bumping into cooker etc."

> "Mrs B suffers from arthritis. Is trying very hard to keep her independence and mobility. Walks with stick and suffers dizzy spells, resulting in falls. Home Care's task is to support her with pension and paying bills."

If sufficient information is already presented clearly in an attached Care Plan, just write "See Care Plan".

Section 2 "Any changes to work towards"
It is expected that this section will be relevant only to a minority of clients. It concerns any specific, fairly short-term goals towards which Home Care staff should be actively working. Examples might be:
- A Home Care plan for encouraging a client to gradually resume particular daily living tasks themselves, following return from hospital.

- Prompting a client to follow a physiotherapist's or an OT's programme of exercises to help regain functioning after accident or illness.

- A plan for reducing hazards in a client's home.

- A plan to reduce a client's home care hours if their functioning improves in specified directions.

If a goal in this section is achieved and the entry ceases to be relevant, it should be deleted.

Section 3 "Any changes to watch for"
For certain clients particular changes are possible - in their health, ability or circumstances - which would require action from staff. This section tells staff to keep an eye open for such developments.

For instance it might warn staff that a particular client is vulnerable to bed sores. Or that a client has suffered falls as a result of balance problems caused by ear infections - and hence that staff should be alert to any sign of such an illness. Or it might instruct staff to periodically check that a client can still undertake certain tasks. Or to check that the client still gets as much assistance from a helpful neighbour as was the case when the Care Plan was written.

Section 4. "Client requests or special needs"

If asked, some clients (though not others) will name one or two strong personal concerns or requests about how Home Care is given them or what Home Care staff do for them. Individuals can vary very widely as to what these are. The purpose of this section is to inform staff about any important requests expressed by a client so that, on some occasions at least, staff might increase service quality by responding to these.

Examples of some such requests: to be served as much as possible by the same two or three Home Care staff; first daily visit at a particular time; help with particular household tasks; time for conversation with particular staff; help to find tradesmen for household maintenance; to be phoned if Home Care staff will be late.

Each client should be asked to their face to name any particular personal concerns or requests about Home Care, however well staff believe they know the person. If a client does not name a request but the staff member is aware of concerns they have raised in the past, the staff member should ask directly about those issues - some older people initially do not give an answer because they believe you already know. However there are also many people who simply do not name a request. If a client says they do not have any request, then write this in rather than leaving Section 4 blank. If a client names more than one request, see if there is one which they regard as clearly more important.

Family carers, sharing the same home, may also be asked to name requests - but it is important to record clearly which requests are from the client and which from the family carer.

Enter in Section 4 the request together with management instructions on how staff should respond to the request. Some requests may entail consultation with a more senior manager before they can be agreed to. Some requests simply cannot be fulfilled. But a case can be made that, whenever possible, instructions to staff should at least try some compromise - like meeting a request on some visits if it cannot be done on all visits, or fulfilling a less important request if the most important cannot be granted.

It may prove worthwhile to delay completing this section until a client has been receiving Home Care for long enough to know what they want. Clearly the more hours of Home Care per week, the sooner a new client will get to know the service well enough to give a meaningful reply.

Section 4 should be revised as circumstances change - either clients' circumstances or staff capacity to meet certain requests.

Section 5. "Additional or practical information"

This records anything else which should be known to anyone working with this client or their family carers. - for instance where cleaning equipment is kept in a client's home, if a client would have difficulty in instructing a new staff member.

Regular updating

Once in operation, the Briefing Sheet should be regularly reviewed to check that each section contains fully up-to-date information. Repeated updating may be needed as clients grow older and their health and social circumstances change. A key point of the Briefing Sheet is to give staff information and instructions which are authoritatively up-to-date. Client reviews offer a helpful opportunity to undertake updating.

CHAPTER FOUR
IMPLEMENTING AN OUTCOMES APPROACH IN CARER ASSESSMENT AND REVIEW

By Elinor Nicholas

1. INTRODUCTION

This project aimed to develop and test tools to assist the practice and recording of carer assessment and review, to enable:

- a clearer and more systematic focus on outcomes intended and achieved at an individual practice level
- the collection and aggregation of information about outcomes with a view to informing service development for carers.

The project involved a collaborative approach with one local authority in which existing research tools were introduced and tested and others were designed and tested specifically for the purposes outlined. Frontline staff, managers and carers contributed to the development process and fed back their views in a variety of ways throughout the project which enabled the product to be refined, and its effectiveness, practicality and potential usefulness to be assessed.

This project was undertaken with the same partner authority whose population is described at the beginning of the second section of Chapter Two.

2. GENESIS
Roots in and links to literature or other research

This project is linked to, and builds, on earlier work in its theoretical understanding of care-giving, conceptualising of outcomes, its practical approaches to working with carers and project development. Key messages from literature and other research studies have influenced the model of care-giving, the tools adopted or specifically designed for the project and ways of using these tools. Issues highlighted in other studies have also assisted reflection on aspects of professional and organisational culture which present significant challenges to the successful implementation of innovation and change, both in general and specifically in relation to the nature of this project.

Building on existing concepts and models

Fundamental to any attempt to define or assess outcomes for carers, must be an understanding of the nature and complexities of caring and the relationship between unpaid carers and those who provide services to support them. A number of studies have highlighted the limitations of current definitions of care-giving and service response models, which tend to focus on carer stress and burden linked primarily to the level of physical care provided and the practical tasks involved (Bowers,1987; Twigg

65

and Atkin, 1994; Aneshensel *et al.*, 1995; Nolan, Grant and Keady, 1996). Conceptual ambiguity has contributed to limited and sometimes unhelpful responses to carers. Twigg and Atkin (1994) suggest four models to describe the various ways in which agencies perceive their relationship to carers:

- to carers as resources
- to carers as co-workers
- to carers as co-clients
- to superseded carers.

These models are not seen as mutually exclusive but ones which agencies can shift between depending on the particular circumstances of the carer, or the role and perspective of the individual worker. They help to explain variations in practice, highlighting the different degrees to which carers are seen as a 'given' resource or a central focus for social care (and other) agencies; and the extent to which carer well-being should be promoted for carers' own sakes or simply as a means of maintaining quality care for the person being cared for.

Evidence suggests that the implementation of the Carers (Recognition and Services) Act 1995 has not made a significant difference to the way carers are currently perceived by agencies, and that inherent confusions and tensions persist and are often most acutely experienced by frontline staff, at the point of interface with the carer (Arksey *et al.*, 1999). These tensions may not be easily resolvable as they are to some extent integral to the very structure of relationships in which paid workers and carers find themselves and the demands placed upon them (Twigg, 1989). Although recent policy developments have given carers a much higher profile, and aim much more explicitly to promote their well-being, in a context of competing demands for finite resources, questions of achieving the right balance between social justice, individual choice, rights and responsibility remain and are even accentuated by the challenge of an ageing population. Nevertheless, the way caring and carers are perceived not only has implications for the relationship between unpaid carers and professional carers but it will inevitably influence the outcomes which are defined and determined through the medium of that relationship. Within this project it was considered important to be explicit about the models and concepts underpinning the approach and the tools used, with a view to enabling practitioners to reflect on and evaluate their own conceptual frameworks, whether implicitly or consciously applied.

A developing understanding of care-giving within the literature has contributed to the frameworks adopted and developed within the project. Nolan, Grant and Keady (1996), building on Bowers work, emphasise the dynamic nature of care-giving: interactive, contextual, temporal, based in relationships and an experience that changes over time. Bowers' (1987) study of female adult children caring for elderly parents with dementia explored carers' definitions of the purpose of caring, which emphasised the complexities of care-giving and the importance of understanding the carer's motivation and purposes in approaching the caring role. The nature and sources of stress are often unrelated to particular tasks of caring (Bowers, 1987) but are influenced both by objective factors and subjective experiences. The relationship between different stressors and the way these are perceived and experienced will be unique to each individual carer (Aneshensel *et al.*, 1995; Nolan *et al.*, 1996). This has implications for the ways in which services respond. Nolan *et al.* (1996) point out that currently, service interventions can range on a spectrum from the *facilitative* to the *obstructive*; the former engaging the carer as active partners, aiming to facilitate the best possible outcome for carer and cared-for, the latter, often inadvertently failing to appreciate the carer's goals or strategies in care-giving and thereby creating more stress or guilt for the carer in accepting help. They suggest that a more explicit partnership with carers is required and propose a new model, *carer as expert*, as a means of reinforcing a facilitative approach towards carers. This model seeks to recognise, promote and sustain a carer's expertise throughout the various stages of care-giving. Through detailed attention to the carer's perspective, minimising difficulties experienced and building on strengths, the aim would be to promote carer well-being in a more balanced way along-side that of the cared-for. This model would appear to go a step beyond the notion of 'co-worker' which seeks primarily to maintain carers in their role as carer, challenges assumptions underpinning 'carer as resource', and offers a more positive frame of reference than 'carer as client' (Twigg and Atkin, 1994; Nolan *et al.*, 1996). As with all models however, it has its limitations and its possible dangers, depending on how it is translated into practice. It would be important, for example, to ensure that the same notions of expertise are applied to the person receiving care and to appreciate that a crucial element in understanding the complexities of care-giving is to see it in the context of a pre-existing relationship which extends beyond, and can be significantly affected by, the caring role.

Based on the traditional concepts of caring and service approaches to carers, earlier attempts to measure outcomes have tended to focus on relieving distress, perceived strain or preventing 'breakdown in caring relationships' assumed to be the result of intolerable pressures. In contrast, achievement of normal life goals (to work or not, enjoy a social life, etc.), choice and independence are as valid for carers as they are for users of services and would offer a more positive framework for measuring outcomes, along with aims to increase the satisfactions of caring (Nocon and Qureshi, 1996). Nolan *et al.* (1996) also take the view, with reference to a study by Smith *et al.* (1991), that current interventions and outcome measures are too general and that 'success' needs to be defined in a more individualistic manner, by the carer themselves, in terms of what works for them. These views were reinforced by our own research findings and form a basic premise for this development project.

Testing and extending the use of existing instrumentation within an outcomes approach
Because an in-depth understanding of a carer's situation was seen as an essential pre-requisite to defining outcomes to be addressed, the project has made explicit use of the Carers' Indices originally designed as research instruments but subsequently offered

for use in practice to assist assessment and individual care planning (Nolan *et al.*, 1998). The Indices comprise three separate questionnaires *(CADI, CASI, CAMI: Carer's Assessment of Difficulties/Satisfactions/Managing)* focusing separately on the carer's own assessment of their difficulties, satisfactions and preferred strategies for managing caring. Although these instruments have not been widely tested in the practice context, they have been well received by carers and proved useful both in fairly substantial, though mainly non-random, postal surveys of carers and in one-to-one situations (Nolan *et al.*, 1995; Nolan *et al.*, 1996).

The purpose and content of these instruments are described more fully later in this chapter. They were not intended to be tools for measuring outcomes. However, by using statements provided by carers (elicited from earlier research) these detailed, self-completion questionnaires reflect the complexities of care-giving and therefore offer a means of assisting an individualised, carer-centred approach to assessment which should lead to a better understanding of desired outcomes. The instruments are also well founded on a strong research-based rationale which links the more familiar themes of stress and coping with an understanding of the rewards of caring, thus promoting a more holistic approach to carer assessment with the potential for more sensitive responses (Nolan *et al.*, 1998). There was significant overlap between the domains covered by the instruments and those identified in stage one of the outcomes programme, and the Indices also reinforced the carer's perspective which is central to the outcomes framework. All these considerations contributed to the decision to use them as tools to assist the identification of desired outcomes as an integral part of carer assessment. An essential component of the project was to find a way of summarising and recording conclusions reached about outcomes so that this information could be tracked through the care management process on an individual level, but also aggregated for management and planning purposes.

Recognising and supporting good practice

Finding or developing appropriate tools or methods for collecting outcomes information in routine care management practice is only part of the task. The effectiveness of even the best tools will be largely determined by the skill and judgement of those who use them. Other studies have noted that sensitive, user/carer-focused assessments, which are essential to effective identification of needs and outcomes, can be compromised by the need to fill in forms (Moriarty and Webb, 2000), reinforcing a routine approach and an agency view of need and eligibility, which ironically can enhance the risk of resources being used inappropriately (Richards, 2000). The importance of the interpersonal skills of assessors has been stressed along with the need for more work in identifying, and promoting, the development of a more reflective approach to assessment which recognises both the individuality and the complexity of the needs and interests of older people and their carers (Moriarty and Webb, 2000; Richards, 2000). Smale *et al.* (1993) put forward three models of assessment: Questioning, Exchange and Procedural. The model underpinning the approach developed in the 'outcomes for carers' project draws on the Exchange model of assessment which emphasises 'expertise in the process of problem solving; the ability to work towards a mutual understanding of 'the problem' with all the major actors'. This is in contrast to the Questioning or Procedural Models of assessment where the professional is expert in identifying the needs and appropriate responses according to certain criteria, focusing on dependencies and problems rather than strengths and possibilities in any situation. These studies highlight issues which support a decision taken early on in the project to pay particular attention to the practice context and beliefs of those who would be using the outcomes tools. At the same time the project aimed to enhance practice through the approach adopted and thus potentially contribute to the outcomes actually achieved for carers.

Tackling recognised obstacles to change

The challenge of implementing an outcomes-focused, carer-centred approach which also produces meaningful management information should not be underestimated. Nolan *et al.* refer to a 'paradigmatic leap' in the professional psyche' in order to operationalise their model, 'carer as expert', requiring 'considerable training and support' (Nolan *et al.*, 1996). The guidance accompanying the Carers' Indices (Nolan *et al.*, 1998) also indicates the potential tension between the therapeutic approach which the instruments require and the more time-limited and functional approach to assessment which has tended to develop in the wake of community care legislation which presents a challenge to their use in routine practice. In addition, Nocon and Qureshi (1996) point out that professional resistance to performance measurement and a view that increasing paperwork impedes professional practice, further indicate the importance of training whereby defining and monitoring outcomes becomes an integral part of practitioners' involvement with users and carers. This also points to the need for a considered approach to development and implementation in order to address these issues.

Roots in policy or practice concerns

The project seeks to address a number of policy and practice concerns which have been highlighted through recent government initiatives. In particular these include three broad intentions: to shift the focus from inputs to outcomes as experienced by individuals, their carers and families and the need to gain more reliable information to demonstrate effectiveness in this respect; to improve the quality and consistency of carers' assessments and the type of support which follows; to encourage partnership with carers at all levels, involving them both in the planning and provision of services.

The National Strategy for Carers places positive outcomes for carers firmly on the policy agenda, aiming to give carers more choice and control over their lives. Drawing on the research phase of the outcomes programme, it outlines what carers most want from services: freedom to have a life of their own; health and well-being maintained; confidence in the standard and reliability of services; a sense of shared responsibility with service providers; and a say in the way services are provided (Department of Health, 1999). At the same time the lack of consistency in undertaking carer assessment, slow progress in developing review systems and the patchy implementation of the Carers (Recognition and Services) Act 1995, have been the cause of concern (Fruin, 1998; Arksey *et al.*, 1999; Department of Health, 1999) leading to the Carers and Disabled Children Act 2000, implemented in April 2001. The government's guidance for practitioners supports a new approach to assessment which should 'recognise the carer's knowledge and expertise' and 'focus on the outcomes the carer would want to see' (Department of Health, 2001)

Partnership is an important principle underpinning many new initiatives in social and health care, with a renewed emphasis on involving users and carers 'in planning services and in tailoring individual packages of care' (Department of Health, 1998). Modernisation agendas have emphasised the need for more reliable information to monitor and compare levels of activity, but at the same time calling for attention to the way information is collected and used. The National Strategy for Carers encourages partnership with carers, and urges local authorities and health authorities to take steps to 'involve carers in assessments, or ask them to assess their own needs'. It also stresses that 'involving carers in service planning and provision must be relevant to carers and aim to achieve something for them'(Department of Health, 1999).

The approach, described in Section 4, seeks to encourage partnership in the process of assessment and review, giving recognition to the carer's expertise, and aiming to be flexible and adaptable to suit individual circumstances. Integrating the collection of outcomes information with routine practice in assessment and review aims to ensure that information about outcomes is meaningful at an individual level, whilst providing maximum opportunity for a range of different perspectives to be heard, recorded and fed into the planning process. Involving carers in this way should also enhance the possibility of achieving something for them at a number of levels. On a one-to-one basis the focus on individualised outcomes in assessment may assist the care plan/package to be more sensitively tailored to each person in the first instance, with the opportunity for adjustments in response to feedback about outcomes at the review stage. Across a population of carers, information about outcomes intended and achieved should help to identify strengths and weaknesses of current services and any shortfalls which need to be addressed within overall provision. This information could be used as a basis for a more informed dialogue with carers in consultation meetings about the nature of service developments which might best achieve the outcomes they would hope for. Recording and aggregating outcomes information in this way may also enable care management staff to influence the commissioning process to a greater extent than happens currently, as was originally envisaged by the community care reforms (Challis *et al.*, 1998).

In summary the 'outcomes for carers' project attempted to address a range of significant policy and practice issues in a way which reflect the purposes and concerns of carers, practitioners and managers. This involved the development of a jointly owned approach to assessment and review in one local authority which focused on and enabled feedback about, outcomes from the carer's perspective. It is hoped that the experience of this project and the tools offered will provide some conceptual and practical ways forward to assist authorities in similar developments within their localities.

Roots in stage one (Research Phase)

The project is grounded in stage one of the outcomes programme, building on three findings from focus groups with carers.

The significance of assessment and review in influencing outcomes for carers

First, it was evident that carers were able to clearly identify the ways in which they would like services to make a difference to their lives. It was also apparent that individual experiences varied in terms of awareness of services available, access to assessment, the quality of assessment received and the type of support and help received which might influence these outcomes. The nature and timing of the assessment, if any, and whether or not a carer's circumstances were reviewed, all seemed to be pivotal factors in achieving the outcomes carers specified.

Carers' preferred methods for providing feedback about outcomes

Secondly, in discussing methods of collecting information about outcomes, three methods emerged as the most likely to engage carers and to elicit useful information: questionnaires which were relevant, clear in purpose and from which they received some feedback of results; face-to-face interviews (held apart from the person they cared for); and occasional group meetings specifically for the purpose of consultation (though separate from regular meetings of carers' groups). It was notable that providing feedback about outcomes made most sense to carers if it was linked to regular reviewing of their individual needs and receiving information about services available. This made it more of a two-way process and enhanced the incentive for participation. It was also important for them to know that action would be taken as a result of the information provided. This feedback from carers contributed to the decision to utilise the Carers' Indices as part of the standard assessment and review arrangements.

An outcomes framework to underpin practice

Thirdly, an analysis of the main themes emerging from focus group discussion suggested a conceptual framework which was felt to offer a useful way of thinking about outcomes from the carer's perspective. This builds on conceptual models referred to earlier, in that it recognises caring as complex and multi-dimensional, and seeks to encourage a holistic, carer-centred approach. The framework was also viewed as potentially fitting with professional ideas of good practice. This was particularly important given that stage one and earlier exploratory work (Nocon and Qureshi, 1996) had also highlighted practitioners' concerns about, and to some extent alienation from, the concept of outcomes, and perceived constraints of the prevailing model of care management with its emphasis on time-limited and task-orientated interventions. The conceptual framework, which has been incorporated into the design of practice tools and provides a basis for outcomes information gathered as a result, encourages practitioners to think systematically about four main dimensions of outcome from the carer's perspective. These four dimensions, summarised in Figure 4.1 below, are worth differentiating in order to consider fully the outcomes which might be relevant to an individual carer, but they are also integrally linked and in some instances could be mutually dependent. Within the general categories presented here, the specific outcomes listed are not intended to be a comprehensive or exclusive list, but simply indicative of the type of outcomes which carers talked about. Not all will be equally important to all carers, but used as a framework for a sensitive assessment and review process in which the carer's expertise is acknowledged and promoted, the relative priorities for each carer should become apparent. These would need to be balanced, and if necessary, negotiated along with the priorities of the person receiving care. Interventions may be directed towards either improving a carer's situation (possibly in line with agreed standards) or maintaining the improvements once these have been achieved. The dimensions are:

i) Achieving quality of life for the person they care for: maintaining the quality of life for the person they cared for was a primary motivation for caring. It was crucial to carers that any external help maintained and complemented their unique, individualised approach and aimed to achieve the specific outcomes they were working towards. These outcomes were generally very similar to those identified by service users themselves: e.g. maintaining comfort, safety, social contact, and meaningful activity, although tensions could arise. Sensitive handling, and where appropriate, negotiation of differences may be dependent on first understanding the nature of the different perspectives.

ii) Achieving quality of life for the carer: attention to the carer's own quality of life, as well as their role as a carer, was greatly valued. Although carers were generally very committed to continuing caring for as long as they could, it was crucial that they were able to retain a positive sense of self, maintain health, well-being, financial security and have sufficient freedom to maintain relationships, employment, interests and other commitments alongside their caring responsibilities. Neglect of this dimension of outcomes for carers could have a negative impact on their ability or willingness to continue caring. Carers of older people with dementia particularly valued sensitive support in negotiating their own needs and interests where the older person's lack of insight led to conflict.

iii) Supported in the caring role: a specific focus on their role as carer was a distinct but related dimension. This included being able to make informed choices about the nature and extent of their caring role; feeling informed, prepared, equipped, and where appropriate, trained for the caring task. Carers stressed the value of a sense of shared responsibility both emotionally and practically. Feeling emotionally supported was often as significant as practical assistance with, or relief from, caring responsibilities. Being able to access such help on an emergency basis was also important.

Figure 4.1: An Outcomes framework for carers - four key dimensions

A: Quality of life for the person they care for

e.g.
- Personally clean, comfortable and well turned-out
- Be as independent as possible
- Feel safe and secure
- Have company/contact (apart from carer)
- Have meaningful activity/stimulation
- Maintain dignity
- Improve mobility, morale

B: Quality of life for carer

e.g.
- Able to maintain physical health and well-being
- Positive morale, emotional/mental health
- Peace of mind (ie. freedom from excessive anxiety about person they are caring for)
- A life of their own (eg. to work if they choose, pursue interests)
- Avoid social isolation
- Maintain a positive relationship with person cared for (and significant others)
- Adequate material circumstances (income/housing)

C: Recognition and support in the caring role

e.g.
- Able to define the limits of their role (level of involvement and nature of task)
- Feel skilled, confident and knowledgeable
- A sense of satisfaction or achievement in caring
- A sense of shared responsibility /being emotionally supported
- Able to manage the physical/practical tasks of caring

D: Service Process outcomes
(impacts of the way help is provided)

e.g.
- Valued/respected as an individual
- Expertise as a carer recognised
- A say in the way help is provided
- A 'good fit' with existing life routines and care giving
- Value for money

iv) Service process outcomes: the way in which services are organised and delivered and the quality of interaction experienced can enhance or inhibit the achievement of desired impacts on the carer's quality of life and may also have serious repercussions for the carer (e.g. refusal of service by user or carer, dealing with additional agitation and distress). Participants valued services which: recognise their needs and expertise; are accessible (e.g. non-bureaucratic and available at the point of need rather than in six months time); treat them as unique individuals; and fit in with their existing routines and patterns of care. Equally important are positive relationships with staff, and value for money, due to the reduced incomes and increased costs often associated with caring. Taking time to establish the processes which are most relevant to individual carers will be an important condition for the achievement of quality of life outcomes.

2. ACCOUNT OF DEVELOPMENT
Initial attitudes and ideas
Initial attitudes of frontline staff and managers played a key role in determining this project and in shaping its subsequent development. Although some scepticism and concern had been expressed by care managers in focus groups about the relevance of outcomes and its application to their work, more positive attitudes were apparent amongst practitioners who attended two one-day courses on outcomes which took place during stage one of the programme. These were planned and co-presented jointly by SPRU and the Social Services Training Unit and provided an extended opportunity for reflection on outcomes in practice, with an introduction to the outcomes framework for users and carers emerging from the research phase. The tentative suggestion of a project to test the use of the Carers' Indices in practice also attracted a number of willing volunteers. It became clear at this stage that there was a high motivation amongst practitioners both to achieve the best possible outcomes for users and carers **and** a desire to improve their own practice and service provision more generally towards this end. Initial exploration of ideas with the managers concerned also revealed a degree of congruence between the basic ideas for the project and management objectives. These are explored more fully in the following section on the development process.

The essential ideas which formed the basis of the project initially were:
• to test the Carer's Indices as a tool to assist the identification and evaluation of outcomes as part of routine assessment and review practice
• to design and try out a method of clearly recording conclusions about outcomes intended and achieved at an individual level with a view to aggregation for strategic planning (with a view to being able to aggregate this information in the longer term).

This was intended to support and supplement the existing general assessment of need, the paperwork for which was currently subject to review. A parallel development sought to introduce an outcomes focus into the assessment summary which formed part of the current assessment documentation for older service users in this authority (see Chapter Two).

Development process

Evidence suggests that many innovations, even the most effective ones, fail to become mainstream practice even when national and local policy support them. Furthermore, the way in which new approaches to practice or new procedures are introduced can influence whether or not it is adopted (Smale, 1996). Smale highlights some key questions for consideration before embarking on the change process: how does the innovation help to fulfil the organisations major aims? How does it fit with prevailing views about good practice and service users' perceptions? In order to find a way of collecting outcomes information as part of routine practice that would be useful and meaningful to all stakeholders, it was considered important to engage key players and achieve their ownership of both the product and the process of development. This required a collaborative process in which ongoing dialogue with stakeholders could inform developments. This would help to elicit a more detailed understanding of the contextual factors, current attitudes and ways of working and ensure that objectives, timescales and ways of working were realistic, mutually agreed, and reviewed at regular intervals.

The development process used in this project was based largely on the 'Coverdale Systematic Approach' to project management, first developed by Ralph Coverdale of the Coverdale Organisation and modified by the Management Centre. It has been used widely in private, public and voluntary sectors and was further adapted by the Management Centre specifically for use by non-profit organisations. A key feature of this approach is its ability to tackle unfamiliar, open situations where there is a high degree of uncertainty. Taking time to clarify and agree with all involved the existing concerns, the nature of the task, the purpose and the success criteria for the project are important initial steps in this approach. The reality of development work, however, is that not all relevant information is available at the start and in a local authority context agendas, priorities and personnel may change over the period of the project. The Systematic Approach allows for the initial understanding gained to be revisited and refined as new information and insights emerge over time. It enables review at any stage, thus providing opportunities to learn from experience, build on successes and adjust arrangements in response to problems (The Management Centre, 1995).

In this project the researcher put forward some initial ideas about tools and a process for developing and testing them, but detailed arrangements and final versions of tools and guidance for each stage of the project evolved through negotiation with key players, using the experience, expertise and information they brought. Although resources did not allow for a second researcher to take the role of independent observer, most planning meetings were taped and detailed minutes produced which facilitated reflection both on the process of development and on the design of tools. Similarly, key points from group discussions within the development workshops were recorded either on tape or flip chart and written up afterwards for circulation to all participants. This was considered important to assist analysis of the factors which helped and hindered progress and end results which might be more widely applicable.

Figure 4.2 below provides a summary of the key stages of the development process and associated objectives. A more detailed breakdown of tasks and mechanisms is provided in appendix C.

Figure 4.2: Key stages and objectives in the development process

Time-scale	Key Stages	Primary objectives
Before July 98	Exploratory	Explore opportunities & initial ideas. Gain agreement. Establish partnership.
July 98 - Jan 99	Planning	Engage key people (managers, practitioners, carers). Establish planning & consultation mechanisms. Understand context & current practice. Develop & test initial ideas and tools with representative stakeholders.
Feb - March 99	Preparation & Training	Establish wider ownership of product and process (consult with staff and carers/amend tools) Brief and equip staff participants. Identify obstacles and concerns. Establish mechanisms for ongoing dialogue, support & evaluation.
April - Oct 99	Experimentation (& further development)	Test assessment tools in routine practice. Develop and test review tools.
Aug 99 - Feb 00	Evaluation	Gain staff's and carers' perspectives on process and impact of tools. Aggregate outcomes information & assess potential usefulness.
Feb 00 - ongoing	Dissemination & Future planning	Review learning gained and identify wider implications.

Mechanisms for involving stakeholders
Involving staff

A steering/planning group was set up comprising up to seven people (numbers varied over the period of the project) representing practitioners and managers from care management/social work and home care in both hospital and community teams. Senior managers' membership of the group was consistent throughout the project although not all were able to attend every meeting. Practitioners' attendance varied slightly as a result of changing job roles and workload pressures but a core membership enabled continuity. All members of the group had existing interests in and/or involvement with carers: two were running separate support groups for carers, one of which was for Asian carers. The senior manager responsible for developments in carers services and care management chaired the planning group, attended all staff development workshops and some Carers' Reference Group meetings and this gave additional legitimation to the project and enabled linkages to be made with other relevant local initiatives.

Considering the time commitment and the duration of the project, the continuity of staff involvement and level of interest in the project was impressive. Over a period of 19 months the planning group met on 18 occasions (two hours duration); during the planning phase meetings were every two or three weeks and later at intervals of four to six weeks. Group members also attended development workshops (eight workshops: seven half days and one whole day) and took on additional tasks, such as arranging a liaison meeting with Asian carers and helping to set up and run the Carers' Reference Group. The researcher took a lead role in planning meetings, in consultation with the chair, producing minutes, draft project plans, tools and practice guidance for consideration by the group. In this sense the researcher acted as project manager/co-ordinator and initiator of developments while the group, on the whole, played an advisory/consultative role, taking on particular tasks where appropriate. This way of working was considered necessary to achieve the objectives of the outcomes programme more generally, and was welcomed by the group, particularly given that no-one within the authority had the time to take on a more active role in the detailed development work. However, subsequent reviews of the process highlighted that a greater degree of shared responsibility for some of these tasks at an earlier stage might have paved the way more effectively for wider implementation.

The development workshops for all participants, held at approximately two-monthly intervals throughout the project were the main mechanism for consulting staff on the products of the planning process. Each workshop contained a mix of input (e.g. on principles and intended use of the tools, update on progress and the next stage of the project) and structured feedback from staff. They provided important opportunities for staff to reflect on their experience, hear others' views, and raise issues and concerns and contribute their ideas. The workshops proved to be a key component in maintaining interest and motivation in the project and provided some valuable insights into practice wisdom which might enable others to make best use of the tools.

Staff were provided with detailed written guidance and were invited to contact the researcher with queries at any stage in the project, although few were received. The researcher made telephone contact with all practitioners in the early stages of the project to offer encouragement and support where needed.

Involving carers

Involvement of carers was seen as vital to ensure that developments were relevant and sensitive to their needs and interests. Consulting with carers as a group on specific aspects of the project was considered a more useful way of working than to have one or two carers as regular representatives on the planning group. This approach, determined by a prior knowledge of and consultation with some of the carers concerned, was thought to offer a more enjoyable, empowering and manageable way of contributing to the project from the carers' point of view.

The Carers' Reference Group, established in January 1999, consisted of five carers who had participated in the original focus groups and three additional volunteers from an existing carers' group. The group met on three occasions to advise on the design and use of the tools and test initial versions (see Terms of Reference in appendix C). The researcher and one or two other members of the planning group facilitated the meetings and represented carers' views to the planning group. Four members of the Carers' Reference Group also contributed to the first training and development workshop for staff and were able to offer their views and experiences first hand in response to issues raised by staff. The group was reconvened in late June 1999 to update them on progress and consult them about the 'Carer's Feedback form', the proposed tool for reviewing outcomes for carers. The Carers' Reference Group was less involved in the latter stages of the project as it was considered important to gain the views of those carers who had received an assessment. A sample of 12 carers who had been assessed were interviewed as part of the evaluation process.

Advised by the senior practitioner involved, it was decided to consult the Asian carers' group separately, as they had not been involved with the project so far. Attempts to set up a focus group for Asian carers during stage one of the outcomes programme had not been successful for a variety of reasons (Patmore et al., 1998). The existing Asian carers' group generally met three or four times a year but this pattern had been interrupted due to the circumstances and time constraints of the worker who coordinated this group in addition to a normal caseload. A special meeting was therefore set up with them later in the development process (June 1999) once initial drafts of the translated versions of the assessment tools (Urdu and Gujarati) were available. The results of these consultations are outlined in Section 5 below.

The perceived need for change - policy, practice and culture

As indicated earlier, an analysis of the context of change was an important aspect of the development process, which could have major implications for what happened later. This included identifying various perspectives on the status quo, and clarifying who felt what needed to change (Smale, 1996).

The policy context

The management imperative for change was provided in part by the need for the authority to respond to a recent SSI inspection of support/services for carers. The inspection had highlighted many strengths in the authority's policies and practice in supporting carers, and some areas for development including carer assessment. As a result motivation and interest in developing an outcomes approach to carer assessment and review was high among managers. These issues were reflected more generally in inspections of other authorities (Fruin, 1998). In addition, a range of other relevant developments and management priorities were anticipated during the coming year including: development of Primary Care Groups; a joint SSI/Audit Commission review; review of community care protocols and care management arrangements.

Although the possible links with these developments were seen as positive, it was also recognised that the same agendas, involving a significant level of management input and potential change for all staff, could detract from the project. In the event, this did not prove to be a major problem, although subsequent developments (e.g. reception of Kosovan refugees, new budget constraints, restructuring of the whole local authority hierarchy with loss of key management posts) created additional pressures on staff, a challenge to project timescales and a degree of uncertainty around the availability of resources and energy for wider implementation. Such concerns, developmental agendas and pressures are by no means unique and are likely to be amongst the pre-occupations of many local authorities, providing an uneasy, though inevitable, juxtaposition of incentives and barriers to developing an outcomes approach to care management.

The practice context

Discovering how the initial ideas for the project fitted with the existing professional and organisational culture and practice was also important in planning the development process. What were the perceptions of current ways of working and the motivation for change? How did practitioners and managers see the task of carer assessment and review, and their role within it? In exploratory discussions with the planning group, a number of issues emerged which could be seen both as potential obstacles to, and factors facilitating, the proposed developments.

Although the authority had produced detailed practice guidance on carer assessment, there did not appear to be a common view about how to apply the guidance in practice. According to practitioners, carers' needs were generally taken into account as part of the older person's assessment. Rather than a separate carer's assessment form, a 'Carers Needs' page within the user's general assessment form, offered the assessor a few prompts and a blank space to summarise the carer's needs in their own words. This was seen as providing freedom and flexibility in recording by some and as an inadequate structure by others. Most planning group members concurred with the latter view. Carer assessment was perceived as a relatively new issue which would benefit from some specific attention, along with a desire to raise awareness of carers' needs and clarify the department's role in supporting them. Some practitioners acknowledged a lack of confidence and skill in undertaking carer assessments which could add to the pressures of doing them. Managers also expressed concern that 'assessment' was sometimes limited to a description of the carer's role without any analysis of difficulties or needs. Overall, within the planning group at least, these factors constituted a fairly high level of motivation for developing a more structured and consistent approach to carer assessment.

The lack of a distinct and explicit process of carer assessment and variability in practice have been identified as issues more generally. In their study of the process and outcomes of carer assessment Arksey *et al.* (1999) comment that many carers interviewed were unaware of having had a formal assessment or of any documentation being completed. Staff also acknowledged that a clear distinction was not always made between assessment of the person receiving care and the carer. The same study highlighted the challenge for practitioners in achieving a distinct focus on the carer *within* a holistic assessment process. While the carer's lack of awareness of and active participation in the process can be a danger of the 'integrated approach', a completely separate carer assessment risks becoming an isolated event with no impact on care planning. Findings suggest that maintaining a balance between the two extremes is both desirable and difficult.

In reflecting on the Carers' Indices as possible assessment tools, the planning group recognised that these presented quite a challenge to the prevailing culture and approach to working with carers in this authority. These instruments aimed to promote recognition of carers' expertise by involving them more explicitly in the assessment process, by reinforcing and building on strengths, and by consciously seeking to elicit the carer's perspective on outcomes to be achieved. While the idea of valuing carer expertise was seen as familiar and integral to social work values, it was suggested that a number of factors militated against pursuing it in practice. The carer was seen variously as a resource, co-worker, or client (Twigg, 1989). For example, care plans commonly recorded the carer's contribution alongside that of paid workers as well as any intervention designed to support carers. On one level this represented, and was sometimes cited as, a hard won shift in the culture towards greater recognition of carers, but it also served to reinforce in some instances the view of the carer as a resource, with the paramount aim of enabling the carer to continue caring. This also seemed to create a degree of confusion for some staff about how to identify and record carers' own needs. Generally it was felt that the concept of 'professional as expert' was a strong, largely unconscious theme which shapes current practice. It was acknowledged that sometimes the carer's expertise was recognised only in as far as providing the organisation with information about the user, thus enabling the organisation to become the expert in working out the best solution for the user. The emphasis on multi-agency working was also seen as reinforcing this tendency to some extent.

Another major culture shift would involve moving from a perception of the user as the main focus of assessment to a more balanced consideration of the needs of both user and carer. The care managers' role in this authority was generally time-limited, with their primary role being to identify the problems and the tasks/services needed to alleviate these problems. Unless circumstances indicated otherwise, care managers would usually cease involvement within six weeks, although practice varied between teams in this respect. Maintaining the 'throughput' necessary to manage the volume of assessments, particularly in a hospital setting, was seen as conflicting with an individualistic, user/carer-centred approach in some instances. A greater focus on carers needs also risked opening up new areas of work, requiring extra time and longer-term contact. Likewise, there was acknowledgement that assessments undertaken within the home care service (where many routine referrals were dealt with) tended to be very prescriptive, in line with standardised/priority tasks, and leaving little room for wider exploration or more flexible responses. The role of home care in assessing and supporting carers was recognised as significant, and worthy of further consideration. For example, how might they be enabled to take a more holistic, preventive and carer-centred approach, in collaboration with care managers. As with the policy context, the practice culture in this authority appears to be very similar to that found elsewhere according to a number of other studies (Fruin, 1998; Seddon, 1999; Arksey *et al.*, 1999)

In conclusion, a deliberate consideration of the local policy context, organisational and professional practice culture, was an essential part of the planning this project. The main implications for the development process included the need for:
- clarity about the principles and practice approaches which underpin the paperwork
- incorporating these into the preparatory training/development workshops
- gaining support from senior and middle managers for a model of practice and its management implications, as well as the forms to be tested in the pilot
- providing regular opportunities for discussion and reflection with all who would be participating in the project
- ensuring the evaluation of the project aims to consider the issues arising, from the perspective of all key stakeholders.

4. THE PRODUCT
Instrumentation - an overview
The product includes a range of instrumentation which seeks to:
- actively involve carers in the process of identifying needs and desired outcomes as part of individual assessment

- vary the level of, and approach to, assessment according to individual circumstances and expressed preferences

- facilitate more overt communication with carers about outcomes intended and achieved and enable these to be recorded clearly to provide a focus for planning and reviewing care arrangements.

- provide a framework for aggregating outcomes information collected as part of individual assessments and reviews with a view to informing service development.

The purpose and nature of each instrument is briefly described below with the full versions attached in appendix C.

Figure 4.3: Summary of tools tested

- **Carer's Needs Form** - a brief introductory questionnaire
- **Carers, Indices**:(CADI: Carer's Assessment of Difficulties Index; CASI: Carer's Assessment of Satisfactions Index; CAMI: Carer's Assessment of Managing Index)
- **Summary of Carer's Outcomes and Needs** (amended to become Carer's Assessment Summary)
- **Carer's Feedback form** - questionnaire to elicit carer's views on the

---

The Carer's Needs Form
This tool is intended as a starting point for discussion and a way of screening for a more in-depth assessment where needed. It is a relatively brief (four sides of A4) and straight-forward document which can be completed by the carer or by the assessor with the carer. With a mixture of 'tick boxes' and space for comments, it is designed to enable the carer to provide information quickly and easily about the level of care provided, how caring affects them, what they would most like to change in relation to difficulties experienced, their wishes regarding assessment and an indication of the type of help that might be useful. It serves to prompt the carer about significant domains drawn from the quality of life outcomes carers had highlighted in stage one of the programme, but locates these within an overall framework of satisfaction, difficulties and

management strategies, so that the use of the Carer's Indices can be a logical next step where a more detailed approach seems useful. The Carer's Needs Form may also serve as a 'stand alone' assessment tool for those carers who do not wish for a more in-depth approach.

The Carer's Indices

Although the Indices can be used for different purposes, their intended purpose within this project was to elicit a detailed profile of a carer's unique difficulties, satisfactions and managing strategies which could be used as a basis for informed discussion with the carer. The additional question this project aimed to answer was whether these instruments could assist the identification of specific outcomes which were relevant and appropriate to the individual concerned. Each questionnaire focuses on one of the three dimensions: difficulty, satisfaction and managing, and contains a list of 30 (or 38 in the case of CAMI) statements about caring from the carer's perspective, with a choice of four response columns to tick. Carers are asked to tick whether the statements apply to them and to rate how stressful, satisfying or helpful (depending on the focus of the questionnaire) they find each item.

The questionnaires, designed for self-completion, take between 10-20 minutes each to complete. They can be used singly or in combination and are ideally completed by the carer prior to the assessment interview. Card versions of the Indices are also available and may offer a simpler format for use in the context of an interview, where the carer does not wish to complete the questionnaires. The cards contain the same statements (one statement per card) which can be easily sorted into piles of relevant and non-relevant cards, the former providing a focus for discussion (Nolan *et al.*, 1998).

Used for the purpose of assessment, Nolan *et al.* stress that it is meaningless to add items to produce a score. Furthermore, planning group members were sceptical about instruments which involved scoring. Both managers and practitioners felt that scores could be used either inclusively or exclusively depending on individual circumstances and resources available. Whereas without a score, each situation had to be judged on its merits.

The Summary of Carer's Outcomes and Needs

This instrument is designed to be incorporated into an existing assessment document and aims to assist a more explicit process of analysis, prioritisation and recording conclusions from the information-gathering process outlined above. This is a critical but often implicit and unexplained part of the assessment process which may help to explain the findings of other studies, Fruin (1998) and Arksey *et al.* (1999), that many carers do not know they have been assessed. The conclusions about desired outcomes for the carer and their priorities and preferences are first recorded in 'freehand' style, the preferred mode of recording amongst care managers in this authority, and then summarised within a standardised 'tick-box' framework based on key aspects of the outcomes framework This was intended to enable information to be aggregated and compared with information about outcomes achieved, collated at the point of review. In line with existing practice, this form was intended primarily as the assessor's summary based on their discussion with the carer, leaving to the discretion of the assessor the way carers were involved in this part of the process. How it was actually used is discussed in Section 7. This summary sheet was subsequently amended taking account of feedback from the project and in order to integrate it more effectively with the assessment summary for older people. Both the revised assessment summaries and the instrumentation for carer assessment and review were further tested by practitioners in a limited trial, as a step towards their wider implementation in this authority.

Guidance on administration

Guidance notes for practitioners were produced for those involved in the second phase of testing, drawing together key learning points from the first phase (see appendix C: 'Key points for Assessors'). These notes, which may be subject to further amendment, were intended as a source of quick reference, supplementing other sources of guidance and reinforced by group briefing/training sessions for staff in which concerns and queries could be addressed. Staff were encouraged to build in extra time to prepare themselves for what may be experienced as quite a different approach to assessment. Key messages highlighted in the guidance are outlined below:

Figure 4.4: Key messages for assessors:

Purpose of tools
- Completion of questionnaires are intended to lead to an informed discussion with the carer.

- The discussion should lead to clarification of outcomes to be achieved and a written summary which will inform care planning and review processes. The written summary should ideally be checked with the carer.

Process of assessment, using the tools
- The assessor acts to facilitate a process which aims to draw out and reinforce the carer's expertise in exploring the complexities of the care-giving situation from their own (ie. the carer's) perspective.

- Explanation and consultation with the carer about the process is important to ensure they have choice and a sense of control about how they are involved and the approach is tailored to their needs and circumstances.

Use of tools
- Tools have their strengths and limitations and need to be used flexibly and with sensitivity to individual carers.

The Carer's Feedback Form

This form is intended to gain the carer's perspective of outcomes achieved and a current indication of their needs at the point of review. The structure of the form relates directly to the elements covered in the Summary of Carer's Outcomes and Needs and is based on the four dimensions of outcome referred to earlier. Carers are asked to comment first on progress towards achieving their priority outcomes (which would be written in by the assessor as a reminder) and the main benefits gained. This is followed by a range of general statements about the various dimensions of outcome written from the carer's perspective. Here the carer is asked to rate the level of impact that service intervention has had on various aspects of their life, ticking one of three options (i.e. greatly improved, a little improved, unchanged) with space to comment if they wish. At the end of the form there is an opportunity for the carer to identify, in their own words, any changed needs and to tick one of five options summing up their overall sense of coping at that point in time. Trial usage within the project has highlighted that additional options/questions might usefully be included to allow carers to indicate any deterioration within specific domains, or where they feel service intervention has actively prevented deterioration.

Although it is more straightforward than the assessment tools, many of the 'key messages for assessors' outlined above would be equally applicable in using this tool. It is intended that the carer's responses should be discussed with the carer, separately from the user where appropriate, and taken into account in deciding on any adjustments to the care plan or new needs to be addressed. Conclusions would be summarised by the worker, in this authority, on their standard review which incorporated an outcome focus.

Both the quantitative and qualitative information provided by carers can be aggregated directly from the Carer's Feedback form, although interpretation may be enhanced if this is combined with an analysis of the worker's conclusions. The type of information elicited and associated issues are discussed in Section Six.

Translated versions

All the tools except for the Summary of Outcomes and Needs were translated into four main languages (Urdu, Gujarati, Polish and Ukrainian), and interpreters (one per language) were briefed both about the purpose of the project and the tools. While these proved helpful in a few instances, there were limited opportunities to test these fully within the project.

5. INITIAL TRIALS, CONSULTATIONS AND AMENDMENTS OF TOOLS

Preliminary testing of the tools with staff and carers provided useful information about how they would be received and highlighted necessary design changes and practice issues which should be taken into account.

The Carers' Indices were initially tested by three members of the planning group with a total of five carers, including one Asian carer, not as part of an assessment but in order to give their views about the questionnaires. This limited trial demonstrated both the potential benefits of these instruments and some concerns. Two of the staff commented on how the tools had enabled the swift gathering of relevant and detailed information which led to new insights into the situations of carers who were previously well known:

> *Example 1:* Identifying the source of the carer's fatigue, i.e. his wife's incontinence at night, meant that this issue could be addressed specifically in addition to the provision of respite which was already planned.

> *Example 2:* The degree of satisfaction gained from caring, revealed through the questionnaires, enabled the worker to understand why the carer continued to refuse help in spite of acute stress.

These carers had found it relatively easy and enjoyable to complete the forms. The third worker, who involved an Asian carer and also someone who was not previously in receipt of services, had more reservations, identifying a degree of wariness from carers about disclosing such personal information and a sense of failure at having to acknowledge their difficulties. This worker was also concerned about the possibility of raising expectations about what could be provided.

As a result of these initial trials two strands of thinking affected the subsequent approach to the project. First it was agreed that the Carer's Indices could be useful tools for enhancing understanding of carers' situations and enabling outcomes to be identified more precisely, if used selectively, with discretion and preferably in the context of a trusting relationship. Guidelines would be needed to assist staff and encourage consistency. Carers needed clear explanations for their use and should have the choice about whether or not to return the form, thus retaining control over the information divulged.

Secondly, while there was an acknowledgement of the importance of developing responsiveness to carer needs, there was also concern about increasing paperwork. Within the current constraints staff felt there were fewer opportunities to develop continuing relationships with carers which might enable best use of the Carers' Indices. Furthermore, not all carers may wish for an in-depth assessment on initial contact. A shorter instrument was seen as desirable, along the lines of the Barthel Index (Mahoney and Barthel, 1965), in current use within this authority. Such a tool would enable a more limited initial assessment and contain an element of screening to identify those carers who would benefit from a more in-depth approach. This led to the development of the Carer's Needs Form as a first stage assessment in order to provide some choice and flexibility for both carer and assessor.

The Carers' Reference Group was invited to complete the Carers' Indices with a view to sharing their views and experiences with staff at the first training and development workshop. Carers' experiences and insights in response to staff's queries and concerns proved to be very helpful in allaying some initial anxieties, reinforcing the potential value of the instruments, and highlighting issues for practice. Most staff involved in this workshop could identify the benefits for practice from the proposed instruments although concerns were expressed about the potential time involved in using them effectively.

The Carer's Needs Form was amended and refined on a number of occasions in response to comments by staff and carers. Members of the Carers' Reference Group felt this form was relevant to their experience, generally straightforward and easy to complete with the potential to help carers consider their situation (as long as they were able to get the support they needed). They emphasised the importance of sensitivity to the carer's situation in introducing and explaining the assessment and the need to adjust the pace of the assessment process accordingly.

Consultations with Asian carers on the Carer's Needs Form: consultation with an existing Asian Carers' Group included their trial completion of, and feedback about, translated versions of the Carer's Needs Form. This reinforced and raised further issues of good practice which generally influenced thinking in the later stages of the project. Three people were not able to read and write in their own language, indicating the importance of the interpreter's role and the need to adapt the approach to the individual. Carers emphasised the importance of a personal approach. Questionnaires were not sufficient by themselves. They felt it was crucial that someone explain what help was available *before* they could answer the questions, although a leaflet in their own language was a helpful back-up. The issue of establishing trust at the start of the assessment was seen as fundamental with many obstacles to be overcome, for example, fears about officialdom, or worries about the charges for services. For this reason, it was considered important that the name and contact number of the person who visits should be left with the carer. Some of the language in the Urdu version of the form was considered too complex or jargon-laden. A simple yes or no answer might be preferable for some questions. Within the time scales and resources available to the project it was not possible to address all suggestions on the forms, but these could usefully be revisited before the translated versions of the tools are made more widely available.

The Summary of Carer's Outcomes and Needs was introduced to staff at the second development workshop and received a positive response from staff. Having tried completing these in the context of a workshop exercise, a number of staff commented at this stage, and demonstrated that the summary helped them to focus on the carer's perspective and distil key points from the assessment.

The Carer's Feedback Form was tested and refined by the Carer's Reference Group in the same way as the Carer's Needs Form. A significant source of confusion was identified at this point arising from different understandings between carers and professionals of the term 'service'. The majority of questions about impacts or outcomes were intended to elicit general feedback from carers about the overall package of care/support with space to comment on which services had been most beneficial. However, when carers were asked to comment on how 'services you or the person you care for have received' had improved their situation, most understood this to mean services which came into the home, excluding day care or other forms of respite. Clearly this would have significantly skewed the results and was easily resolved by including a list of the type of services which might be received.

Staff also had the opportunity to comment on draft versions of the Carer's Feedback Form before they were finalised.

5. TESTING OF FINALISED VERSIONS - WHAT AND WHO WAS INVOLVED?

While initial consultations and trials had indicated both the potential value and challenges of using the proposed instrumentation, more systematic testing within routine practice was intended to identify how the tools might be applied to best effect, highlight any further amendments needed and implications for practice or policy.

Staff involved and work undertaken

A total of 14 staff located in three different community offices and one hospital team were involved in voluntarily testing these instruments in the course of their ordinary work. This included nine social workers and five home care organisers with differing levels of experience. Eleven of the 14 participants provided information about their professional experience and qualifications, indicating that five had been in their present job for between one and five years, four between six and ten years and two for over ten years. All social workers were qualified except one (a social work assistant). Unqualified social workers in this authority, as in many others, have a very similar role to qualified staff.

Each person undertook up to four assessments, although several people managed only two or three due to a variety of factors. Overall they tested some or all of the assessment instruments with 37 carers over a six-month period. It was intended that each assessor would follow the carers they assessed to the point of review, whilst recognising that there would be an inevitable drop-out rate determined by carers', users' and staff's circumstances. In the event, only 15 of the total number of carers assessed were followed up with a review using the Carer's Feedback Form, between two and six months of their assessment. This was a lower number than intended due to a combination of carers' circumstances, staff constraints arising to some extent from changes in the environment and project timescales.

Although the limited number of reviews may be partly due to the constraints of the project, the extent to which carers' reviews take place in routine practice will be an important factor in determining the usefulness of aggregated information gathered in this way. This is discussed further in Section 7.

Tables 4.1 and 4.2 below summarise the work undertaken.

Table 4.1: Work undertaken and number of staff involved

	WORK UNDERTAKEN		NO OF STAFF INVOLVED	
Location	Total No Assessments	Total No Reviews	Total No HCOs	Total No SWs
Community. Team 1	12	9	0	3
Community Team 2	12	4	2	2
Community Team 3	10	1	2	3*
Hospital Team	3	1	1	1
Totals	37	15	5	9

[*1 person took on one assessment only on behalf of another worker/but was unable to attend workshops]

Table 4.2: Level of involvement by occupational group

	Assessments	Reviews
HCO	13	4
SW	24	11
Total	37	15

Documents tested

Table 4.3 below indicates the number of instances in which each of the tools were used. The different levels of usage indicate that not all tools were deemed appropriate by the worker in all circumstances or that carers themselves expressed a preference which was respected by the assessor. This was an important and intended part of the process of using the tools. It is likely that there was a tendency to do more in-depth assessments than would normally have been the case within ordinary practice for a number of reasons: a target for the project was to test the Carer's Indices in at least 50 per cent of assessments; the fact that 20 of the carers assessed were previously known to the assessor (15 were new referrals and for two, previous contact was not known) with a degree of trust already established; and, assessors needed to familiarise themselves with using these tools before assessors could become more selective.

Table 4.3: Number of carers for whom each document was used

Instrument	Number of carers (Total possible = 37)
Carers Needs Form	35
CADI	28
CASI	30
CAMI	37
Summary of Outcomes	35
Carer's Feedback Form	15

Profile of carers assessed and reviewed

There were a number of concerns at the start of the project regarding selection of carers to participate in the project. Although the project was keen to test the instruments in 'routine practice', it was uncertain whether there would be sufficient new cases referred within the target timescales which would warrant a carer's assessment. The authority concerned did not, at that stage, keep records on the number of carers' assessments undertaken. The staff involved were also keen that the overall sample should include a reasonable cross-section of caring situations that they were likely to encounter within their work. At the same time, it was felt to be important that at the point of initial contact carers were made aware of the nature of the project and given some choice as to whether or not they participated, and the level at which they participated. Another important aim was to try and ensure that the end sample reflected the ethnically mixed population, with significant proportions from Asian and Eastern European communities. For example, within this authority there were estimated to be 50,000 carers, 20,000 of whom take prime responsibility for someone else. Approximately 2,000 are likely to be of Asian origin, with 40 per cent of the latter estimated to be caring for older people. However, recognised obstacles to accessing services, including language barriers, lack of information and culturally appropriate services were thought likely to inhibit carers coming forward for assessment in the usual way.

In response to these concerns, the planning group attempted to avoid undue bias by identifying a target profile of characteristics against which selection of carers for the project could be broadly monitored. As a step towards this, the senior manager involved with the project instigated a limited audit of carers in which basic information was provided by all project participants (social workers and home care organisers) about those cases on their existing workloads which involved a carer, regardless of whether or not they had had an assessment. Home care organisers undertook the audit for only one of the 'patch' teams they were responsible for, as it would have been too time-consuming to do more. This exercise provided a useful 'snapshot' of carers currently in touch with the authority, covering 130 'cases' in which there was a carer (including 148 individual carers). Figures revealed that cases involving carers featured in between 20 per cent and 50 per cent of each individual's caseload; approximately 62 per cent of carers were over 60 years of age; 16 per cent were from black and ethnic minorities (representing individuals from 12 different ethnic origins and 10 different first languages other than English). Managers expressed some surprise at the relatively high numbers, that is two out of three carers in this sample, who were estimated to be providing more than 20 hours care per week, and understood this to be in part a result of successful targeting policies. In addition, data from the General Household Survey 1995, Office for National Statistics (1997) analysed within SPRU provided another point of reference in which the characteristics of carers of older people who were caring for 20 or more hours a week were identified. Both these sources of data enabled the development of a target profile to guide staff selection of carers for the project, whilst recognising that rigid adherence to this would not be sensible or useful. It was decided to include both new referrals and existing cases where carer assessment seemed appropriate, as this was likely to reflect the reality of routine practice, at least to some extent.

The characteristics of our sample seemed to reflect to a reasonable extent the characteristics of the target profile, although efforts were made midway through the project to encourage staff to seek out carers from black and minority ethnic groups, who fell short of the desired target. Characteristics of the overall sample of carers assessed and those who were reviewed are included appendix C. In the event, our sample included a higher proportion of partners than either the local 'carer's audit' or the General Household Survey data had included, and also, partly in consequence, it is assumed, slightly higher proportions of carers living in the same household.

6. RESULTS OF EVALUATION

The evaluation process was designed to elicit an understanding of the views of carers and practitioners about the ease of use or practicality of the tools and their potential value within mainstream practice. Methods used included interviews with a sample of carers (no=12) who had been assessed, interviews with all staff participants (no=14), an analysis of completed documentation and ongoing feedback from both staff and managers through the development workshops, planning group and written reflections after individual assessments and reviews. Interviews with staff and carers were conducted by two separate researchers who had not been involved with the development process, although the researcher who led the developmental aspects of the work contributed to the analysis of these interviews and other documents. Information from all these sources have informed the conclusions outlined below.

The assessment process - identifying outcomes
Carers' views

Carers' views need to be understood in the context of their understanding of the purpose of the assessment. Most saw the use of the tools primarily as a research exercise and were motivated by the desire to help other carers rather than have their own needs considered, although many indicated that they found the process provided a useful opportunity to talk things over and reflect on their situation. Carers spoke about it giving a release for the feelings they had been bottling up, new insights into why they were caring and what they were getting from the role, and an opportunity to be more truthful about the difficulties they were having and what they wanted for the future. Others said it might be useful where carers wanted some help **and** Social Services were prepared to assist.

Carers had different views on how the forms should be administered, indicating that there was no one right way to use them. Some carers appreciated being able to complete the forms on their own whereas others welcomed help with them, reinforcing the need for a flexible, individualistic approach. There were equally mixed views about who should, or should not, be present. Although carers were not specifically asked how they felt about this, three carers did express a preference for **not** having the cared-for person present while they were being interviewed. Two people said they found it useful to have their partner (who was not a recipient of care) present: one because the partner brought up issues the carer had not thought to mention; the other, because it gave them an opportunity to discuss their situation, which is something they usually avoid.

Some carers suggested changes could usefully be made to the content and layout of forms, for example, reducing perceived repetition to CADI, CASI, and CAMI and simplifying the response options on these forms to 'yes' and 'no'. Most carers who had used the Carers' Indices valued the additional scope and detail they offered, commenting that they felt the Carer's Needs Form was too basic by itself and should be supplemented with other questionnaires. The issue of 'satisfaction in caring' presented difficulties for a number of carers who felt they were not experiencing any and were quite shocked to think that others might be. This had a particularly negative impact on one person who was confronted with this realisation through the use of the CASI form.

> It made me think ... up until then it had never crossed my mind ... it was something I was doing, had to be done. It made me think that I wasn't enjoying it, and should I enjoy it? And then you think, is there something wrong with me, that I don't care, I don't enjoy it. I think it was not helpful actually because it made me question myself.

Two others, however, became aware for the first time that they were gaining more satisfaction than they had thought which provided a boost to morale.

> It pulled me out of the doldrums really 'cos I was getting down in the dumps about what I was doing, how much I was doing, how much time I was spending there.

Overall this suggests that assessors need to take particular care in the use of CASI and the Carer's Needs Form (which includes questions on satisfaction), emphasising that they understand that not all carers will be gaining personal satisfaction from their role. The issue of satisfaction in caring may also be an important element to include in staff training.

None of the carers who took part felt that it had been an intrusion on their privacy. Reasons for this included: being told that they could stop at any time; being comfortable with speaking their own mind; feeling that doing something that will help others is worth it; being familiar, as a carer, with professionals visiting their home; being glad that someone had listened; feeling that social services cannot help if they do not know about the situation.

It could be an emotional process but only one person saw this as problematic (as illustrated above). Carers expressed a range of views about whether or not the exercise was worthwhile, depending on their experience of the process, what they gained as a result, and their perceptions of Social Services' intentions and abilities to meet carers' needs in general. Carers had mixed views on whether the forms were difficult or easy to complete. Reasons why some people had difficulty with the forms were: that it required them to think about things they had not considered before; that they did not like writing and therefore struggled with the sections which required them to do more than tick a box; and that their feelings about caring changed from day to day, making it difficult to know how to respond. The time involved in completing forms did not seem to be a major issue for carers with only a couple of people bringing this issue up. One carer reported that she had initially set the forms aside because she did not feel she could complete them in an evening. Another carer, commenting on the fact that she had completed the forms in one session lasting one and half hours, described it as 'fairly gruesome'. A few people commented that the forms were interesting: they made them think; gave them an insight into why they had been feeling bitter about caring; or made them aware of the satisfaction they were getting from the role.

In recalling the results of the assessment, seven carers had experienced changes in services since the assessment although only three attributed these to the assessment rather than to other events or circumstances which had been more significant factors in bringing about the changes. Only four of the carers interviewed indicated that an explicit agreement had been reached with them that there was a need to change the arrangements for support and only in one of these was it put in writing. Carers generally did not feel their expectations had been raised and not met (another concern expressed by staff) but this may be connected with their perception that this was primarily a research exercise.

In summary, the feedback from carers highlights the potential value of these tools in enabling the carer to express their views on their role and circumstances, an important step towards defining outcomes to be achieved. However, much will depend on the way they are used: the skills and sensitivity of the assessor in determining when they are likely to be most helpful and in dealing with the issues which will inevitably arise for carers, and the way they reach and share agreements about outcomes to be achieved.

Staff's views
Interviews with the 14 practitioners who participated focused on feedback about the assessment process as few had undertaken reviews by that stage. The assessment 'tools' were intended to assist staff in understanding the carer's needs and identifying and recording desired outcomes in such a way that progress towards these could be later reviewed. Staff were asked about the impact of the tools on their understanding, their practice and their recording, and their views about practicality in terms of routine practice.

Impact on service provision. Before considering staff's views it is worth noting the results of the assessments in terms of service provision. Separately from interviews, staff provided data on service provision before and after the assessment for 35 of the 37 carers assessed. Twenty-two caring situations assessed had some services and 13 had no services in place prior to the assessment. As a result of assessment assessors reported the following impact on service provision:

Table 4.4: Reported impact on service provision

	Total *
	(*out of 35 unless otherwise indicated)
No change in existing service/support required:	6
Fine-tuning of services (e.g. adjustment to timing, task, etc.)	9
Those where existing services had been adjusted **and** increased	17
Those without an existing package for whom new services were provided	13#
	(# Out of 15 who were not previously in receipt of services)
Total number resulting in increased or new service provision	28
(Note: Eight assessments resulted in both fine-tuning and increased/new service provision)	

Given the large proportion of this sample who were in receipt of some services at the point of assessment, it is notable that so many assessments resulted in additional or changed input, perhaps reinforcing the value of regular reviews/re-assessments of carers' circumstances. These results would also suggest that a more specific focus on the carer within the assessment process can highlight areas of need and desired outcomes which may not have been thoroughly addressed in the initial assessment of the older person. The absence of a control group and lack of more detailed information about the nature and timing of the initial assessment make it difficult to draw too many conclusions from this data. Here it is intended to provide contextual information, the meaning of which may be further elucidated by staff's views.

Figure 4.5: Impact on awareness and understanding

Key points:
From staff's perspective, use of tools helped to:
- Raise general awareness of the complexities of care-giving
- Challenge expectations and assumptions about carers
- Encourage a more comprehensive and pro-active approach to assessment
- Shift thinking and orientation of work towards outcomes (for some staff)

Impact on awareness and understanding. The use of the questionnaires in particular seemed to have made a noticeable impact on general awareness of carers' needs, encouraging a more comprehensive and specific approach to the assessment process. Ten people commented that the use of the forms had helped in this respect, some being quite surprised themselves at this impact:

> It's sharpened me up a bit ... because I'd actually been a carer you can easily get into thinking 'Oh yeah I've done it, you know, because I've been one I know it, but I realised that I didn't know as much as I thought I did ... it's perhaps changed in some of the questions I might ask or even if I don't ask, some of the things I might look for.

> It helped me understand where she was coming from ... I understood a lot more of what her issues were.

> It's made me more aware that there's not just what is physically obvious to anybody ... you know, it might just be stress and tearing their hair out or struggling to actually give physical care for somebody.

For others it helped to change expectations and assumptions about carers and the authority's role in supporting them:

> I have thought I was aware of carers needs prior to this ... I think like I'm more aware that, although they're carers it doesn't mean to say that they have to provide or we should expect them to provide care. So ... it has certainly raised my awareness.

> I'm now aware to actually ask directly to the carer how she's coping or how he's coping whereas I might not have done before.

Although there was some evidence of continuing confusion between the concepts of need and outcome, with the terms being used interchangeably, many (eight staff) indicated that there had been a significant shift in their thinking or orientation which was

95

sometimes quite subtle, for example:

> ... I wouldn't have thought about that ... as a result of services ... you know, having the ability to go out and enjoy ... have social time for themselves. I wouldn't have seen that as an outcome ...

> We may have been doing it [meeting carers needs] but not in a way that was either so focused or so able to be evaluated as an outcome. It's a different way of thinking about things, and thinking is the crucial word.

Figure 4.6 Impact on practice

Key points:

From examples given, use of tools helped many staff to:

- identify outcomes which were specific and relevant to the individual
- develop care plans which were more focused, creative, and tailored to achieve individualised outcomes identified
- target respite and relief services more effectively
- open up new opportunities for carers with potential to enhance quality of life
- highlight aspects of assessment practice which they would approach differently in future

---

Impact on practice. Two staff did not feel there had been much impact on their awareness or practice. Many others however gave examples of how existing care plans had been changed and new care plans had become more specific, focused or creative than they might have been previously, and for one or two people crises had been averted as a result of the explicit attention to carers' desired outcomes. As one assessor explained, it is not just a matter of:

> giving them a break but giving them a chance to do something for themselves ... before it might have just been, as we write, 'carer relief'.

Several assessors highlighted the value of exploring the potential use of respite which emerged from a focus on outcomes:

> ... to look at what a good outcome for them was. I mean some people would just like to go and lie on a bed for a couple of hours if they had carer relief but may not feel that was a valid thing to do. Some people may have thought they would have to actually physically leave the house if somebody was there caring for the person.

More effective targeting of respite/relief services according to specific outcomes was evident in a number of examples given. Two assessors spoke of tailoring various respite services to enable carers to take up interests again, attend specific classes or meet up with people at more sociable times, for example, one person to join a yoga class, another to have an early Saturday morning swim. As well as a much needed break, the 'carer relief' provided was therefore much more likely to achieve other outcomes identified, e.g. improved morale, sense of well-being, social integration or reduced stress.

> I'd never have thought of suggesting that, you know, and she would never have thought of saying: 'I would like to go for an early morning swim', I mean that's purely come out of that ... I wouldn't have said before 'Look if you can find a class we can actually get a sitter to cover those specific times' ... which I would do now.

Many carers find it difficult to make best use of respite services due to the loss of social contacts and giving up interests as caring gradually takes up more and more of their time. They may also get out of the habit of thinking about their own needs and can benefit from encouragement to do so. Sensitive assessments where the carer is given the opportunity to think more broadly about their situation can open up whole new opportunities for carers. For one carer completing CADI, CASI and CAMI stimulated ideas about how he could use his free time as well as giving attention to his own deteriorating health:

> He got quite excited about doing courses at the local college in the evenings and using a sitter at a particular time so he could study ... [instead of] to just go off and do the shopping and collect the pensions when his wife was being looked after. We also tinkered around with a private service so that we offered both sitting and hoovering, vacuuming. Because I don't think he would even have said that doing the vacuuming was a difficulty for him had we not been sitting down and taking him through these forms. It was a small thing and it certainly made no difference in cost to the care package but it was enormous psychological benefit to him not to have to do the vacuuming.

In summary most staff saw the process of assessment as enabling for carers. It provided recognition, an opportunity to reflect on their needs, gain new insights, express themselves and for some the encouragement they needed to accept help or develop new coping strategies which the care package was then designed to support. Carers' comments at the review stage also reinforced the value of the assessment process in contributing to improved emotional or mental health and a sense of shared responsibility or being emotionally supported.

Several staff indicated how their experience of using these forms would affect their future approach to carers' assessment, for example: alerting them to issues which might be covered; generally increasing the assessor's level of confidence in assessing carers;

ensuring carers are seen separately; spending more time in building a rapport with the carer; following up with carers after the initial client assessment (this is currently done less often where a carer is involved according to one home care organiser); sharing agreed outcomes in writing. One person particularly welcomed the more holistic approach and would not want to return to a focus on difficulties alone.

Figure 4.7: Practice issues and concerns

Key points
Use of tools raised a number of issues and concerns:
• Staff and carers need to be prepared for the possible emotional impact of using the tools, and the assessment planned accordingly
• Danger of over-reliance on the carer's perspective
• Process may be culturally biassed towards those who are literate and used to discussing feelings
• Use with black and minority ethnic carers can be effective though further testing would be beneficial
• Professional judgement, sensitivity and skill are of paramount importance

Practice issues and concerns. The very strengths outlined previously also raised some difficulties and concerns for staff. A few comments indicated the danger of 'over-exposure' for carers, or getting into an unplanned counselling session which staff may not have the time or the skills to deal with effectively (both social work and home care staff raised concerns about this). The reliance on the carer's perspective was seen as problematic in some circumstances and one person questioned the value of this approach to assessment in situations where the carer's ability to provide adequate care is being challenged. Others suggested that the process may be best suited to those who are literate, comfortable with the written word and used to discussing their feelings. It may need to be adapted for those who are not. Once again this highlights the need for sensitivity and professional judgement in the application of the tools.

The approach and paperwork were positively used with, and experienced by, a few carers from black and minority ethnic communities, involving staff who spoke the same language or an interpreter. Translated forms were important for those who could make use of them. They appeared to be culturally relevant for some, and indeed helped one assessor gain new insights into a different cultural perspective of dementia. At the same time staff commented that two carers (both male) from black and minority ethnic communities had found the questions too personal. More extensive use with the translated versions of the tools, which did not prove possible within this project, will help to establish the strengths and limitations and circumstances in which they are most effectively used.

Impact on recording outcomes

The 'Summary of Carer's Outcomes and Needs' was the main tool for the assessor to summarise and record the conclusions from the assessment process. This is a single A4 sheet intended to be incorporated into the user's assessment form, with the purpose of informing the care planning process. Feedback from staff and an examination of the completed summary sheets indicated that for many, this had been an important and useful tool in distilling the information gleaned from the questionnaires and subsequent discussion with the carer. The process of using this tool assisted reflection and analysis as well as recording, clarifying outcomes, priorities and preferences from the carer's perspective which helped to focus care planning and maintain a distinct and clear view of the carer's perspective. At the same time it was apparent that some staff still struggled with the concept of 'outcomes' and commented on the challenge of recording these on the summary sheet, although some said this became easier with experience. Difficulties appeared to be partly due to the nature of the form (although only one person suggested change was needed) and partly due to the challenge of separating outcomes from needs and services, and distilling the wealth of information provided by carers on the other questionnaires. Several staff indicated that they would have welcomed more opportunities to 'try out' the forms and discuss them in a training context.

A further dimension of recording outcomes is the way in which carers might be involved in this stage of the assessment. Evidence from this study and others suggest that the process of decision making is often implicit rather than explicit and the results of assessment and review processes are not always clearly communicated to carers. This means that carers may not always have the opportunity to say whether or not they agree with the assessor's conclusions; they may be left wondering what the point of the exercise was, or whether they have even had an assessment in the first place (Arksey et al., 1999). It was interesting to note that although this tool was designed for completion by the assessor, in line with existing practice in this authority, staff varied considerably in how they perceived its purpose and use. Only a few people chose to show, or verbally check with carers their written conclusions about desired outcomes they had recorded in writing, although on reflection others indicated that they would be more likely to do so in future. For some assessments, this seemed less appropriate to assessors given that the user's assessment had been already completed and no changes were deemed necessary. Others indicated that they felt that a copy of the care plan, which would generally have been given to the older person and carer, was sufficient, although few plans actually specified the specific outcomes intended for the carer. A degree of reticence was expressed, and some confusion apparent in relation to sharing written agreements with carers due to concerns about how these may be used in situations of dispute.

The experience of this project suggests that it would be useful for any training to support the implementation of an outcomes approach to include opportunities to practice defining and recording outcomes in relation to case material. Attention should also be given to the *purpose* and the *process* of recording, aiming to encourage a more explicit and participative process in which assessors seek as far as possible to gain a common understanding (if not agreement) with carer and cared for about the specific impacts or outcomes the care package should aim to achieve, and not just the services agreed. This would help to make the review a more meaningful and focused exercise for all concerned. It may also be helpful to include within the summary of outcomes a trigger question to encourage assessors to elicit the carer's verbal or written agreement to the assessors conclusions and to provide clear guidelines about this, setting it in the context of the local agency's policy about open records.

Practicality and fit with routine practice

The assessment questionnaires were used in a variety of ways to facilitate the assessment depending on carers' preferences, staff judgement and to some extent time available. These included: use in the context of face-to-face interviews; self-completion by carers alone; and by combined self-completion and interviews. Face-to-face interviews were the most frequently used mode of assessment, and enabled carers to talk about their feelings but were very time-consuming. Self-completion was chosen by some carers and provided mostly adequate but less in-depth information. Several staff commented on the value of discussing the carer's responses to gain a fuller understanding. However, some carers who had completed forms, returned them without further discussion with the assessor, and indicated that they would have welcomed this opportunity. This also highlights the dangers of self-assessment forms already referred to by other studies where self-completion can become a short-cut to assessment, experienced by carers as an alienating or pointless exercise (Arksey *et al.*, 1999). Some forms were also left with carers and not returned. Combined self-completion followed by an interview, which was the intended, but least used mode seemed to work well, focusing the discussion around the issues identified by the carer. Levels of self-completion were lower than anticipated which may have been partly due to the novelty of the approach, some staff having not appreciated fully at the start the intended use, and partly to the high proportion of older carers in this study a factor evident in other authorities where such an approach is used (Arksey *et al.*, 1999).

The time available for carer assessment presented the main issue for staff. Feedback from interviews with staff indicated that the entire assessment of the carer, using one or more of the questionnaires, took between 30 minutes and almost two hours, and could involve more than one visit. This was generally perceived as being longer than normal, although exactly how much longer was difficult to ascertain. Some staff estimated that assessments using the new forms would 'double' or 'treble' the time currently spent on this, or add two hours. Very few staff specified the actual time currently spent on this activity; where it was mentioned it ranged from 15 minutes to over two hours. It was not always clear if this referred to the assessment of the carer only or the assessment of the user *and* the carer. It seemed that the issue of time might be prominent because it was not common practice to offer carers a separate interview. The time staff spent on these assessments, including personal contact, administration and follow-up work, tended to be regarded as 'special' time in that the carers concerned were given more time than the staff believed they could routinely give people. Consequently the general view expressed by staff was that a more condensed version, or selective application, of the tools (CADI, CASI, and CAMI in particular) would be more realistic to use in the context of routine practice. Some staff considered a system of leaving the forms for carers to complete *and* giving them the option of deciding whether to discuss this in person would be ideal, while having some flexibility to adopt other methods where this was not ideal or practicable. However, as indicated earlier, positive choice for carers needs to be balanced with a pro-active and enabling approach to facilitating the assessment process. A conscious effort may be needed both by the assessor and the organisations in monitoring practice, to avoid the unhelpful practice of self-assessment forms being left for the carer to complete as a substitute for personal discussion with the assessor with the inherent dangers of limited understanding, misinterpretation or failure to respond to the needs expressed.

Organisational issues

Staff were asked what organisational issues or obstacles needed to be addressed in order to implement such an approach more widely. Whilst recognising the need for a modified approach, several people expressed the view that the current model of care management was too task and problem orientated, affording insufficient time to listen and respond to carers' needs as effectively as practitioners would wish. This imposed constraints on the breadth and depth of assessments to a degree which was seen as unhelpful, leaving little room for an individualised approach. Recognition of the nature of carers' assessments (often more emotional in content and process than that of the service user) and the time involved in personal contact, administration and follow-up were seen to be of vital importance. Other practical issues raised included the question of whether a carer's record should be separated from the user's file, and whether the roles of different staff groups in carer assessment should be further differentiated, for example acknowledging the respective strengths, emphases and functions of home care and care management staff. For example, should home care organisers focus on initial assessments, using Carer's Needs forms, and refer on to social work teams if a more in-depth approach is indicated?

There is a considerable challenge for managers and practitioners in finding the right balance between allowing sufficient time for individual carers to receive unhurried, sensitive, comprehensive assessments and ensuring that time as a resource is managed fairly and carer assessments targeted appropriately overall. Determining eligibility for assessment and ensuring fair and equitable access both to assessment and services are not straightforward issues. Rationing can happen implicitly and unconsciously through a failure to make insufficient time available for detailed and separate assessments. This issue needs to be addressed at two levels: at a policy level, clarifying the circumstances in which a detailed or in-depth assessment should be offered, and at an individual level, ensuring staff ask the right questions as part of an initial assessment or screening process to identify whether those circumstances exist. Although screening for assessment did not receive a high profile in this project, a series of trigger questions have since been developed and tested as part of the process of integrating the paperwork for service users and carers. Staff who participated in this latter phase of testing reported that these questions led to a more informed decision-making process in many cases.

In summary, the results of the evaluation indicate that the assessment tools have the potential to enhance practice, and can help carers and assessors communicate more effectively about outcomes, although some modifications may be necessary to enable their incorporation into mainstream practice. In addition, assuming that this authority is not unusual, current models of care management, the resources allowed and priority given to carer assessment may need to be reviewed to ensure that the assessment process and outcomes identified are sensitive to the individuals concerned. Clear guidelines and training should be essential components in introducing them into mainstream practice to assist professional judgements on when, where and how they might be used most effectively.

The review process - evaluating outcomes achieved (using the Carer's Feedback Form)
Staff's views on the tool and process of using it
Although it was intended to interview carers following reviews to gain their views about the process this did not prove possible for two reasons. Research time was not available at this point in the project, partly due to the extended deadlines, and also staff involved in the project felt that it might be too confusing for many of the carers who had already been through an assessment, a review and a research interview. Instead staff fed back their views and observations of carers' experience through workshops and through written feedback after each review. As with the assessment questionnaires, this form was completed variously by carers alone, mostly initiated or followed up with personal discussion, or by the assessor in conjunction with the carer. Neither assessors, nor carers (according to staff) had significant difficulty using the Carer's Feedback Form. Most found it a straightforward and useful tool in the review process which gave further recognition and validation to the carer's perspective. In approximately half the reviews, assessors found that the process either revealed positive outcomes which they had not fully expected, or highlighted necessary adjustments to the care package which would assist achievement of desired outcomes. It also indicated strengths and weaknesses in the way that services were delivered which could affect achievement of outcomes.

In a number of situations staff cited significant benefits arising from the *process* of using this tool for their work with carers, both in terms of helping to achieve desired outcomes, or bringing about a new perspective on the carer's situation (for the carer, the user, or the worker). It was felt that a focus on outcomes at the review stage helped in clarifying risks and highlighting how care plans could be amended in order to achieve maximum benefits for both user and carer. In one instance the assessor felt that explicit attention to outcomes achieved for the carers, discussed openly at the review in the presence of the service user, helped to manage a conflict of interest which had arisen. Other assessors commented on the high degree of satisfaction with services which emerged through using the form or the way it reinforced the importance to carers of particular services. Receiving such positive feedback was both a surprise and boost to individual assessors' morale.

From the information available, 60 per cent of reviews undertaken using the Carer's Feedback Form took either no extra time or less than half an hour longer than an ordinary review would have taken. Nevertheless, discussions in the wider group (not all of whom had used the form) indicated mixed views about how easily this approach could and should be incorporated into the routine practice of assessors, within the resources available, particularly if it involves a separate interview with the carer which was not widely seen as a routine part of existing practice. Some tension would seem inevitable on this issue, given the difficulty for social services at a national level in undertaking reviews routinely (Challis *et al.*, 1998). One person reported that they would have closed some cases if it had not been a requirement to review outcomes for the project. If a case is closed, within current practice, staff would not be expected to check the outcome of the work beyond ascertaining at the point of closure (usually within four to six weeks) that the situation is stable and the services are satisfactory. It was suggested that there is insufficient time to do more than this. Others felt strongly that reviews should be a regular, ongoing process, with results fed back into the system. There was also acknowledgement that it is not responsible to provide services without reviewing whether they are effective. A compromise suggestion was that it may be possible to regularly review a sub-sample, perhaps those who had the most expensive package of care.

Analysis of the results
The feedback from carers elicited through these forms was analysed manually by the researcher involved in the development process. Data from such a small sample is not statistically significant and caution is therefore advised about drawing too many conclusions from the results. The aim of analysis was rather to demonstrate *the type* of information that might be elicited from such an exercise and to consider different ways of presenting and using it. Further consideration and resources would be needed to enable larger samples to be collated and analysed. However, until the potential benefits are recognised there may be little incentive or motivation to engage with such an exercise.

This small-scale exercise did appear to elicit some potentially useful outcomes information, the value of which could be extended if such an exercise was carried out regularly or routinely in a manner that attempted to ensure a degree of representativeness across the spectrum of carers. The Carer's Feedback Form would also lend itself, with some modification, to periodic surveys of carers as well as use within reviews, preferably linking it to opportunities for review or re-assessment for those who needed it. The analysis of feedback from this group of 15 carers also highlighted some interesting issues.

Variation between outcomes anticipated and outcomes achieved
The majority of outcomes prioritised by carers at the point of assessment had been achieved at least to some extent by the review stage. Overall a greater level of impact was reported by carers than was anticipated by workers (though not always for the same individuals). At the same time, for all domains, there were a few carers reporting no positive impact when assessors had anticipated one. Overall, 70 per cent of the outcomes anticipated by assessors were reported by carers to be achieved at least to some extent at the point of review. Those domains for which there was most frequent variation (i.e. in three or more instances) between the outcomes anticipated by assessors and the improvements reported by carers are listed in Table 4.5. The figures indicate the number of carers out of the total of 15 reviewed.

Table 4.5: Variation in outcomes anticipated and achieved

Improvement to:	Anticipated by assessor but not achieved	Not anticipated by assessor but achieved
Physical health or well-being	6	3
Significant relationships	3	7
Sense of expertise in caring	3	6
Satisfaction/reward in caring	3	4
Ability to cope with physical/ practical tasks of caring	3	4

Reasons for variation between the outcomes predicted and those achieved are not clear and may be varied. Firstly, given that the comparison is between different perceptions of outcomes, at different points in time a degree of variation is inevitable. These differences may be accentuated due to the fact, as indicated earlier, that very few assessors chose to check their conclusions about desired outcomes with carers. In addition, assessors may be cautious about raising expectations about what might be achieved, and may be particularly reticent about specifying more sensitive areas of impact such as relationships. The positive impact on relationships reported by carers may sometimes be a by-product of other anticipated outcomes, such as 'time to self' or 'ability to have a life of one's own' which would feature more prominently in assessors' thinking. Similarly, a sense of satisfaction and expertise in caring may be less familiar as explicit targets of intervention for assessors, with these impacts arising from other outcomes achieved, for example a sense of shared responsibility, which was achieved in nine of the ten instances anticipated. The lack of achievement of certain outcomes, for example health improvements, may be to do with the timing of the review (not sufficient time for improvements to have occurred) or different subjective interpretations as to what would constitute improvement in health. Bringing about a greater sense of expertise or increasing satisfaction in care-giving may also call for some less standardised responses which may not always have been possible for the assessor to provide, such as training, ongoing support or counselling. While all these explanations may have some basis in reality, it may also be that outcomes are genuinely hard to predict with any accuracy. Nonetheless, it would seem to be important that assessors aim as far as possible to gear services to achieve the impacts that carers and service users feel are of greatest significance, and that review processes are not restricted to evaluating only the outcomes which were intended at assessment.

Carers' views about outcomes achieved - the type of information elicited
Carers' own comments about the benefits of services were diverse in nature, reflecting their own subjective interpretation and often relating to the package of care received rather than to single services. However, some clear themes emerged. The type of help most frequently cited as beneficial from carers' points of view were the range of services which provided a break from caring, enabling carers to enjoy more time to themselves, relaxing, seeing friends and family, going to the theatre or on holiday and generally alleviating stress. These benefits closely relate to the outcomes framework referred to in this report.

When asked about impacts on specific aspects of their quality of life or capacity to manage caring, the most frequently cited outcomes achieved for carers were those relating to improvements in emotional health and well-being:
• feeling emotionally supported (not alone/having someone to talk to if needed) improved emotional/mental health (feelings of reduced stress, anxiety, depression)
• peace of mind (being less worried about the well-being of the person cared for).

It is suggested by some comments from carers both through the feedback form and the evaluation interviews, that these outcomes may be in part due to the assessment process and the sense of recognition and being valued that was gained, as well as to services provided subsequently. Almost as frequently, carers cited improvements which were conceivably linked to improved emotional/mental health, including: an increased ability to have a life of their own, a sense of shared responsibility, more positive relationships, an improved sense of expertise and ability to manage practical tasks.

Generally this group of carers were very positive about the quality of services received and the way they were delivered, and felt that they were good value for money. They particularly valued punctuality, reliability and flexibility in a number of services and conversely it was the lack of these qualities which were the main source of negative comment in a minority of instances. Some 'process outcomes' were highlighted, which might indicate a need for improvement in some aspects of service delivery, or at least further consultation:

- recognising the carer's expertise
- achieving a better 'fit' with their lives and routines
- allowing carers more of a say in the way help is provided.

Comparing carers, own overall sense of coping at two points in time (as indicated on the Carer's Needs Form and the Carer's Feedback Form) may provide further evidence of the impact of services, if seen in context. For this group of carers, two people were not coping as well as they would like at the review stage, but it would appear that some stability had been maintained for seven people and definite improvement in overall coping for five. Although there may be a variety of reasons for these results, the general feedback from carers suggested that service intervention had made a significant contribution towards either maintaining or improving both their quality of life and their capacity to continue caring.

Comments on analysis

The process of analysis indicated that some changes to the form might facilitate aggregation in future and that some aspects of the content are more easily aggregated than others. Interpretation of carers' ratings and comments was assisted by the researcher's broader knowledge of the cases and written feedback from staff as part of the evaluation. This points to the value of including some factual information about the carer's circumstances, and staff's perspectives on outcomes achieved in order to put the carer's feedback in some context.

Staff reactions to aggregated information and issues in interpretation

Initial presentation of this aggregate feedback to staff and managers who had participated in the project received mixed reactions (managers being more positive than staff). Some staff questioned whether carers can be honest about their views if reviews are undertaken by those responsible for assessing and providing services. A number of people thought it might be better to have someone independent of services undertaking reviews. This may indeed be possible within this authority which is about to follow the practice adopted elsewhere, of appointing reviewing officers (Challis *et al.*, 1998). Concerns were also raised about the possible interpretation and use of data from the forms particularly if there is a low response rate or a low level of reviewing. In a small sample such as this, positive results may lead to complacency whereas as some staff suggested, those who do not respond may include carers who have not had such a good experience of services, or those who have most difficulty accessing services. Therefore, efforts need to be made to ensure a balanced and representative cross-section of carers for the results to be meaningful and acceptable to staff whose cooperation is a vital element in a successful monitoring system. The importance of an effective 'feedback loop' was thus reinforced in this discussion (Nocon and Qureshi, 1996).

Bearing in mind some of the practical considerations raised, the limited evidence from this project would suggest that the Carer's Feedback Form could provide the basis of a useful and manageable tool both from a practice point of view and for collecting outcomes information. Further work would be needed to test response rates and the usefulness of information elicited in a more systematic way.

8. GENERALISABILITY

The development process - staff views

Feedback from staff on the process of development was considered important in order to identify the factors which might help and hinder the introduction of similar systems elsewhere. In a context of continuous change and development and acute pressure on staff, anticipating obstacles and opportunities to change will be a vital component in planning for successful implementation of an outcomes approach.

Figure 4.8: Staff views on the development process

Key points

- Staff were motivated by an interest in improving practice
- Staff most enjoyed meeting with other colleagues and carers, having time to think, and being able to influence developments for carers
- The biggest source of difficulty was individual time constraints making it difficult to fulfill their original commitment to the project
- Sharing experiences, views and difficulties in the workshops was crucial in maintaining interest and participation
- To integrate an outcomes approach into mainstream practice, staff need:
  - information, training, opportunities to reflect on practice
  - ongoing support and an enthusiastic lead from managers

Overall approach

In considering the extent to which the approach and tools used and developed in the project are more widely applicable, it is important to differentiate between key principles, core elements of a system and particular methods. It would not be necessary for agencies to adopt all the tools wholesale if there were existing methods of achieving the same purposes. The process of introducing such a change would ideally include consultation with all relevant stakeholders, with a view to tackling practical concerns and obstacles and gaining ownership. This process may well lead to adaptation so that tools are seen to fit with existing practices and procedures. In adapting the tools it would be important to bear in mind the key principles and core elements outlined below (see Figures 4.9 and 4.10). Neglect of these (rather than the precise methods) may risk a more mechanistic approach perceived as an administrative chore, unrelated to good practice, thus alienating staff and carers.

Figure 4: Key principles underpinning an integrated outcomes approach (At an individual level)

- The definition and recording of outcomes are carer-centred, specific and relevant to the individual concerned

- Evaluation of outcomes achieved should begin with clarity about outcomes intended

- Reaching a common understanding about outcomes to be aimed for needs thorough and sensitive exploration at assessment

- The carer is actively engaged as 'expert' in the process of identifying and reviewing outcomes

- The professional offers the carer choice about the level of assessment and means of participation, and facilitates the process accordingly (eg taking into account language, help with forms, privacy, time to think about their needs in advance)

- A distinct, though not necessarily separate, focus on the carer's desired outcomes is a starting point for understanding and mediating any differing interests from those of the user

**Figure 4.10: Core elements of an integrated outcomes system
(At a service/organisational level)**

> ▸ **A clear conceptual framework**

> ▸ **An effective screening process** to determine who should be assessed and at what level

> ▸ **A method (or methods) of clarifying and agreeing outcomes** to be achieved with individual carers within the assessment process

> ▸ **A method (or methods) of gaining feedback from carers** about progress towards outcomes identified, other impacts (ie those not specifically intended) and changing needs

> ▸ **A means of summarising and clearly recording** outcomes to be achieved (at an individual level) in order that they can tracked at an individual level and also aggregated for management/planning purposes

> ▸ **A system for aggregating, analysing and feeding back outcomes** information collected at assessment and review

> ▸ **Training and support for staff** in understanding and implementing the system and the underpinning principles and approach

Wider applicability of the specific tools
Wider applicability of the Carers' Indices

Where authorities do not have separate, detailed carer-assessment documentation these tools, used selectively, would offer a useful tool for an in-depth assessment to assist the task of identifying outcomes to be achieved. They may also be used to supplement existing carer-assessment forms in some instances, for example, where carers would welcome the chance to prepare for an assessment interview or as a means of offering greater depth. For some carers these questionnaires may have some advantages over more open-ended styles of 'self-assessment' forms which require a lot more descriptive writing, also offering a more rounded view of the positive as well as difficult aspects of their situations. Incorporation into assessment processes should be accompanied by guidance (Nolan et al., 1998) and training for staff. However, where existing detailed assessment forms are in place and seen to be working well agencies may decide these will fulfil the same purpose, perhaps with some minor adjustments.

Wider applicability of the Carer's Needs Form

A tool for a first stage assessment, or more basic assessment (for carers who may not wish, or be ready to engage in, a detailed exploration of their needs) may be less commonly available to practitioners and the Carer's Needs Form may therefore offer a useful supplement to existing documentation. The opportunity for carers to comment directly about desired outcomes, the differences they would like services to make, may be an important component to incorporate into existing assessment forms (if such exist). The value of a first stage assessment in screening for an in-depth approach has been highlighted within the COPE project (Carers of Older People in Europe) (Nolan and Philp, 1999).

Wider applicability of the Summary of Carer's Outcomes and Needs

This tool, or something similar, is an essential component to ensure conclusions are documented both for individual care planning and monitoring and for the purposes of aggregation. Experience suggests that a combination of qualitative and quantitative information is most helpful to practitioners and will assist interpretation of the information at the point of aggregation. The following qualitative components have proved useful in this project:

- an analysis/summary of the main difficulties, satisfactions and preferred coping strategies
- a descriptive summary of outcomes intended in relation to these carers' priority outcomes, and preferences about services and the way these should be delivered.

The qualitative information can then be summarised in a checklist (tick-box) format, using a predetermined list of outcome domains which services are intended to impact. This can act both as an aide-memoire to staff and a source of reference for monitoring/reviewing outcomes.

Wider applicability of the Carer's Feedback Form

Evidence suggests that existing review systems do not generally incorporate a focus on outcomes, and there is less likely to be documentation which allows the carer to give specific feedback, beyond overall satisfaction with services (Challis *et al.*, 1998). This tool should therefore be readily adoptable (adjusted for local considerations where necessary). It should easily supplement existing review procedures although these might be revisited to ensure conclusions about outcomes can be clearly recorded.

110

Training and development

Some training and a process of planned change and development for staff are considered essential to successful implementation of an outcomes approach to carer assessment and review. This would ideally include or lead to:

Knowledge/understanding of:

- the complexities of care-giving and helpful models to support practice (e.g. the Exchange model of assessment)
- the outcomes framework described in Section 2
- the purpose/value of an outcomes approach in practice
- reasons for collecting outcomes information and its potential use
- the theory underpinning the specific tools (eg stress, coping and satisfaction in caring).

Opportunities to:

- influence the process of introduction/adaptation of tools alongside existing systems
- comment on the tools, try them out in a safe environment, or on a trial basis in routine practice
- reflect on their experience, feed back issues and concerns and learn from the experience of others
- listen to/learn from carers' experiences.

In addition it may be useful for agencies to review existing induction/training opportunities in relation to working with carers and the extent to which these equip staff at all levels to provide an effective service for carers. There is a range of useful sources of guidance for practitioners and managers which may assist this task.

8. CONCLUSION

It is of the utmost importance to recognise that the tools are designed to assist sensitive and skilled practice in carer assessment rather than being standardised instruments which can be uniformly applied for the purpose of data collection. Much will depend on the extent to which practitioners perceive congruence with their practice or can be enabled to adapt their practice accordingly. The more the tools can be integrated with effective practice, the greater the likelihood of services being targeted to achieve individualised outcomes and meaningful outcomes information being collected.

The emphasis of this project has been to develop a method of collecting outcomes information which could work in routine practice, and which the authority concerned could implement. The indications are that this approach has been valued overall and that it makes a difference. Following further developments to refine paperwork and integrate the approach with the user assessment, this authority hopes to implement the approach more widely.

The next logical step would be to test the use of this approach more systematically within a number of different settings to ascertain:

- the extent to which the tools can be easily adopted/adapted by other authorities
- what difference the use of the tools make to practice and outcomes compared to more traditional approaches
- how outcomes information collected as part of routine practice can be utilised within broader systems of performance management and service planning and development.

The potential benefits of introducing an outcomes approach into carer assessment and review for all stakeholders must be balanced with an appreciation of the real obstacles and likely costs. This will require a subtle but significant shift in the existing culture of Social Services Departments, which will be assisted by pro-active, systematic and enabling change management. It may also require a review of the resources (staff time and skill in particular) currently available to achieve high quality carer assessment and review. If an outcomes approach is to become a driving force for continual improvement in practice, rather than simply a dry and detached monitoring exercise, it must be based on thorough, sensitive assessment and review processes which enable individualised outcomes to be clearly identified, negotiated and recorded in a way that actively involves the carer (and service user) as experts in their own situation.

SUMMARY OF CHAPTER FOUR

Aims and purpose of project

This project aimed to address a number of current policy and practice concerns by developing and testing tools with a view to:
- assisting outcomes-focused practice in carer assessment and review
- enabling information about outcomes to be collected as part of routine practice.

Integrating an outcomes focus into practice was seen as a crucial step towards facilitating the routine collection of outcomes information which would be meaningful and useful to all concerned. Building on the findings of the research phase of this programme and other studies, carers' views of valued outcomes are central to the framework developed in this project. The tools are designed to encourage a more systematic, explicit and participative approach to carer assessment and review in which clear communication about, and recording of, outcomes intended and achieved are seen as integral to good practice.

Methods

The approach emerging from this project was developed collaboratively with carers, frontline staff, and managers in one authority. The emphasis was on understanding the possible barriers and facilitators to achieving the aims outlined above and finding methods which worked and were seen to be useful to all stakeholders. The project adopted some existing research-based instruments and developed others, including a range of self-completion questionnaires for carers, to assist informed discussion with assessors about outcomes, and a summary tool for assessors to record conclusions. These tools were tested by 14 practitioners within assessment of 37 carers (some already known to the authority and some who were newly referred) and 15 reviews. Ongoing dialogue and in-depth interviews with staff and carers enabled both the benefits and the challenges of implementing such an approach to be highlighted.

Barriers and facilitators to implementing a carer-centred, outcomes approach

A number of aspects within the organisational context and professional/practice culture were identified as potential barriers or challenges to the proposed approach:
- The significant change agenda, increasing budget constraints and plans for restructuring which emerged as the project progressed
- The existing model of care management which tends to be user focused, task-orientated (towards identifying need and providing services) and time-limited (aiming to withdraw within six weeks)
- The additional burden on limited care management resources created by the more distinct and detailed approach to carer assessment
- The emphasis on the expertise of the carer could require a significant shift in orientation and approach.

At the same time a number of key factors both within the context and culture of the participating authority and in the chosen approach to development had a positive impact:

- Carers' participation and influence at various stages ensured tools were relevant and useful and helped to address staff's initial concerns
- Frontline staff were motivated to improve practice, and perceived the need for more structured recording for carers
- Opportunities for regular discussion and reflection on experience throughout the project, helped to reinforce the value of an outcomes approach, maintain interest and tackle problems and concerns as they arose
- Managers viewed these developments as contributing to a range of key agendas; their active involvement and support was appreciated by staff, and provided legitimation.

Key messages emerging so far
At an individual level:
- Carers felt recognised and 'listened to'
- Many staff have valued the clearer focus in their work and the feedback gained
- Awareness and understanding of carers' needs and desired outcomes was enhanced
- There was evidence of care plans becoming more targeted or creative
- The tools can assist an outcomes focus within skilled and sensitive practice
- Professional judgement and flexibility are essential to determine for whom, when and how the tools might be used most effectively (within agreed criteria).

At an organisational level:
- Aggregated information is potentially useful - more systematic testing needed
- Limited resources and pressures on care management may jeopardise the definition and effective monitoring of individualised outcomes and make information collected less meaningful
- Integrating an outcomes focus into mainstream practice requires a subtle but significant shift in orientation at an individual and organisational level
- This will best be achieved by a planned and participatory process of change, in which staff receive training and support and all stakeholders are able to influence and own the detailed developments.

What next?
The evidence from this project suggests that an outcomes approach in carer assessment and review can make a difference at a number of levels, but now needs to be tested more systematically in a variety of settings, along with the practicalities of implementation. The development of a training resource pack is planned to assist authorities with this task.

References

Aneshensel, C.S., Pearlin, L.I., Mullan, J.T., Zarit, S.H. and Whitlatch, C.J. (1995) *Profiles in Caregiving. The Unexpected Career,* London: Academic Press Inc.

Arksey, H., Hepworth, D. and Qureshi, H. (1999) *Carers' needs and the Carers (Recognition and Services) Act 1995: an evaluation of the process and outcomes of assessment,* York: SPRU.

Bowers, B. J. (1987) *Inter-generational care giving: adult caregivers and their ageing parents, Advances in Nursing Science,* 9 (2), 20-31.

Challis, D., Darton, R., Hughes, J., Stewart, K. and Weiner, K. (1998) *Care management study: report on national data,* and *Care management study: care management arrangements,* London: Department of Health.

Department of Health (1998) *Modernising Social Services,* London: Department of Health.

Department of Health (1999) *Caring about Carers: A National Strategy for Carers,* London: Department of Health.

Department of Health (2001) *A Practitioner's Guide to Carers' Assessments under the Carers and Disabled Children Act 2000,* London: Department of Health.

Fruin, D. (1998) *A matter of chance for carers? Inspection of local authority support for carers,* London: Department of Health.

Mahoney, F.I. and Barthel, D.W. (1965) 'Functional evaluation: the Barthel Index', *Maryland State Medical Journal* 14, 61-5.

(The) Management Centre (1995*) Project Management Handbook,* The Management Centre: London

Moriarty, J. and Webb, S. (2000) *Part of their lives: community care for older people with dementia,* Bristol: The Policy Press.

Nocon, A. and Qureshi, H. (1996) *Outcomes of community care for users and carers: a social services perspective,* Buckingham: Open University Press.

Nolan, M., Keady, J. and Grant, G. (1995) 'CAMI: A basis for assessment and support with family carers', *British Journal of Nursing* 4 (14).

Nolan, M., Grant, G. and Keady, J. (1996) *Understanding family care: a multidimensional model of caring and coping,* Buckingham: Open University Press.

115

Nolan, M., Grant, G. and Keady, J. (1998) *Assessing the needs of family carers: a guide for practitioners*, Brighton: Pavilion Publishing.

Nolan, M. and Philp, I. (1999) 'COPE: Towards a comprehensive assessment of a caregiver need', *British Journal of Nursing* 8 (20), 1364-72.

Office for National Statistics, Social Survey Division (1997) *Living in Britain: results from the 1995 General Household Survey*, London: The Stationery Office.

Patmore, C., Qureshi, H., Nicholas, E. and Bamford, C. (1998) *Outcomes for older people and their family carers: stage 1* Report to Department of Health DH 1537 York: University of York, Social Policy Research Unit.

Richards, S. (2000) 'Bridging the Divide: Elders and the Assessment Process', *British Journal of Social Work* 30, 37-49.

Seddon, D. (1999) *Carers of elderly people with dementia: assessment and the Carers (Recognition and Services) Act 1995*, Bangor: Centre for Social Policy Research and Development.

Smale, G. (1996) *Mapping change & innovation*, London: HMSO.

Smale, G., Tuson, G., Biehal, N. and Marsh, P. (1993) *Empowerment, Assessment, Care Management and the Skilled Worker,* National Institute for Social Work Practice and Development Exchange, London: HMSO.

Smith, G.C., Smith, M.F. and Toseland, R.W. (1991) Problems identified by family caregivers in counselling, *The Gerontologist* 31(1), 15-22.

Twigg, J. (1989) 'Models of carers: how do social care agencies conceptualise their relationship with informal carers?', *Journal of Social Policy* 18 (1), 53-66.

Twigg, J. and Atkin, K. (1994) *Carers perceived: policy and practice in informal care*, Buckingham: Open University Press.

APPENDICES TO CHAPTER FOUR

The following are supplied as appendices:

- **Table A4.1: Outcomes for Carers - Development Process**
- **Carers' Reference Group: Terms of Reference**

Assessment Tools:

- **Carer's Needs Form** (Carer's Needs - How can we help you)

- **The Carers' Indices:**
  - ▸ Carers' Assessment of Difficulties Index (CADI)
  - ▸ Carers' Assessment of Satisfactions Index (CASI)
  - ▸ Carers' Assessment of Managing Index (CAMI)

- **Summary of Carer's Outcomes and Needs**

Revised/additional Assessment Tools:

Following evaluation and feedback from the project, some tools were revised, in the light of experience and subject to a second phase of trial use by a small group of practitioners.

- **Summary of Carer's Assessment**
  - intended for use where a separate carer's assessment has been undertaken whether or not the user is present. This replaces the Summary of Carer's Outcomes and Needs, and is used in conjunction with the Assessment Summary (see Chapter 2)

- **Revised Carer's Needs Page**
  - a page within the 'general assessment of need' for the user aiming to assist decision making about who should receive a carer's assessment

- **Key Points for Assessors** - Guidance Notes

Review documentation:

- **Sample letter to accompany the Carer's Feedback form**

- **Carer's Feedback form**

- **Profile of carers**

Table A4.1 Outcomes for Carers – Development Process

KEY STAGES/ DATES	TASKS	MECHANISMS TO ACHIEVE TASKS
1. Exploratory (prior to July 98)	Establish interest, explore initial ideas, gain agreement from Senior Managers	Research phase of project. Meetings with key people. Overall Advisory group for Outcomes work
2. Planning July 98 - Jan 99	• Set up Planning/Steering group for project (staff members and SPRU) • Check out initial ideas for "fit" with current practice • Develop project plan • Design tools (SPRU) in consultation with Planning Group and Carers' Reference Group • Recruit carers for Carers' Reference Group • Engage operational managers and recruit staff for participation in pilot • Initial testing of tools	• Project Planning Group • Carers' Reference Group • Meeting with operational managers • Publicity leaflets for staff and carers
3. Training and Preparation Feb - March 99	• Training and preparation of staff volunteers • Consultation on tools/amendments • Carers Audit (to discover number and type of carer currently on caseloads) • Preparation of written guidance (about tools and project requirements) • Mechanisms for ongoing support, feedback and evaluation established	3.2.99 — Introductory Briefing Session — ½ day staff; 15.2.99 — Training and development workshop *(focus on use of tools)* — for staff with carer input; 16.3.99 — Development workshop *(focus on evaluation/ support mechanisms)* — ½ day - staff; & Planning Group meetings
4. Experimentation April - Oct 99	• Testing of assessment tools in routine practice • Design and testing of tool for reviewing outcomes Carer's Feedback form • Ongoing dialogue with staff	• three development workshops for staff - May, July, October • telephone calls by researcher and individual staff and offer support/resolve difficulties • Newsletters and update staff on overall progress

Table A4. 1   Outcomes for Carers – Development Process

KEY STAGES/ DATES	TASKS	MECHANISMS TO ACHIEVE TASKS
5. Evaluation and feedback Aug 99 - Feb 00	• (Aug/Sept) Evaluation interviews with carers (re assessment process) • (Oct/Nov) Evaluation interviews with staff (overall experience of project) • Analysis and feedback to staff of key findings	• Undertaken by independent researcher (i.e. not involved with development process) • Independent researcher (i.e. not involved with development process) • Two development workshops (Dec 99 & Feb 2000) involved all researchers
6. Dissemination/Future Planning Feb - onwards	• Distilling learning from the experience of the project • Further revision of documentation and integration with user assessment • [Wider dissemination]	• Joint Planning Group (reps from each project) • Overall Outcomes Advisory Group • Briefing of Senior Manager

CARERS' REFERENCE GROUP
Terms of Reference

Role and Purpose

1. To enable carers' expertise and experience to influence all key stages of project development and implementation.

2. To ensure that the work of the project will be as relevant and as helpful as possible for carers.

3. To test, and give views on, some of the proposed new ways of working.

4. To contribute, where appropriate, to project development workshops, along with staff and managers in Social Services.

Setting the Scene for Working Together

Points agreed with carers at first meeting:

1. Carers' experience and expertise is essential to the project. (Your views count)

2. All experiences and views shared in the group meetings will remain confidential to the group. This means that any verbal reports or written record of these experiences will ensure that the identity of individuals is protected.

3. We will stick to agreed times for beginning and ending meetings (recognising carers' other commitments).

4. We will try to ensure a balance between getting through the tasks that need to be done to move the project forward and allowing enough time for discussion of experiences which relate to these.

5. Carers should feel free to ask if anything is not made clear (eg. Social Services jargon)

6. Carers may say 'No' to participating in any aspect of the project they do not feel happy about.

7. Feed back is welcome at any stage on the Carers' Reference Group or the way the project is developing.

**Confidential**

CARER'S NEEDS - HOW CAN WE HELP YOU?

This questionnaire, and any information you provide is intended to help the Social Services Department talk with you about the type of help which would be most useful to you at this point in time (*see back page for more information*).

Carers' situations vary. Some may provide regular physical care, some may need to do a lot of prompting and encouraging. Others may have to respond to unpredictable behaviour. Each situation presents its own particular challenges. Whatever your situation, the questions below aim to highlight the more difficult areas with which you might like some help. However, knowing about the positive aspects can also help to work out how to tackle the difficulties!

Please answer the questions as they apply to you generally at the moment - we know that things can change over time and fluctuate from day to day. **You don't have to fill in any parts of the form you don't wish to. If you would prefer that someone fill it in with you please let us know.**

A. About you and the person/people you care for

Your name (carer) ....

Your address ....

.... Postcode ....

Phone number   Home   ....

                 Other (day) ....

Date of birth ....

Ethnic origin ....

Language used ....

....

....

Name of the main person(s) you support/care for .... Their d.o.b. ....

Your relationship to them ....

Their address (if different from above) ....

....

Do you support/care for other people who are disabled or ill?

Name	Age	Your relationship to them
....	....	....
....	....	....

Your other commitments

☐ I am working full-time   ☐ I am working part-time

☐ I am studying full-time   ☐ I am studying part-time

☐ I care for children   ☐ Other commitments

Comments

B. About the care/support you provide

The care/support I provide includes:

☐ Physical care (e.g. help to wash, dress, use toilet) ☐ Financial management

☐ Practical help (e.g. cooking, cleaning, shopping) ☐ Emotional support

☐ Generally keeping an eye on them (e.g. checking on ☐ Other ....
safety, well being)

Comments ....
....

To provide this care means I am involved:

☐ All the time (can't leave the person alone) ☐ Several times a week

☐ Several times a day ☐ Once a week or less

☐ Once a day (on average)

Comments ....
....

C. How caring affects you

1. **I find caring gives me:**

A great deal of satisfaction	Some satisfaction	No real satisfaction
☐	☐	☐

Comments: ....
....

2. **I find caring creates:**

No major difficulties	Some difficulty	A lot of difficulties
☐	☐	☐

Comments: ....
....

3. **At the moment I feel:**

Able to cope with most/all aspects of caring	I'm not coping as well as I'd like to	It can be up and down from day to day	I can't carry on as things are
☐	☐	☐	☐

Comments: ....
....

4a. The biggest difficulties I have right now are related to:

Physical/practical aspects of caring	My health	Not getting enough sleep	Emotional stress	Finances	Other
☐	☐	☐	☐	☐	☐

Comments:

Form A2/C1

4b. I am concerned about how my caring responsibilities affect

My relationship with the person I care for	My relationship with others	My work/studies	My other commitments	Social life and interests
☐	☐	☐	☐	☐

Comments: ....

....

4c. What I would like most to change in relation to these difficulties is:

....

....

....

....

D. What type of help would be most useful?

1. The opportunity to talk to someone about my situation   ☐

   a. I would prefer to talk separately from the person I care for   ☐

   b. I would prefer the person I care for to be present   ☐

2. More information/advice about: Please say if there is anything in particular in the space below

a. the health or condition of the person I care for   ☐   ....

b. the services available to help   ☐   ....

c. other   ☐   ....

3. Practical help or advice with aspects of caring   ☐

   In particular   ....

....

4. Help to maintain my own health, quality of life or other commitments   ☐

   In particular   ....

....

5. Time off/a break from caring (regular or occasional)   ☐

   The sort of break (or time off) I would find most helpful is   ....

....

6. Other type of help   ....

....

....

....

E. Please use the space provided below to add any other comments, concerns or suggestions.

FURTHER INFORMATION

1. **About your rights**

   If the care or support you are providing, or intend to provide, is of a 'regular and substantial' nature, you have a right, under the Carers' (Recognition and Services) Act 1995, to ask for an assessment of your own needs as a carer. The local authority has a duty to take this assessment into consideration when they are deciding how best to help the person you care for. Ask for a leaflet about this if you have not received one already. An 'assessment' simply means that a member of Social Services Staff (usually a Social Worker or Home Care Organiser) would arrange to talk to you about your situation to find out how we might help. This questionnaire is a first step in that process.

2. **What to do with the form once completed**

   When you have completed this form, please hand it in person or send it by post to the person who gave it to you.

3. **What happens next?**

   If you have indicated on the form that you would like some help, or would like to talk to someone, we will contact you as soon as possible to arrange a time to meet with you. The information you provide on this form will be a helpful starting point for discussion about your situation. We will then tell you about the range of help which might be offered and do our best to make arrangements which suit you. Sometimes financial constraints or service limitations may prevent us from meeting all your requirements. If so, we will explain fully the reasons and suggest any alternative options.

4. **What happens to the information you provide?**

   With your permission, it would be helpful if we can keep a copy of the completed form for our files. This will be useful to refer to at a later date when we check how any arrangements we make are working for you. The information will not be shared with any one else without asking you first.

IF THERE IS ANYTHING ELSE YOU WOULD LIKE TO KNOW, PLEASE ASK.

THANK YOU VERY MUCH FOR TAKING
THE TIME TO COMPLETE THIS FORM.

THE CARERS' INDICES
(CADI, CASI, CAMI)

These instruments have been included by kind permission of the authors.

They are available for copying on purchase of the following publication:

"Assessing the Needs of Family Carers: A guide for practitioners"
by Mike Nolan, Gordon Grant, John Keady

Pavilion Publishing (Brighton) Ltd
The Ironworks, Cheapside,
Brighton, East Sussex, BN1 4GD
Telephone 01273 623222
Fax 01273 625526
E-mail: pavpub@pavilion.co.uk

The above publication includes the Carers' Indices in questionnaire and card
format together with permission for photocopying, more detailed guidance on
how to use the instruments and the theory behind them.

Thank you for your co-operation.

Social Policy Research Unit
University of York
August 2001

Carers' Assessment of Difficulties Index   (CADI)

CADI is a 30-item index and contains a series of statements which carers have made about the difficulties they face. Carefully read each statement and show if it applies by placing a tick in the space available. Together, responses can be used as the basis for discussing an agreed programme of support with the carer.

THIS STATEMENT APPLIES TO ME AND I FIND IT:

CARING CAN BE DIFFICULT BECAUSE:	This does not apply to me	Not stressful	Stressful	Very stressful
1 I don't have enough private time for myself.				
2 I can feel helpless/not in control of the situation.				
3 I can't devote enough time to other family members.				
4 It causes financial difficulties.				
5 The person I care for can play me up.				
6 The person I care for is immobile/has problems getting about.				
7 Professional workers don't seem to appreciate the problems carers face.				
8 It restricts my social life/outside interests.				
9 It can put a strain on family relationships.				
10 It is physically tiring.				
11 The person I care for can demand too much of me.				
12 I no longer have a meaningful relationship with the person I care for.				
13 The person I care for needs a lot of help with personal care.				
14 The person I care for doesn't always help as much as they could.				
15 My sleep is affected.				
16 Relatives don't keep in touch as often as I'd like.				
17 I feel angry about the situation.				
18 I can't see friends as often as I'd like.				
19 My emotional well-being suffers.				
20 I can't have a break or take a holiday.				

Continued/...

Assessing the Needs of Family Carers © Mike Nolan, Gordon Grant, John Keady, 1998.

THIS STATEMENT APPLIES TO ME AND I FIND IT:

CARING CAN BE DIFFICULT BECAUSE:

	This does not apply to me	Not stressful	Stressful	Very stressful
21 My standard of living has fallen.				
22 The person I care for doesn't always appreciate what I do.				
23 My physical health has suffered.				
24 The person I care for is incontinent.				
25 The behaviour of the person I care for is a problem.				
26 There is no satisfaction to be gained from caring.				
27 I don't get enough help from health and social services.				
28 Some family members don't help as much as they could.				
29 I can't relax because I worry about caring.				
30 I feel guilty about the situation.				

Please add below any further difficulties you face and indicate how stressful you find them:

Carers' Assessment of Satisfactions Index (CASI)

CASI is a 30-item index and contains a series of statements which carers have made about the satisfactions they have experienced. Carefully read each statement and show if it applies by placing a tick in the space available. Together, responses can be used as the basis for discussing an agreed programme of support with the carer.

THIS APPLIES TO ME AND PROVIDES ME WITH:

CARING CAN BE SATISFYING BECAUSE:	This does not apply to me	No real satisfaction	Quite a lot of satisfaction	A great deal of satisfaction
1 Caring has allowed me to develop new skills and abilities.				
2 The person I care for is appreciative of what I do.				
3 Caring has brought me closer to the person I care for.				
4 It's good to see small improvements in their condition.				
5 I am able to help the person I care for reach their full potential.				
6 I am able to repay their past acts of kindness.				
7 Caring provides a challenge.				
8 Despite all their problems the person I care for does not grumble or moan.				
9 It is nice to see the person I care for clean, comfortable and well turned out.				
10 Caring enables me to fulfil my sense of duty.				
11 I am the sort of person who enjoys helping people.				
12 I get pleasure from seeing the person I care for happy.				
13 It's good to help the person I care for overcome difficulties and problems.				
14 It's nice when something I do gives the person I care for pleasure.				
15 Knowing the person I care for the way I do, means I can give better care than anyone else.				
16 Caring has helped me to grow and develop as a person.				
17 It's nice to feel appreciated by those family and friends I value.				

Continued/...

NOT TO BE COPIED OR USED WITHOUT PERMISSION FROM AUTHORS BELOW

Assessing the Needs of Family Carers © Mike Nolan, Gordon Grant, John Keady, 1998.

THIS APPLIES TO ME
AND PROVIDES ME WITH:

CARING CAN BE SATISFYING BECAUSE:	This does not apply to me	No real satisfaction	Quite a lot of satisfaction	A great deal of satisfaction
18 Caring has strengthened close family ties and relationships.				
19 It helps to stop me from feeling guilty.				
20 I am able to keep the person I care for out of an institution.				
21 I feel that if the situation were reversed, the person I care for would do the same for me.				
22 I am able to ensure that the person I care for has their needs tended to.				
23 Caring has given me the chance to widen my interests and contacts.				
24 Maintaining the dignity of the person I care for is important to me.				
25 I am able to test myself and overcome difficulties.				
26 Caring is one way of showing my faith.				
27 Caring has provided a purpose in my life that I did not have before.				
28 At the end of the day I know I will have done the best I could.				
29 Caring is one way of expressing my love for the person I care for.				
30 Caring makes me feel needed and wanted.				

Please add below any other aspects of caring that you find satisfying and indicate how much satisfaction they give you:

© Mike Nolan, Gordon Grant, John Keady, 1998. Assessing the Needs of Family Carers

Carers' Assessment of Managing Index (CAMI)

CAMI is a 38-item index and contains a series of statements which carers have made about the coping strategies they use. Carefully read each statement and show if it applies to you by placing a tick in the space available. Together, responses can be used as the basis for discussing an agreed programme of support with the carer.

I USE THIS AND FIND IT

ONE WAY OF DEALING WITH DEMANDS OF CARING IS BY:	I do not use this	Not really helpful	Quite helpful	Very helpful
1 Establishing a regular routine and sticking to it.				
2 Letting off steam in some way – shouting, yelling or the like.				
3 Talking over my problems with someone I trust.				
4 Keeping a little free time for myself.				
5 Keeping one step ahead of things by planning in advance.				
6 Seeing the funny side of the situation.				
7 Realising there's always someone worse off than me.				
8 Gritting my teeth and just getting on with it.				
9 Remembering all the good times I used to have with the person I care for.				
10 Finding out as much information as I can about the problem.				
11 Realising that the person I care for is not to blame for the way they are.				
12 Taking life one day at a time.				
13 Getting as much practical help as I can from my family.				
14 Keeping the person I care for as active as possible.				
15 Altering my home environment to make things as easy as possible.				
16 Realising that things are better now than they used to be.				
17 Getting as much help as I can from professionals and other service providers.				
18 Thinking about the problem and finding a way to overcome it.				
19 Having a good cry.				
20 Accepting the situation as it is.				
21 Taking my mind off things in some way, by reading, watching TV or the like.				
22 Ignoring the problem and hoping it will go away.				
23 Preventing problems before they happen.				

Continued/...

NOT TO BE COPIED OR USED WITHOUT PERMISSION FROM AUTHORS BELOW

Assessing the Needs of Family Carers © Mike Nolan, Gordon Grant, John Keady, 1998.

ONE WAY OF DEALING WITH DEMANDS OF CARING IS BY:	I do not use this	Not really helpful	Quite helpful	Very helpful
24 Drawing on strong personal or religious beliefs.				
25 Believing in myself and my ability to handle the situation.				
26 Forgetting about my problems for a short while by day-dreaming or the like.				
27 Keeping my emotions and feelings tightly under control.				
28 Trying to cheer myself up by eating, having a drink, smoking or the like.				
29 Relying on my own experience and the expertise I have built up.				
30 Trying out a number of solutions until I find one that works.				
31 Establishing priorities and concentrating on them.				
32 Looking for the positive things in each situation.				
33 Being firm and pointing out to the person I care for what I expect of them.				
34 Realising that no one is to blame for things.				
35 Getting rid of excess energy and feelings by walking, swimming or other exercise.				
36 Attending a self-help group.				
37 Using relaxation techniques, meditation or the like.				
36 Maintaining interests outside caring.				

Please add below any other coping methods you use and indicate how helpful you find them:

SUMMARY OF CARERS' OUTCOMES AND NEEDS

(This form replaces the "Carers' Needs page" within the general assessment form
which, in the participating authority, focuses mainly on the user)

Note to assessors: The purpose of this page is for the assessor to summarise their conclusions following discussion with the carer (with the assistance of either the Carers Needs Questionnaire or the Carers' Indices: CADI, CASI, CAMI). This should highlight what the carer and assessor feel the care plan should ideally aim to achieve from the carer's perspective (and if appropriate the type of help which may achieve it). *Actual services or support agreed with carer and older person, should be recorded separately on the care plan.*

1. What are the main sources of satisfaction/ reward for the carer in their present situation?	To what extent might these be maintained or increased as a result of any help offered?
2. What are the main sources of difficulty or stress for the carer?	What would the carer hope to achieve in relation to these (ie. as a result of any help offered?)
3. What strategies does the carer find most helpful in dealing with these difficulties?	In what ways (or aspects of caring) would the carer hope to maintain or increase their sense of expertise and coping?

Priorities (carer's perspective)

From the carer's point of view what is most important for the care plan to achieve:

In relation to the person they care for:

In relation to their own needs:

Any preferences about aspects of service delivery (e.g. Timing, ways of doing things) to ensure a good fit with existing routines and care patterns.

Priorities (assessor's perspective - if different from above)

Reasons

SUMMARY OF OUTCOMES FOR THE CARER

Please tick the main impacts on the carer you would hope to achieve in relation to both A and B:

A   Carers Quality of life:
Improving or maintaining:

- ☐ Physical health or well-being
- ☐ Emotional/mental health
- ☐ Time to themselves/a life of their own
- ☐ Relationships/social integration
- ☐ Financial/material circumstances
- ☐ A sense of control of their life
- ☐ Peace of mind

B   Their role as carer:
Achieving, maintaining or increasing:

- ☐ Expertise or confidence (incl. knowledge & skills) in caring
- ☐ Satisfaction/reward in caring
- ☐ Sense of shared responsibility/being emotionally supported
- ☐ Ability to cope with physical caring tasks
  (May include relief from, equipment, or practical help with tasks)
- ☐ Ability to manage particular difficulties or stress

OVERALL OUTCOMES FOR CARE PACKAGE	Client Ref Nº:
Please indicate the main outcomes for the care package overall to which the outcomes identified above will contribute:	Assessor:
☐ Maintenance ☐ Prevention ☐ Rehabilitation	Date of completion:

SUMMARY OF CARER'S ASSESSMENT

This summary is intended for the assessor to summarise and check out their conclusions from their discussion with the carer, following completion of the appropriate questionnaires in this pack. See "Key Points for Assessors" and "Checklist - Approaching Assessment"

1. CURRENT SITUATION

Brief description of care/support provided................and by whom.................
(Carers Needs Form may assist or A2/S2 if more detail on network is needed)

2. CARER'S (or Carers') PERSPECTIVE(S) ON CURRENT SITUATION

2a. What are the main difficulties from the carer's (s') perspective(s)?
(Summary of main points from Carer's Needs Form and/or CADI if appropriate)

2.b. What (if anything) do they find most satisfying or rewarding about the caring role? *(Summary of main points from CASI, where appropriate)*

2.c. What are the carer(s) preferred ways of dealing with the demands of caring, which services should take into account? *(Summary of main points from CAMI, where appropriate)*

3. DESIRED OUTCOMES TO AIM FOR

What are the most important things the carer(s) would hope to achieve in relation to :

3.a **The quality of life of the person they care for** (*eg. Improved mobility/morale, more social contact/company/activities, maintain independence/sense of dignity, safety*)

3.b. **The Carer's own quality of life** (*eg. Improved health or morale, less tired, less anxious/stressed, keep working, reduce tensions in relationships, more time to self/take up interests, improve finances, more control over their life*)

3.c. **Managing the caring role** (*eg. increasing confidence/skills/satisfaction, reducing or sharing caring responsibilities, having someone to talk to*)

---

3. **Are there any major differences in perspective within the caring network about desired outcome?** *Please specify, and indicate any action needed/ agreement reached*

Carer's agreement and consent to share information

Has the carer....

■ Checked and agreed with the above conclusions since they were written?   Yes/No
■ Given consent for these conclusions to be discussed with:
  ▸ the person they care for?   Yes/No
  ▸ with others who may be able to provide help?   Yes/No

Assessor's Signature: .... **Date** ....

Carer's Signature (where possible) .... **Date** ....

For conclusions on overall outcomes to be aimed for and preferred ways of achieving these - see combined assessment summary in the A2. For services/support to be provided - see Care Plan.

CARER'S NEEDS

1.   CURRENT SITUATION

1.1 Please describe briefly the nature of carer support currently being provided, and by whom:

1.2 Do any of the above people act   Yes ☐ No ☐ If Yes, who is this? _____
as the main carer ?

2.2   ELIGIBILITY FOR A SEPARATE CARER'S ASSESSMENT

2.1   Are any of the people above likely to provide care for:

20 Hours or more per week	Yes ☐	No ☐
80 hours or more in any given four week period	Yes ☐	No ☐

2.2   Does/Do the carer(s) wish to: Have more information about help available   Yes ☐   No ☐
Talk with someone about their needs   Yes ☐   No ☐

2.3 Are there likely to be differing/conflicting interests within the caring network ?   Yes ☐   No ☐

2.4 Are there any other reasons that indicate a separate carer's assessment is needed ?   Yes ☐   No ☐

If yes, please outline these reasons:

ASSESSOR'S CONCLUSION

2.1 In the assessor's view, should a separate carer's assessment be offered ?   Yes ☐   No ☐

(If yes, then Home Care refer to the Care Management Team, Care Management refer to Carer Assessment
Documentation/Line Management).

2.2 Assessment Priority ? ☐ Same day ☐ Within 3 days ☐ Within 10 days ☐ Within 4 weeks

---

NOTE: This is an extract from the participating authority's general assessment
of need form (A2), developed for the second phase of testing.

KEY POINTS FOR ASSESSORS

INTRODUCTION

The tools and notes included in this pack are offered for use on the basis of experience in the pilot project, "Outcomes for Carers". The range of tools included are intended to support the task of skilled assessment, not to replace it, recognising that different approaches will be needed in different circumstances. They will need to be used with professional judgement, sensitivity and understanding of their purpose and underlying principles. As with many tools they have their strengths and limitations. Training and experience of using them will assist judgements about when and how to make best use of them. These brief notes are therefore intended to offer a framework for understanding them and some key points to guide their use in practice. They are not intended to be a comprehensive guide to carer assessment (See other sources of guidance listed overleaf).

PLEASE NOTE that until you are familiar with the contents of this pack and have used the tools a few times, the process of assessment may take longer and feel more cumbersome than usual. When approaching your first assessment using this pack please take time to read the guidance and prepare yourself as this may be slightly different from the way you have done assessments previously. The pilot has also shown that used with care, the tools can help to enhance practice and be a rewarding experience for carers and assessors alike.

PURPOSE OF TOOLS

The overall approach to assessment is designed to assist assessors in discovering the carer's perspective on their situation, at a level which is appropriate and acceptable to the carer, with a view to finding out what **effects** or **impacts** they would like services to have on their own quality of life and the quality of life of the person they care for. Greater clarity about the desired effects (ie. outcomes) of any help to be offered should help in:

- ▸ tailoring care packages specifically to individual needs
- ▸ improving accountability - ie. making it easier to check with carers at the review stage, whether services have achieved what they set out to achieve
- ▸ providing useful information to inform development of services for carers

It is hoped that information about outcomes for carers recorded on assessment and review forms will eventually be collated through SSID.

☐ The aim of the different questionnaires is to help the carer express their views on their situation in varying levels of detail. They are designed for completion by carer, although clearly this will not always be appropriate and they may be used in other ways (more details below). The questionnaires may be used singly or in combination depending on what makes most sense for the individual carer and the circumstances of the assessment.

☐ The completed questionnaires are **not**, in themselves, the assessment - once completed, they are intended to provide a focus for discussion with the carer, preferably in person, in which the carer's needs and desired outcomes are identified and clarified/checked with the carer.

☐ The **Summary of Carer's Assessment** (Amended since the pilot, to complement the A2 summary). After a discussion with the carer, this summary is intended to help the assessor draw out the key points from discussion, highlighting the carer's perspective on their situation and outcomes they would hope services to achieve, and to record these clearly and distinctly from the user's needs and views. The two perspectives may then be brought together, and if necessary negotiated before and agreed outcomes for user and carer are recorded on the A2 Assessment Summary. In some circumstances, where the carer's needs are being assessed at the same time as the user, the A2 Assessment Summary may be sufficient.

To assist recording, see also - SPRU's Checklist of Outcomes for Assessment Summary - which outlines the sort of outcomes which older people and carers have said are important.

PRINCIPLES UNDERPINNING THE APPROACH (1)

☐ *Promoting carer expertise*
This approach aims to acknowledge and promote the carer's expertise in their own situation. The assessor is seen as an enabler or facilitator in the assessment process.

☐ *A person-centred approach*
The approach is intended to be person-centred and holistic, acknowledging that a carer's experience and perceptions of their caring role (and their ability/willingness to continue), are not necessarily related to the level of physical care provided alone, but to the way caring affects the whole of their life.

☐ *Caring is seen as a process.*
The way in which the caring role is acquired (either suddenly or over a longer period) and the impact this has on the carer will also be an important considerations in determining the approach in individual situations. Carers may be looking for different outcomes at different stages of caring. For example, being fully informed, prepared and equipped for caring and knowing where to turn in the event of difficulties may be more important in the early stages than any practical help.

☐ *Acknowledging the complexities of care-giving*
The framework of 'difficulties, satisfactions and managing' recognises the complexities of care-giving which in some situations may be appropriate to explore more fully. The theory underpinning this framework is well grounded in many years of research and practice with carers by those who designed the tools: CADI, CASI and CAMI. Understanding the thinking behind these tools should enhance their use in practice. A short practical guide has been produced for practitioners, including examples, and is recommended reading for anyone preparing to use the tools for the first time:

"Assessing the Needs of Family Carers: A Guide for Practitioners"
Mike Nolan, Gordon Grant and John Keady

PLANNING THE ASSESSMENT

Experience from the pilot indicate that it is important to:

☐   Consider from the information available, the best approach for the carer concerned. Timing of assessment meeting and choice of tool will depend on a variety of factors including carer's relationship with assessor and/or the department, the stage of the caring, their current emotional state, the urgency of the user's situation, carer's literacy skills, preferred means of communication, etc.

☐   Consider whether translated versions of the tools and/or interpreter may be appropriate and ensure these are available.

☐   It may not always be appropriate to carry out the carer's assessment at the same time as the user's assessment (even if the carer doesn't mind the user being present). The Carer's Needs form might be introduced at this stage and a follow-up appointment made to focus on the carer's needs more fully.

☐   **Offer** the carer an opportunity for a private discussion (apart from the person they care for) and a choice about where and when this takes place. This will be important for some carers and not for others.

☐   **Explain** the nature of assessment, suggesting use of one of the questionnaires, where appropriate, as a way of informing the discussion about the help that might be offered. Explain what will happen to completed questionnaire (offer carer a choice about whether they keep it for own reference or allow copy to be kept on file). Reinforce the message that they can choose how much information to share, with whom and at what point.

☐   **Offer** the carer choice about whether they complete the suggested questionnaire in their own time (prior to a meeting) or with your help.

☐   Establish a rapport before introducing CADI, CASI, or CAMI. This may be possible within the first meeting or may take longer.

USE OF THE TOOLS

For use of CADI, CASI and CAMI please see guidance pack, "Assessing Needs of Family Carers", referred to above. In addition, some key messages from the pilot were:

☐   **The Carer's Needs** form is a useful introduction or starting point and can help to indicate whether a more in depth assessment is needed. A number of carers who had used CADI, CASI, and CAMI within the pilot said they valued the opportunity for a more in depth focus on their needs and suggested that the Carers Needs form was not sufficient by itself. However it may be sufficient where a limited assessment is considered more appropriate or the carer's choice.

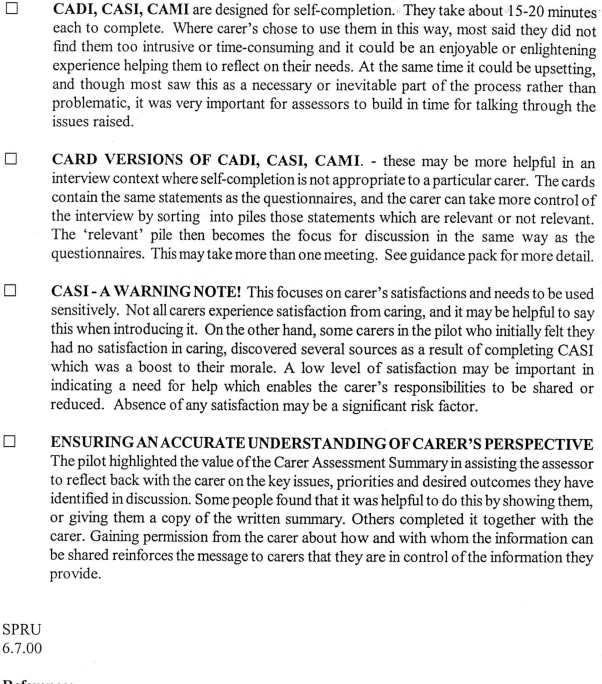

☐ **CADI, CASI, CAMI** are designed for self-completion. They take about 15-20 minutes each to complete. Where carer's chose to use them in this way, most said they did not find them too intrusive or time-consuming and it could be an enjoyable or enlightening experience helping them to reflect on their needs. At the same time it could be upsetting, and though most saw this as a necessary or inevitable part of the process rather than problematic, it was very important for assessors to build in time for talking through the issues raised.

☐ **CARD VERSIONS OF CADI, CASI, CAMI.** - these may be more helpful in an interview context where self-completion is not appropriate to a particular carer. The cards contain the same statements as the questionnaires, and the carer can take more control of the interview by sorting into piles those statements which are relevant or not relevant. The 'relevant' pile then becomes the focus for discussion in the same way as the questionnaires. This may take more than one meeting. See guidance pack for more detail.

☐ **CASI - A WARNING NOTE!** This focuses on carer's satisfactions and needs to be used sensitively. Not all carers experience satisfaction from caring, and it may be helpful to say this when introducing it. On the other hand, some carers in the pilot who initially felt they had no satisfaction in caring, discovered several sources as a result of completing CASI which was a boost to their morale. A low level of satisfaction may be important in indicating a need for help which enables the carer's responsibilities to be shared or reduced. Absence of any satisfaction may be a significant risk factor.

☐ **ENSURING AN ACCURATE UNDERSTANDING OF CARER'S PERSPECTIVE**
The pilot highlighted the value of the Carer Assessment Summary in assisting the assessor to reflect back with the carer on the key issues, priorities and desired outcomes they have identified in discussion. Some people found that it was helpful to do this by showing them, or giving them a copy of the written summary. Others completed it together with the carer. Gaining permission from the carer about how and with whom the information can be shared reinforces the message to carers that they are in control of the information they provide.

SPRU
6.7.00

Reference:

(1)   *"Understanding Family Care: A multidimensional model of caring and coping"* (1996) by Mike Nolan, Gordon Grant and John Keady. Open University Press *(The book on which the above guide is based)*

SAMPLE LETTER TO ACCOMPANY THE 'CARER'S FEEDBACK FORM'

Dear

CARER'S FEEDBACK

A while ago we assessed your needs as a carer. We would now like to check with you how things are going from your point of view and to review any arrangements we made at that time to see whether these are still suitable for you.

The enclosed questionnaire is intended to help you tell us your views about any services or support we are providing to you or the person you care for. **These are listed in your care plan - a copy of which is attached.** Through your answers to the questions in this form we hope to learn from you:

- Is the help you are receiving achieving what you hoped it would achieve?
- Is it provided in the right way?
- Have your needs changed at all since the help was first provided?

If you would like someone to fill this questionnaire in with you, please let me know. Either way, we will arrange to talk with you about your responses in order to consider any changes or additional help needed. We will do our best to meet your needs within the resources available and if we are unable to do so we will always give you the reasons.

Thank you very much for your co-operation. Please do not hesitate to contact me if you have any queries about this letter, or the questionnaire.

Yours sincerely,

(Name of worker)

CONFIDENTIAL

For office use only

Client Ref Nº		Worker Initials		Office Base	
Date of assessment/last review:					

CARER'S FEEDBACK
Carers' views about the help and support provided

Your name (carer): ....

Your address: ....

Your Phone No: ....

Name of person(s) you care for: ....

Their address (if different): ....

A. WHAT HAS BEEN ACHIEVED FOR YOU AND YOUR LIFE?

1. Below we have listed YOUR priorities at the time the help was arranged (or last reviewed). Please tick the column which applies to indicate how far these things have been achieved. Add any other priorities you think we have missed out.

The things you said were most important to achieve	Fully achieved	Partly achieved	Not achieved
....			
....			
....			
....			

2. What has been the most important service or aspect of the help provided from your point of view?

....

....

2. What has been the *main* benefit FOR YOU of this help (what difference, if any, has it made to your life)?

....

....

1

3.   YOUR QUALITY OF LIFE

Please tick the column which applies to you:

As a result of the services/support received. . . (This may include home care, equipment in the home, day care, sitting service, respite breaks, carer's group, someone to talk to/emotional support, and other help)	Has / have greatly improved	Has / have improved a little	Has / have not changed
a. My physical health or well-being (including sleep, rest, exercise etc.)			
b. My emotional/mental health (e.g. feelings of stress, anxiety, depression)			
c. Time to myself /to have a life of my own (e.g. work, studies, interests, other commitments)			
d. My relationships (with the person I care for or other people)			
e. My financial or material circumstances (e.g. income, housing)			
f. My feeling of control over my life (eg. my ability to make plans for myself and stick to them)			
g. My peace of mind (being less worried about the well being of the person I care for)			

Any comments *(to explain the above)* ....
....
....

4.   MANAGING CARING

The services and support...

	Have helped a lot with this	Have helped a little with this	Have made no difference
a. I feel more confident and knowledgeable in what I do as a carer			
b. I gain a sense of satisfaction or achievement in caring			
c. My caring responsibilities have been reduced or shared (to an acceptable level)			
d. I feel I'm not alone in caring - I have someone to talk to if needed			
e. I am able to manage the physical/practical caring tasks			

Any comments *(to explain the above)*...
....
....

2

B IS THE HELP PROVIDED IN THE RIGHT WAY?

The questions below are about THE WAY THE HELP IS PROVIDED and how it affects YOU. Please feel free to say what you think. If you have indicated that there is room for improvement, we would always discuss with you first the best way of tackling this.

		Always	Mostly	Not at all
1.	Are you and the person you care for treated with respect?			
2.	Is your expertise as a carer recognised?			
3.	Do you feel you have a say in the way the help is provided?			
4.	Is the help provided in ways which fit in with your life and routines?			
5.	Do you get on with the staff you have contact with *(eg. do you feel at ease with them, are they approachable and helpful? Are you able to understand/communicate with them?)*			
6.	Do you feel the service(s) provided is (are) value for money?			

Any other comments *(For example, what you particularly value about THE WAY the help has been provided, or how it could be improved)*

....
....
....
....

C. COMMENTS ABOUT OTHER AGENCIES e.g. Housing, Health Service, Voluntary bodies

Do you have any comments about help received (or not received) from other agencies which affect you or the caring situation? *(We may not have the power to change this, but we can discuss this with you to see whether or not we can help)*

D. WHAT HAS BEEN ACHIEVED FOR THE PERSON YOU CARE FOR?

1. From your point of view, what have been the main benefits of the help received, for the PERSON YOU CARE FOR?

2. **Do you have any comments about the WAY the help is provided to the PERSON YOU CARE FOR?** *(For example, timing, reliability, the general approach of staff - things that are positive or things which could be improved)*

E. CHANGES IN YOUR SITUATION OR NEEDS

1. Please describe below, any changes in your situation or needs which you think we should know about?

2. What are the main concerns or difficulties which you have at the moment for which additional (or different) help might be needed?

F. TO SUM UP EVERYTHING YOU HAVE SAID ...

1. At the moment, overall I feel:

Able to cope with most/all aspects of caring	I'm not coping as well as I'd like to	It can be up and down from day to day	I can't carry on as things are	Overall I am coping better than I was
☐	☐	☐	☐	☐

2. Please tick the statements which best apply to you:

☐ I am happy with the current arrangements

☐ I would like to talk to someone to see what changes/other help might be possible

☐ I would prefer to contact you if I need to in future

Signed... Date:...

☐ Carer   ☐ On behalf of carer

PLEASE RETURN THIS QUESTIONNAIRE TO:

Name: Job title:

Address: Phone:

4

PROFILE OF CARERS

	Carers Assessed (37)	Carers Reviewed (15)
Age of Carer		
80+	1	0
70-79	9	6
60-69	13	5
40-59	9	3
20-39	2	0
Under 20	0	0
Not known	3	1
Gender of Carer		
Females	24	9
Males	13	6
Ethnicity		
Afro-Caribbean	2	0
White British	30	13
Indian	2	1
Latvian	1	1
Polish	1	0
Not known	1	0
Relationship of Carer to Cared For		
Spouse	20	10
Daughter/Son (+ daughter in laws)	12 (+3)	3 (+1)
Other	2	1
Residence of Carer		
With cared for	25	11
Apart from cared for	9	4
Not known	4	0
Level of carer involvement		
Full time (person cared for can't be left alone)	19	8
Several times a day	10	3
Once a day	1	0
Several times a week	4	3
Not known	3	1
Prior contact between carer and assessor		
Yes	20	15
No	15	0
Not known	2	0

CHAPTER FIVE
PROGRAMME OF INTERVIEWS BY SERVICE MANAGERS: TO UNDERSTAND EXPERIENCES AND OUTCOMES AMONG SERVICE USERS

By Charles Patmore

1. INTRODUCTION

This chapter describes a programme of home interviews with a small random sample of older users of Social Services. The interviews were conducted by the managers who had overall responsibility for the interviewees' services. The interview programme was intended to assist these managers in making decisions on policy and service development through providing a fuller, fact-based understanding of the strengths and weaknesses of current services and policies, as a result of directly perceiving their outcomes in clients' everyday lives. During 1999 a test of this interview programme, using a purpose-designed interview schedule (shown as an appendix), was carried out with 30 older users of community social services, in total. They were interviewed by two teams of managers at two different area offices. Reports were produced which made some common recommendations and also identified different challenges facing each area office.

This project was undertaken with the same partner authority whose population is described at the beginning of the second chapter.

2. ORIGINS OF THE INTERVIEW PROGRAMME

Three separate sets of findings from the stage one research combined to inspire this project (Patmore *et al.*, 1998). These were: the views of managers on how and why service outcomes should be investigated; older service users' expressed preferences for face-to-face interview as a method of data collection; and users' concerns that information should be conveyed in the most direct way possible to senior managers who were responsible for services, and who would have some power to take action. These findings are explored in more detail below.

The views of the senior managers on how service outcomes should be investigated

Interviews with senior managers - an Assistant Director, area managers, principal care managers and home care managers - communicated the following sentiments.

- In view of heavy workloads, the service would only have time for methods of studying outcomes which clearly helped senior managers with important management tasks. For instance they wanted information about the benefits from different services to help them assign budgets between different services. They wanted to know which components or aspects of their services were bringing most benefit, so that they could concentrate resources there. Some managers seemed to be seeking a series of one-off investigations into issues where decisions currently needed to be taken.

- The experiences and views of clients were regarded as crucial indicators of outcome, as the best means for ascertaining benefits from services. Among all staff clients' satisfaction with service was regarded as a key outcome. Thus particular value was placed on effective, sensitive means for reaching clients' views.

- In-depth individual interview at home was prized by staff as the effective, meaningful way to obtain client's views. Noting the time-costs of individual interview, senior managers argued for interviewing small samples of clients in order to ensure high quality in-depth interviews.

Thus senior managers supported investigation of outcomes through periodic rounds of in-depth interviews with small samples of clients, focused round questions which were of immediate practical importance to management. Conversely, they rejected in particular any system which would require managers to continuously monitor the whole social care case-list, thousands of clients strong. This was regarded as probably unproductive and impossibly burdensome.

There were two viewpoints about who should carry out such interviews. Some managers argued for researchers from an independent agency, so clients could speak freely without fearing their services might be affected. Others saw benefits through care managers or more senior staff conducting the interviews, so they would gain wide-ranging feedback about services which could inform their own future decisions. An area manager felt the interviews' findings would gain authority and credibility among the managers in an area office if they, rather than an independent agency, had conducted the interviews themselves.

Evidence emerged that Social Services needed home interviews to consult service users effectively

The report from stage one described how individual interview at home was consistently named by older service users as the most appropriate means for consulting them. Major reasons were that it could reach a much wider range of older people than other methods - people too frail to travel to group discussions, people who could not see well enough to fill in written questionnaires, people who felt uncomfortable with interview by telephone. Written questionnaires in particular were strongly criticised by many older people interviewed in the stage one research. One reason was the problems experienced by many frail older people in reading or writing. Other reasons were dislike of closed questions or the impersonality of written questionnaires.

Further analysis produced additional evidence for using individual interview at home. Individual interviews appeared more likely to engage people aged over 80 years than group discussions (Patmore et al., 2000). While the latter certainly suited service users in the 65 - 80 year age range, a clear majority among older community service users were aged over 80 years and could be seriously under-represented if consultation were based on focus groups alone.

These findings had major implications for the authority. As mentioned, there was a strong culture of respect for consulting service users. Significant effort had been invested in consulting older people through a series of regular focus groups, through large annual conferences for older people and through a citizens' panel whereby some older people were consulted in writing. Some managers noted how none of these seemed appropriate for the bulk of the home care clientele, who were too frail or too old for such vehicles. One senior manager cited the relatively young age of those older people who could be enlisted in his group consultations; they were the service users of tomorrow, he said, rather than service users of today. A case was acknowledged for using interview at home to reach the service users of today.

Service users expressed desire for individual interview by senior managers
Unexpectedly, one particular notion of home interview was especially favoured by many sets of older service users interviewed during stage one. This was that a senior Social Services manager should conduct the interview in person. Phrases like 'the men at the top' were often used for senior managers; interviewees were very unclear about Social Services job titles. The following are reasons why this idea appeals to older people so much.

- Interviewees wished to be interviewed by someone who was a sufficiently senior manager to ensure that something was actually done with the information they heard. They worried that otherwise results would not reach senior staff or be acted on.

- They believed that conducting this interview at home would add meaning to the interviewee's words because the manager would be able to see their problems and living circumstances directly. Repeatedly these home interviews were envisaged as a means for educating managers who were so senior that they did not often see the realities of older people's lives.

- Another theme was a feeling that senior managers had a moral obligation to witness first hand the results of the services for which they were responsible.

- Such visits, it was also said, would encourage older people through showing that senior managers cared about them enough to investigate their services' end results.

- Another aspect was that if a senior manager would visibly invest time in asking the questions, then it was worth older people investing their own time in answering them. This contrasted with postal questionnaires which, some interviewees suggested, took older people much trouble to complete but could be easily ignored.

Thus the service managers' interview programme had multiple origins. It was not solely the fulfilment of a request from service users. It had also emerged that there would have to be some sort of programme of home interviews, if Social Services were to hear the views of their many very old or infirm home care clients. Senior managers themselves had affirmed a case for in-depth individual interview of small samples of service users as the method for investigating outcomes which was most likely to be useful to them. Service users' clear request for a senior manager supplied a rationale for who should conduct the interviews.

Influences from national policy

There were other factors which probably promoted the project, though less explicit. The interview programme's potential for bringing service users' views into the service commissioning process attracted at least one influential manager. This may reflect the fact that during the project Department of Health guidance on service commissioning promoted the same theme (Department of Health, 1998; Gazdar, 1999). Links between Best Value and the interview programme were discussed on a number of counts. While nothing explicit came of this, Best Value may have still promoted participation in the project. The authority's own pilot Best Value Review had involved Council staff from outside Social Services interviewing home care clients at home and making recommendations. Best Value heralded an era of service reviews which were to include similar feedback from users. Accordingly some service managers saw the advantage of an interview programme which would put them closer in touch with their own clients' views and show how to 'add value' to their service in Best Value reviews of the future.

The concept of the interview programme

The development of the programme of interviews followed quite closely the ideas expressed by senior managers in the stage one interviews. It was intended to include only a small sample of service users to ensure that sufficient time was available to conduct high quality interviews. Managers would interview users of their own area office's services, so as to provide feedback to assist decision-making. It was anticipated that there would be some emphasis on investigating topical issues facing managers. There would be a general focus on enabling managers to witness first-hand the results of their services - or the absence of services. Indeed, essential to the focus on outcomes was attention to the interviewee's life situation, whether or not relevant services were supplied. Thus, for instance, interviewees would be asked about the satisfactoriness of their meals and how these were provided, regardless whether they were provided by Social Services, by relatives or were self-prepared. Attention would be paid to dimensions of outcomes which had been identified in stage one.

This attention to outcomes from all sources, rather than only those resulting from services, makes this interview programme somewhat different from other uses of in-depth interviews to guide service development in Social Services, like the interviews of older service users described in Saunders et al. (1992). Another distinctive feature was, of course, the use of service managers to conduct the interviews. A helpful comparator for the latter can be found in McQuarrie's (1998) description of the evolution of short interview programmes by managers in the American computer software industry. Small teams of operational managers developed programmes of semi-structured interviews with samples of between 12 and 30 randomly selected customers (these customers were themselves managers in firms which used computers) in each customer's workplace. The aim was to directly acquaint managers with customers' aspirations, preferences and current practical challenges so as to inspire the development of new or improved products. One rationale for using managers was that their practical knowledge made them more effective than independent researchers for understanding the wide variety of problems raised by customers, while their authority equipped them to personally investigate the issues raised. Another rationale was that, if a manager were used, the experience of these interviews could directly inform everyday decision-making. Furthermore, the final report would carry particular conviction among managers - indeed, part of its audience would be the same team who had undertaken the interviews. Some guiding principles from these interview programmes in industry proved very relevant to the Social Services interview programme.

3. DEVELOPMENT OF THE PROJECT

Two area offices in the Social Services department had agreed to participate in the interviews. Each area office served a general population of around 90,000 people. Area office A served a small town which was geographically completely separate from the city where the bulk of the authority's population lived. Area office B served around a quarter of the latter city. It had been expected that in each area office the interview programme would be conducted by four managers. These would be the overall manager for the area office and the managers with local responsibility for care management, home care, and service development.

The two teams of interviewers

Significant differences between the two area offices emerged. At the beginning, area office B had fewer managers available for the interview programme. The service development manager was acting as home care manager, since the latter was on long-term sick-leave. Partly for this reason, area office B was much less confident about participation in this project, although at the outset managers in both Areas expressed strong fears about demands on their time.

In area office A the area manager did not undertake any interviews. To share out the interviewing, area A's local coordinator involved principal care manager from the local hospital-based social work service, plus two administrative managers. In this office the interviewing was shared evenly among six managers. In area B, the area manager participated actively in the planning of the project but, owing to time constraints, conducted only one interview. To compensate for its shortfall in managers, area office B involved as an additional interviewer the coordinator for authority-wide dementia services, who was based there. However it was only the appointment of an extra manager late in 1999 that enabled area office B to complete sufficient interviews. Five managers were involved in interviews altogether and the new manager (who knew this area office very well) undertook a large proportion. There are important issues, which will be discussed later, about the appropriate number and seniority of interviewers, and desirable number of interviews per interviewer.

Developing an interview schedule

Work on the schedule for the Social Services interview programme began in July 1998. One concern was how to limit the length of the interview and soften its structure so as to make it suitable for the very old people who were a large proportion of the authority's social care clientele. The possible subject-matter for questions was very large, noting the many dimensions of quality of life and the number of different social care services which an interviewee might be using. Other researchers have argued that interviews with very old people must be short and streamlined in view of how burdensome they can find interviews (Wallace *et al.*, 1992). Similarly, it seemed important to avoid the high level of structure and direction of an interview by the interviewer, which often occurs when many topics need to be covered. The older people interviewed in SPRU's stage one research did not wish an interview which was controlled by the interviewer: they wished at least some space to present their own prepared views at their own pace (Patmore *et al.*, 1998). Likewise, Fisk (1997) recommends a loose, conversational approach to interviewing with very old people. A continuing tension throughout this interview project was reconciling comprehensive information-gathering with sensitivity to the needs of very old interviewees.

Piloting the interview schedule

By November 1998 SPRU was piloting an initial interview schedule. Some older service users, who had been interviewed in stage one research and who had indicated readiness to help in this way, were paid by SPRU to act as consultants who would experience the interview and advise on improvements. First the schedule was piloted by a SPRU researcher with three such former stage one interviewees. Then, after modifications, it was piloted successfully with two more former interviewees by a Social Services staff member who had not previously used interview schedules but who was used to visiting older Social Services clients at home. If she could use the schedule, it was reasoned, then the same might be expected from the managers in the interview programme. Principles learned from stage one interviews were applied, like sending interviewees advance written summaries of questions and ensuring that women interviewers were available for women. Modifications made during this period comprised reduction in length of interview, a more conversational opening, and expanding a section which the interviewer filled in on their own after the interview. The latter change was made because pilot interviews sometimes raised unexpected, rather global issues which needed description at length afterwards. All recording from interviews was through notes completed by the interviewer during the interview or by the interviewer on their own soon afterwards. It was reasoned that tape-recording would not suit routine use by service managers, notably because of the lack of resources for transcription and analysis.

In early 1999 the resulting interview schedule was examined by the managers who acted as project coordinators at each area office. The coordinators then engaged managers to participate as interviewers, resulting in somewhat different interviewer teams at each office, as mentioned earlier. Steps were taken to arrange one pilot interview by each prospective interviewer. SPRU produced extensive guidance notes and met with interviewers beforehand. By early April eight interviews had been completed and written up by interviewers, who also supplied feedback on their experiences. SPRU then produced a model of an overall report on the service based on notes from just these eight pilot interviews. This was intended both to test the amenability of interviewers' notes to analysis and to show Social Services the type of information which was being generated. Social Services was generally pleased and wished to press ahead. There was some difference of opinion between managers who wished to shorten the interviews, so that they became primarily an assessment of different services' quality, and those who wished to also include some holistic attention to outcomes. The latter opinion prevailed.

Much concern to reduce the length of the interview was expressed as a result of this pilot. Social Services produced a new, shorter introduction piece. Various reductions were made - but also some additions. Social Services now wished to use the interviews to answer some questions relating to new quality standards. These were incorporated accordingly. Specially for this initial interview programme SPRU added a short section which reflected recent government emphasis on promoting independence among older people (Fiedler, 1999). Each interviewee was to be asked to name any extra help which might promote their own contribution to management of their needs and affairs. Also, after each interview the interviewer was asked for any observations from the interview about promoting independence or self-support.

When interview times were calculated at the end of the series, this revised interview took on average ten minutes less than the original schedule, though practice may also have been a factor. This interview schedule is presented in the appendices; the guidance notes explain its different components. The interview schedule's contents are summarised in Figures 5.1 - 5.3 below.

Figure 5.1 Main topics within interview schedule for comment from interviewee

- Review of outcomes in areas of daily living (including areas where no services are received)
- Home Care Service
- Day centres
- Other significant social care services used by interviewee
- Care following any recent hospital discharges
- Family carer views
- Any additional help sought from Social Services, other Council Services or Health Service
- Rating of satisfactoriness of help received

Figure 5.2 Contents of interviewee's review of satisfactoriness of outcome in areas of daily living (including areas where no services are received)

- Meals / refreshment
- Shopping
- Laundry
- House cleaning
- Household repairs / decoration / gardening
- Swift access to help in emergency
- Feeling safe from crime and nuisance
- Managing with money, bill, pensions, benefits and legal matters
- Personal care
- Getting out of the house
- Social life
- Sources of interest in everyday life

Figure 5.3   Main topics within interview schedule for post-interview write-up by interviewer

- Aspects of service particularly praised or approved
- Aspects of service linked to major dissatisfaction
- Any post-interview interventions by interviewer
- Issues which the interviewer wishes raised in the Report
- Interviewer's rating of satisfactoriness of help provided
- Interviewer's additional reflections from the interview

The programme of interviews

The two areas sought to complete a total of 16 interviews each. SPRU organised the random selection of interviewees, drawing names from the authority's computerised database for community care charges. For each of the authority's 'Priority' categories for home care clients a number of interviewees was prescribed, together with specifications for the age and gender of interviewees and the balance between recent and long-term clients. The specifications reflected the relevant population on the database. There was concern, for instance, to represent appropriately the large proportion of very old service users. SPRU supplied each area office with a list of names to approach, plus procedures. Assessment of clients' suitability for interview was then conducted by home care organisers on lines similar to those used in stage one (Patmore *et al.*, 2000): home care organisers were asked to exclude any proposed interviewees if specified barriers to interview existed - for example severe communication difficulties, illness or recent emotional distress. (The screening document used, together with the guidance notes, is supplied as an appendix). In the event of moderate communication difficulties, they were expected to inform the interviewer in advance. In actual practice, the latter did not always occur but the interviewers proved well able to cope with some unexpected situations. Each interview record included space for comment by the interviewer on such problems. Generally the interviews took place very smoothly, which probably reflects the experience and knowledge of the managers concerned.

Once names had been screened by the home care organisers, potential interviewees were written to with a request for interview. (This letter, together with the enclosed advance information on interview topics, is supplied as an appendix.) Home care staff were also informed about the interview programme, lest they be worried through first hearing of it from a client. (A letter for this purpose is also supplied as an appendix.) The identity of interviewees, however, remained confidential.

Analysis

By January 2000, later than expected, 30 interviews had been completed. Area office B found their task harder than did area office A. They completed fewer interviews, 13 compared to 17, and took longer. Analysis and report-writing was conducted by SPRU - an important consideration, noting that the procedure is intended eventually for operation solely by Social Services staff. Each catchment's interview notes were first analysed separately. Responses were collated for each section of the interview schedule. Then the two catchments were compared for common and contrasting themes. In addition, for each interviewee SPRU compiled some notes concerning any general messages emerging from that interview as a whole, since it was important that analysis did not fragment interviewees' responses simply into comments on a list of topics. Effort had been made to encourage interviewers to likewise make some general reflections in their post-interview write-ups, since this had proved important in the pilots.

Reporting the findings

Late in 1999 major disruption occurred to the intended reporting back process owing to changes among top social services management and a reorganisation which called into question the future management structures for Elderly Division. It had been intended to produce a report from the interview series which could be presented to management team for at the end of 1999, so that it could inform service-planning decisions scheduled for January 2000. Reorganisation however created a hiatus when it was not known what would be the new decision-making body for services for older people. Accordingly a short summary report, which presented recommendations only, was delivered for the beginning of an annual round of service-planning in January 2000, as requested by Social Services. A much longer full report was then prepared for presentation when a new management structure for older people's services had been determined.

In March 2000, after seeing drafts of the full report, the interviewers at area office A met to discuss setting up another interview programme. This reflected the value they ascribed to the experience. But first, they agreed, they must conduct a planning exercise for applying findings from the reports to their own area. Independent from any eventual authority-wide implementation of the findings, in the coming months they would meet with junior colleagues to plan action on findings felt to be relevant to their catchment.

Table 5.1 Facts about the interview programme

	Area "A"	Area "B"	Both catchments
Number interviewers	6	5	11
Number interviewees	17	13	30
Age range interviewees	66 - 95 years	74 - 92 years	66 - 95 years
Mean age interviewees	84 years	83 years	83 years
No. aged over 85 years	8	7	15
Number of men	5	4	9
Number of women	12	9	21
Home Care Priority 1	9	8	17
Home Care Priority 2/1	3	2	5
Home Care Priority 3	4	3	7
Day centre only (no Home Care)	1	-	1
Range of Home Care hours provided per week	15 minutes - 33 hours	45 minutes - 14 hours	15 minutes - 33 hours
Mean Home Care hours	10.21 hours	7 hours	8.8 hours
Living alone	12	12	24
Living with spouse	5	1	6
In sheltered housing	9	6	15
In ordinary housing	8	7	15
Range of length of interview	Shortest: 25 minutes Longest: 1 hour and 50 minutes	Shortest: 45 minutes Longest: 1 hour and 30 minutes	Shortest: 25 minutes Longest: 1 hour and 50 minutes
Mean length of interview	1 hour and 4 minutes	1 hour and 10 minutes	1 hour and 7 minutes

4. WHAT WAS ACHIEVED THROUGH THIS INTERVIEW PROGRAMME?

A variety of questions need to be considered. What changes to services will result from the interview programme? While the reports can be reviewed for their comprehensiveness and potential usefulness, their true usefulness depends on how much they occasion actual changes in practice, a question which will take time to resolve.

If benefits are eventually delivered, there are questions about which aspects of this interview programme set in motion the process of service improvement. How important was the use of managers as interviewers? Would this particular interview schedule have produced the same end-results if the interviews had been conducted instead by independent researchers? If the role of managers was a crucial element, might similar end results have occurred had managers used a much simpler, less structured interview method, or greatly simplified reporting procedures?

Only limited comment can be made on these issues. But there are some questions which can be usefully explored at this stage.

Did these interviews reach very old service users, as intended?

These interviews were intended to reach very old people, who formed a large proportion of the home care clientele but whose views were rarely obtained through current consultation methods. Here the interview programme was very successful. As Table 5.1 shows, half the interviewees in each catchment were aged over 85 years. It proved possible to obtain samples which matched closely the age distribution of the local home care clientele.

What were interviewers' opinions about the interview programme?

One source for interviewers' views is the questionnaires completed by the interviewer immediately after each interview, rating its usefulness. These showed that half the 30 interviews were rated as 'Clearly worthwhile'. Eleven were rated 'Probably worthwhile', while there were four where the interviewer was uncertain whether the interview had been worthwhile. No interviews were rated as either probably or definitely not worthwhile.

These ratings do not convey interviewers' experience of the programme as a whole. Information on this is available from a set of individual telephone interviews with all the interviewers, conducted soon after the draft of the full report was circulated. These interviews were conducted by a researcher who had never been involved with the interview programme. The results of these telephone interviews are presented at the end of this section.

What did the reports provide?

Both reports presented 16 recommendations - shown in Fig 5.4. In addition, at least eight other important specific messages about services can be discerned in the full report, though these did not constitute recommendations. Some particularly important findings can be singled out.

Figure 5.4: SUMMARY LIST OF SPECIFIC RECOMMENDATIONS

Proposals for new types of service
(To be piloted and evaluated on a limited scale, for wider application if successful)
1) Measures to enable supportive one-to-one relationships for selected Home Care clients, identified on grounds of social isolation, to supplement their help from Home Care.

2) A service to improve quality of life for older people who feel markedly frustrated by difficulties caused by mobility or sensory losses. It should address both travel outside one's home and rewarding activities inside it.

Modifications to established services
3) There should be a programme of general guidance to Home Care staff on working with people who are depressed or isolated.

4) People who wish household cleaning additional to hygiene and safety requirements - i.e. for quality of life reasons - should be actively helped to obtain their own private cleaners at their own cost.

5) People who at present receive cleaning on an 'unplanned' basis should instead be actively helped to obtain their own private cleaners at their own cost.

6) Home Care should extend to all isolated clients the help with small household maintenance tasks which it currently often gives to people who are both isolated and very frail.

7) Home Care clients, who wish help to access good maintenance, repair or gardening services, should be actively helped to find providers on a private basis just as for extra cleaning.

8) There should be a review of what is expected from day centres in terms of activities for clients and of the resources needed for such service.

9) Steps should be taken to identify people who should be offered more bathing.

10) A programme should be organised to offer prompt installation of showers in the homes of people for whom this would extend the years for which they can bathe themselves.

11) Procedures for obtaining aids and adaptations should be revised so as to enable much swifter delivery.

12) The management of overpayments by clients to their Community Care Accounts should be reviewed.

13) The Housing Department's agreement should be sought that it is a responsibility of Sheltered Housing Wardens to reduce risk of residents suffering crime and to help them feel safe.

14) There should be a review of possibilities for making more use of Sheltered Housing Wardens to assist social care tasks.

Proposals for new information gathering
15) Differences between different catchments should be investigated concerning the amount of help given to older people by family and friends. Resource distribution within Social Services should be adjusted to recognise any marked variations.

16) The new procedures for annual reviews by Reviewing Officers should include questions which help to identify people who may need the responses in Paras 4, 5, 6, 7 or 8 and which can also identify outcomes from implementing those Paragraphs.

A major theme

- To an extent older people's satisfaction with their services seemed something they constructed according to their underlying level of morale. Some older people seemed to emphasise the good aspects of the help they received and to consistently overlook or play down its shortcomings. They felt cared for and expressed appreciation and friendliness concerning people who helped them. Other interviewees, who seemed distressed concerning matters not connected with their services, seemed especially affected by the deficiencies in their services and inclined to dwell on shortcomings. It seemed possible that these service user attitudes could affect the behaviour of service givers in ways which might compound the service user's feelings about their services - whether feelings of appreciation or feelings of distress.

- There was a clear connection between interviewees being depressed or otherwise distressed and the use of frequent negative ratings and strong negative ratings about their services and their life-situations. A service's overall satisfaction ratings could be significantly affected if it had especially many clients who were distressed or depressed. The question was raised as to through what agencies and by what methods steps should be taken to respond to such distress.

- Illustration was given of factors which commonly distress older people - social isolation, problems in travelling outside the home, loss of valued activities like reading, knitting or needlework owing to disorders affecting vision, hearing or manual dexterity. Many interviewees received no help with such problems.

- There were signs that both social isolation and depression were more common in area office B's catchment. There, support from family and neighbours seemed less available than in area A. Also, very isolated, depressed or distressed older people seemed more common in area B.

- Satisfaction with Social Services help differed substantially between the two catchments. A case could be seen for conducting this interview programme in every catchment area in the authority to identify differences in satisfaction. However, understanding and responding to such differences appeared a complex task. Poorer satisfaction ratings might very well reflect that Social Services faced a more difficult task in that area and that local resources had not been adjusted sufficiently to recognise this. As just mentioned, area office B seemed to encounter two aspects of local disadvantage, each of which could lower satisfaction ratings. It seemed in fact to address more problems on behalf of home care clients than the area A service, because less informal help seemed available in this community. Also there were signs that the general shortage of informal social support in this catchment might mean more home care clients with low morale and a depressed outlook, who were inclined to give lower ratings of satisfaction.

A central conclusion was that an important opportunity might exist to improve the outcomes from Social Services help, as experienced by clients, through addressing the problems of low morale and depression which seemed to undermine the impact of conventional Social Services practical help. Moreover it seemed that these problems might be concentrated in particular geographical parts of the authority, possibly in quite small localities so that the home care teams assigned to certain 'patches' might be particularly affected. As follows, the full report proposed the testing of special measures for addressing the problem in relevant localities.

In this programme of interviews, negative ratings about outcomes and satisfaction with services were pronounced among a small group of depressed or unhappy interviewees, some of whom were very isolated. Arguably a direct step for improving the results of Social Services help would be to try to address the factors which prevent this minority from experiencing the same benefits as do other clients. Even though opportunities are limited, this problem seems sufficiently marked that responses should be thoroughly explored. Sometimes it may be appropriate to address depression through links to mental health specialists. Sometimes it may be possible to tackle an underlying practical problem. For instance, one interviewer arranged the rehousing of a very depressed interviewee, whose mood seemed affected by how her housing amplified her limitations from arthritis. Some recommendations likewise relate to factors which can affect mood. For instance, there are measures for helping people who are very troubled by being unable to leave their home, or by loss of valued leisure activities through vision disorders or arthritis, or by the decline in the cleanliness and attractiveness of their home. Importantly, there is evidence from other sources that sometimes depression can be prevented by supportive relationships which can help people get over distressing events like episodes of illness or advancing disability which are now so common among the home care clientele. Also, there are researchers who believe that such relationships can sometimes help to alleviate depression. In this respect the isolation of some interviewees, aside from paid service-givers, demands attention. Arguably, some sort of emotional support should be available for every older person who is facing the health adversities which are becoming the norm on today's home care list. Appropriate paid staff should perhaps attempt this role where relatives or friends are not undertaking it. Another desirable step would be training for home care staff in how to approach everyday contacts with clients who appear depressed or uncommunicative, and training for Senior home care assistants in ways of supporting staff when they find clients distressing. Also important could be training in recognising depression and when to involve other workers.
(Patmore, 2000)

Both the findings and the recommendations are supported by the work of researchers elsewhere. Vetter *et al.* (1988) studied satisfaction ratings on different aspects of life among people aged over 70 years. People whose scores on mental health questionnaires suggested anxiety and depression gave much lower satisfaction ratings on all topics than did the overall sample. The researchers concluded that satisfaction ratings are closely related to psychological state. It seems plausible that satisfaction ratings for social care services would likewise be affected.

Grundy and Bowling (1999) conducted interviews to investigate quality of life among people aged over 85 from a single London borough. Among these, they identified a small group of particularly dissatisfied people. The latter used community care services on account of illness or disability and were socially isolated and lonely. They gave very negative ratings on all aspects of quality of life. They had General Health Questionnaire scores clearly indicating psychiatric problems but, while they made comments which the researchers believed indicated depression, they were not receiving treatment for depression.

Social networks and social support can strongly affect older people's morale, according to a number of researchers. Tinker (1982) noted significantly lower morale among older people who lived alone and Wenger (1992) stated that older people's morale benefitted if they had a 'confidante' within their network, 'someone with whom one can talk about the joys, sorrows and problems of life'. Wenger (1992) also found that networks which comprised both many relatives and many friends all living close by were of particular benefit, and that having this type of network was linked to high levels of satisfaction among older people.

Other research findings are also broadly consistent with the interpretations made in the full report concerning isolated, distressed or depressed home care clients. There is very widespread evidence that episodes of physical ill-health are a common trigger for the onset of depression in older people (Denihan *et al.*, 2000). More specifically, Prince *et al.* (1998) and Copeland *et al.* (1999) emphasise the impact of physical ill-health which leads to handicap like loss of accustomed roles or functions - for instance loss of mobility. Such disabling health conditions were in fact mentioned by SPRU interviewees as major dissatisfactions. Vetter *et al.* (1986) found a strong association between severity of disability and both anxiety and depression among older people.

As might be expected from the high proportion of home care clients with disabling illnesses, depression can be widespread among them. Banerjee & Macdonald (1996) found that a quarter of their sample of older home care clients were depressed and 84 per cent of these were not receiving appropriate treatment. Failure to treat depression in older people appropriately has also been noted in general community surveys (Copeland *et al.*, 1999; Denihan *et al.*, 2000), even though effective methods of treatment do exist (Banerjee *et al.*, 1996; Denihan *et al.*, 2000). Proportions of older people who suffer from depression can vary substantially between communities (Vetter *et al.*, 1986). Murphy (1982) found a much higher prevalence of depression among working-class than middle-class older people.

Thus there is support from findings elsewhere for key constructs in the full report, such as the linkages between an older person's social world, their satisfaction with services and the possibility of important differences between Social Services catchments in terms of the social networks most common among their older service users. The latter would have implications for how resources are assigned and for conclusions drawn from comparisons between satisfaction ratings. There is support too for the notion that some home care clients are conspicuously vulnerable to depression on account of illness, handicap, isolation and lack of help with emotional or mental health. The SPRU recommendations also have parallels in conclusions drawn by some of the studies previously cited.

Other themes in the reports from the interview programme by service managers

- Day centres were clearly facing challenges in meeting needs for stimulating, interesting activities for a significant number of their users.

- There was a case for opening dialogue with sheltered housing providers on ways in which housing staff and Social Services staff could work together to fulfil the goals of social care. Sheltered housing staff appeared a major under-utilised resource for achieving the latter.

- There was a case for investigating and challenging whatever system for providing aids and adaptations could result in the delays which had been discovered during some interviews. In fact, unwarranted delays in provision of aids and adaptations are a widespread problem nationally (Audit Commission, 2000).

The views of the managers who conducted the interviews

Telephone interviews with the interviewers were conducted by a SPRU researcher who otherwise was independent from the project. The telephone interviews were taped, transcribed and analysed.

All managers interviewed in the evaluation found the experience enjoyable, valuable for practice and interesting for service planning. Most managers had been approached by someone senior to them and invited to take part, and all said they were happy to do so. Some had initially been apprehensive about the possible reactions of older service users, anticipating that they would meet substantial complaints, for example about cleaning, and would have to spend considerable time justifying the department's policies. In the event, direct contact with users proved to be the most enjoyable aspect of the experience. Although a few managers anticipated that the process would not yield new information, this concern proved unfounded.

All managers had enjoyed the process of interviewing. Reasons included: positive reception by older people, and their obvious enjoyment of the occasion in many cases; the reminder that some service packages were excellent and much valued; admiration for the way in which some older people coped with difficulties and problems; a holistic view of services and people's lives; being reminded about the fundamental purposes of services.

Occasional difficulties encountered during interviewing included: coping with digression; interviewee fatigue; being unable to offer a service that would resolve problems presented; a depressed person who did not want the interviewer to leave; worry about older people who had high expectations about the pace of likely change following the interview.

All managers expressed willingness to conduct further interviews, despite continuing pressure on their time. However a majority would desire some changes to the interview schedule. Many, but not all, had found it repetitive and felt it could be shortened or streamlined. One suggestion was a shorter schedule for those receiving lower levels of service. There seemed to be some variation in the way that interviewers had used the schedule, with some taking a more flexible approach, but others not feeling confident enough to do so. This suggests that, in any future usage, there would be benefits from additional training or briefing sessions with interviewers.

Most managers felt that there were gains for the department in enabling senior managers to keep in touch with the issues which really matter in users' lives. One staff member stated a preference for independent interviews, perhaps conducted by the voluntary sector. Another suggested a newly appointed reviewing officer. Three favoured a mixture of in-house and independent researchers, with the latter perhaps having an overall role in relation to reviewing the information gathered. When asked whether doing these interviews was a good way of gathering information on topics that matter to customers, there was an overwhelmingly positive response.

One member of staff was concerned that in their area office the responsibility for interviews had been devolved to less senior managers. This is certainly of importance because the presumed benefits of being interviewed by someone with the power to achieve change, and to analyse organisational failings, will be reduced as the responsibility for interviewing is devolved. In fact, more senior managers were more likely to raise inter-agency issues, which was a very useful consequence of some interviews.

Staff were asked whether the process of doing the interviews had had any impact upon them or stimulated them to change their practice. Many positive responses were made. Two staff felt that it was helpful in keeping them in touch with 'the real world' of service users, and one described this as 're-grounding'. One staff member subsequently gave more thought to assessment of depressed people and how well they were served. One re-examined the meals service and revised their view of the importance of sheltered housing wardens in service users' lives. One subsequently took steps to direct junior staff to systematically ascertain the wishes of service users. Another manager was made acutely aware of the importance and value of some services to service users, like home cleaning. Four staff did not note any impact. Overall, the capacity to positively affect professional practice was the area in which staff reported the most positive change and was without doubt, the most useful aspect of the interviews to staff members.

In thinking about the changes which might result from the exercise, some interviewers pointed out that certain interviewees had experienced changes to services as a result, and some managers had acted on their own initiative to tackle more general problems which had become visible. In general participants felt that they had gained valuable information on their services and opportunities for improving these. However, wider impact on the organisation as a whole, and the development of new services, was still uncertain. This uncertainty was attributed to local changes taking place in the structure and operation of social services as mentioned earlier.

5. SOME LESSONS FOR FUTURE INTERVIEW PROGRAMMES

The quantity, variety and detail in the reports produced from the interviews, is so extensive that they would stimulate some years of development work, even if only partially implemented. This is true even of the summary report. It is clear that this is not a method which it would make sense to repeat annually in exactly the same way with the same service user groups in the same catchment - though repetition after four or five years or after any major changes to services could be appropriate.

This interview programme is a tool for stimulating initiatives to improve services. Monitoring the progress of the initiatives suggested by the interview programme could be undertaken through a routine client review system, like the new annual review system, operated by review officers, which is scheduled for introduction by this authority. It is important to recognise that the interview programme, which takes an in-depth approach with a very small sample, is a qualitative method intended to inspire a possible programme of action. It is not an appropriate method for monitoring successful implementation of that programme of action. For the latter, much larger samples are needed and it should be possible to harness the routine review procedure for this purpose. This interview programme and a routine client review system are both needed. They are complementary and support each other.

The interview programme fulfils well the wish expressed by senior managers in stage one for a means for occasional in-depth investigations which could supply guidance for developing their services. It would also appear promising as an element in the process of commissioning services promoted in *Modernising Social Services* (Department of Health, 1998).

There are grounds for a degree of confidence that a report on 16 interviewees in a single catchment area, similar in length and content to the summary report, could be produced by interviewers in an area office with four weeks FTE staff time devoted wholly to analysis and report-writing. But such a report would obviously not include the inter-catchment comparisons which feature in the reports from this exercise, which drew on two catchments. The inter-catchment comparisons proved a very helpful aspect of this exercise.

In contrast, the full report was so time-consuming that it cannot be suggested that a senior Social Services staff member could be seconded from other duties for long enough to produce such a detailed report. Either research personnel are needed or the report must be much simpler. The latter would definitely mean a loss of information. However, a full report is only useful if it can be read and acted on. Some interviewers commented that the full report was too long and detailed for busy managers to read. There seem inevitable limits to the number of recommendations which management can work on. Possibly a shorter report would make high priority information more salient. However, the comparisons between catchments were extremely useful and it would seem a clear mistake to miss this opportunity.

Consequences of using managers as interviewers

Some important expected gains from the exercise cannot be assessed until there has been opportunity for implementation. However signs of certain gains from using managers as interviewers can be identified already.

McQuarrie (1998) cites the ability of manager interviewers to probe topics whose importance an independent researcher might not recognise or not be equipped to discuss. There were certainly instances in this interview programme where interviewers used their knowledge as managers to make recommendations on subjects where an independent researcher might not have felt competent to identify a problem. For instance, managers identified certain time-frames for supplying aids or adaptations as constituting unacceptable delays. A home care manager pointed out an opportunity for easy financial abuse and urged counter-measures. A manager with an administrative role probed for mistakes in the charging system and identified a problem with the policy on overpayments by clients. Some managers assessed whether the cleanliness of an interviewee's home met organisational standards - and sometimes commissioned extra service. Some managers made discreet appraisals of how well-stocked was an interviewee's larder in order to assess the general standard of care.

The most conspicuous application of managers' knowledge was direct intervention by interviewers in response to issues raised in the interview. It had been agreed that, while information gathering was the core purpose, interviewers could intervene whenever their Social Services commitments required them to do so. Interventions were recorded, as requested, in the interview notes. Interventions included, for instance, referrals to Welfare Rights to check eligibility for unclaimed benefits, referral for physiotherapy investigations, for extra home care for specific purposes, referral to day centres, to voluntary sector gardening services, or for rehousing in accommodation adapted to an interviewee's disabilities.

The most interesting interventions were those which would affect many other service users besides the interviewee who had inspired the intervention. This type of intervention seems a means whereby the interview programme can directly bring changes to services. For instance an interviewer witnessed a meals-on-wheels delivery during an interview with a partially sighted client. The interviewee had to ask her interviewer what was on her plate because the meals-on-wheels worker had failed to tell her. The interviewer raised this incident with the meals-on-wheels management and was told all staff would now receive reminders about communicating with people with vision problems. Another interviewee's complaint about a type of alarm used throughout a block of sheltered flats led to an enquiry which would cover all its residents. In one area office home care staff were given mass briefings about two issues which had been raised during interviews by their home care manager. When interviewers in one area heard complaints about lack of activities at a day centre, they began regular visits to observe the centre, which adjoined their own offices. If changes are now made, clients additional to their interviewees will benefit. When some interviewees complained about the relief wardens in their sheltered housing, an interviewer placed this on the agenda for a forthcoming meeting between managers from Social Services and Housing. She would be able to speak at this meeting from what she had heard for herself. These interventions, which affect many more service users than one fortunate interviewee, are made more effective by interviewers' authority within their own agency and their status in discussions with other agencies. They add to the case for using managers as interviewers.

There were some other gains from using Social Services managers as interviewers. They had easier access to interviewees than independent researchers. They seemed to handle confidently some unexpected situations. For instance, they could recognise communication or cognitive difficulties (when home care organisers had not identified these during the screening process) and make swift judgements about the best course of action. Not least, some managers seemed to feel strongly encouraged in their commitment to Social Services through hearing first-hand how much Social Services had achieved for certain interviewees and how greatly this was appreciated. Normally, some commented, they never met service users except when there were complaints or difficulties. These interviews had shown them the service's successes as well.

Alternative ways of using managers as interviewers
As mentioned, some area A interviewers wished to conduct further interview programmes. One suggestion was to interview Social Services clients about different sheltered housing projects. The idea was to follow up issues from the initial interview programme about collaboration with sheltered housing staff and differences in quality between different sheltered housing schemes. One possibility was for these interviews be conducted jointly by pairs of Social Services and Housing Department managers so

that ensuing discussions between the two agencies might be based on shared experience of the interviews. Another suggestion for a second interview programme was interviews with a sample of users of a rehabilitation service, which managers wished to understand better. For both suggestions, a new interview schedule would need to be devised.

An issue raised by SPRU concerning further programmes was the possibility of verbal, rather than written, reporting procedures. If an interview programme is intended to inform particular management decisions, an interview schedule could focus on these alone and the reporting procedure could occur verbally, the interviewers reporting together to a meeting where those decisions would be made. This would be much less time-consuming. Such a modification would require that all interviews be conducted within a short time-frame, soon before they were discussed. However, while the reporting of interviews would be verbal in this model, there still should be a written summary of the conclusions reached and a written plan for action. As with the original form of this interview programme, the summary of conclusions and the action plan should be made public.

Some issues concerning future use of managers as interviewers

The following emerged as important considerations, in any form of interview programme which uses managers.

1. After the interview programme, some interviewers expressed concern that future interviews must not use managers less senior than themselves. They worried that the procedure might become undermined by use, say, of care managers, rather than principal care managers in order to limit the latter's workload. They felt that it was decision-makers of their rank and above who should interview service users. Some argued that Area Managers and, indeed, Assistant Directors, should be required to act as interviewers. SPRU concluded that readiness to raise inter-agency issues as a result of interviews seemed likely to increase with an interviewer's seniority.

2. SPRU would especially welcome an interview programme where managers interviewed four service users each. There are hazards from managers interviewing too few clients, in that they become excessively influenced by one or two examples (McQuarrie, 1998). A particular hazard is a single interview by the most senior manager, on account of the latter's shortage of time, which may then over-influence the key decision-maker. Within a 16 interview programme, involving each interviewer with four interviews would help by inviting the number of managers involved, which should make for easier discussion of the results within the interview team. Intuitively, it would seem productive for a small team of managers to undertake equal amounts of interviewing so as to feel equally informed when discussing information from the interviews.

3.   It might make it easier for very senior managers to participate as interviewers if they interviewed jointly with other managers. The latter could save the former's time by making all preliminary arrangements and completing all interview notes. Such joint interviewing is recommended by McQuarrie (1998) both on practical grounds and as an easy means for increasing the number of interviews in which each manager participates. However, we do not know how older Social Services clients might view joint interviews.

4.   Some area A interviewers said that, with hindsight, they thought a well-planned interview programme could be conducted within little more than a month. They suggested that a coordinator should organise the checks of willingness and suitability of prospective interviewees *en masse* in advance of the interview programme. Such checks conducted one at a time had involved avoidable delay. It is hard to estimate how rapidly an interview programme can be completed without a practical test of measures to speed progress. But it seems likely that improvement could be made on the timescale of this initial programme.

6.   CONCLUSIONS

This interview programme demonstrates a promising method for appraisal, planning and management of services. Both its components - the use of service managers as interviewers and this particular interview schedule - can be used in a wide range of community social services for older people.

In any community it should be constructive to conduct the interview programme described here. Results seem capable of providing inspiration for years of service development. It can apply to many situations. A lone manager in an isolated rural community could apply it on their own if they had time to interview, say, 12 randomly selected clients, and could analyse results in a structured fashion. It will be easier to persuade managers to undertake an interview programme if they can envisage useful results and are confident that they can actually complete it despite other demands on their time. While such an interview programme requires substantial work it may well be swifter and easier to organise than alternative methods of gathering views of frail older service users (Patmore, 2001).

The interview schedule (see the appendices) was designed with widespread applicability in mind. The central section on outcomes, Section 3, can apply to any older person living in the community - including older people who do not use services, for whom Section 3 could be used on its own. The optional sections on particular services, Supplementary Sheets 4 - 6, were designed to embrace any combination of services in an individual's care package in any authority. They can include care packages which use more than one home care provider or more than one day centre. The Supplementary Sheets for *Other Significant Social Care Services* can be used for any additional, locality-specific services which a team of managers wishes to investigate. During the programme these sheets were used, on the interviewers' own initiative, to investigate two unusual types of service which have been developed within this authority. A team of managers could also devise further Supplementary Sheets of their own choice using the same simple format.

If SPRU were to make any modification to the interview schedule as a result of the trial, it would be to add a Supplementary Sheet about sheltered housing. Despite interviewers' comments about repetition, it is felt that, on balance, more would be lost than gained from reducing the schedule further. Experience of using the schedule and knowledge about how useful responses can prove, when aggregated, would, it is hoped, reduce such reservations.

It had always been hoped that interview programmes by managers could eventually include a true cross-section of Social Services clients, including people who could not communicate at all well with interviewers. It had also been hoped that in such situations managers could learn something from whatever communication was possible, from observation, and from any family members present. However, for this trial interview programme, on grounds of caution, Social Services had been instructed to exclude any of the clients randomly selected for interview if communication would be 'very difficult' on grounds of dementia or speech or hearing problems. But, as mentioned earlier, some interviews did take place with people with moderate communication difficulties, who were interviewed jointly with a spouse who supplied substantial information for the interviewee. These interviews all proved productive. For a more complete picture to result, it would seem desirable in future to include people with pronounced communication difficulties within an interview programme. It should also be possible to include people who do not speak English through interviewing with an interpreter, though no such clients were encountered during the trial interview programme.

One remaining area of uncertainty is how easily a manager team could handle the analysis and reporting stage. Another is how faithfully a manager team could practice stratified random sampling to select interviewees. These were both areas where SPRU retained control during the interview programme, while delegating other procedures to Social Services via written instructions. Testing Social Services' ability to manage these steps is a major priority in any future development.

Discussion of the interview programme here has dwelt on its use to guide service commissioning by a statutory authority. However, it could also be used to guide a provider service, be it Social Services or independent sector, on improving customer satisfaction or developing new types of service. For an enterprising independent sector provider, much of the wide-ranging SPRU interview schedule could still have relevance - for instance to identify opportunities for developing new services. Indeed this would be a usage similar to McQuarrie's programmes of visits to customers in private sector industries (McQuarrie, 1998).

Alongside the particular interview programme described here, it would also seem constructive for Social Services managers to develop other manager interview programmes, perhaps to make such structured investigations a routine tool for management. Such additional programmes might include investigations of specific services or programmes on inter-agency collaboration, where both agencies conducted interviews jointly. A challenge would be for managers to innovate and customise when designing fresh interview programmes, while maintaining an appropriate structure to ensure well-focused, comparable and informative answers.

SUMMARY OF CHAPTER FIVE

A programme of home interviews with a small random sample of older users of Social Services community care was designed. It was intended to assist managers in making decisions on policy and service development through providing a fuller, fact-based understanding of the strengths and weaknesses of current services and policies, as a result of directly perceiving their outcomes in clients' everyday lives. The interviewers were the local managers who had overall responsibility for the interviewees' services. The design of the interview programme reflected information learned during stage one research.

During 1999 a test of this interview programme was carried out with 30 older users of community social services, who were interviewed by 11 managers from two different Area Offices. An interview schedule was devised by SPRU which examined both outcomes in various areas of daily living (regardless of whether interviewees received help with these) and, also, interviewees' experience of the impact of each service which they received.

Reports were produced which identified particular areas for development in each catchment. They made a general case for a greater role for Social Services in addressing threats to the morale of older community care clients - like isolation and social consequences of disabling illnesses - in part because service users' morale seemed to influence whether outcomes from services like home care were experienced as satisfactory. The interview programme showed potential as an qualitative tool for service review and for inspiring plans for service development.

Despite initial reservation about time costs, the managers who acted as interviewers were generally positive about the experience and willing to continue. Some felt better informed through their personal experience of these interviews. Before the reports had been produced, some interviewers had felt moved to investigate and address a wide range of problems raised by their interviewees. A significant number of these interventions would affect many service users besides the interviewee who inspired it - for instance, review of a day centre's activity programme or of the roles of the Housing Department's sheltered housing wardens. These benefits from using managers as interviewers need not be specific to the interview schedule used in this instance. There is a general case for managers engaging personally in structured investigations of the services which they manage or purchase.

The reporting process used in this first test of the interview programme was too time-consuming for routine use. A streamlined approach needs to be developed and tested. Likewise, examination is needed of how such an interview programme could be routinely completed using only Social Services resources. Since this was an initial test of the interview programme, some key functions like random selection of interviewees, analysis of interview notes and production of the report were conducted by SPRU. Investigation is needed into how a Social Services Department can best undertake these functions using only its own resources.

There are also challenges which are intrinsic to the method. By their nature, these interviews produce recommendations which reflect older people's global experience. They are wide-ranging and do not neatly fit the compartments of management responsibilities within Social Services - or, indeed, the boundaries between the responsibilities of Social Services, Health and Housing. This global character of feedback from older service users was expected and was seen as a gain from the method. But it does make the report harder to process and act on when there are many competing demands on senior management time.

Acknowledgement
The interviews, which evaluated the managers' experience of interviewing service users, were conducted by Jennifer Harris, Senior Research Fellow at SPRU, independently from the rest of this project. She also wrote the passages in this chapter which report this evaluation.

References

Audit Commission (2000) *Fully Equipped*, Audit Commission, London

Banerjee, S. and Macdonald, A. (1996) 'Mental Disorder in an Elderly home care Population: Associations with Health and Social Service Use', *British Journal of Psychiatry* 168, 750 - 756

Banerjee, S., Shamash, K., Macdonald, A. and Mann, A. (1996) 'Randomised controlled trial of effect of intervention by psychogeriatric team on depression in frail elderly people at home', *British Medical Journal* 313, 1058 - 1061

Copeland, J., Chen, R., Dewey, M., McCracken, C., Gilmore, C., Larkin, B. and Wilson, K. (1999) 'Community -based case-control study of depression in older people', *British Journal of Psychiatry* 175, 340 - 347

Denihan, A., Kirby, M., Bruce, I., Cunningham, C., Coakley, D. and Lawlor, B. (2000) 'Three year prognosis of depression in the community-dwelling elderly', *British Journal of Psychiatry* 176, 453-457

Department of Health (1998) *Modernising Social Services*, Social Care White Paper, Cm4169, London: The Stationery Office

Fiedler, B. (1999) *Promoting independence: preventative strategies and support for older people: report of the SSI study,* London: Department of Health

Fisk, M. (1997) 'Older People as Researchers', in Roger Sykes (Ed) *Putting Older People in the Picture: a conference report*, 54 - 61, Kidlington: Anchor Trust

Gazdar, C. (1999) *That's the way the money goes: inspection of commissioning arrangements for community care services*, London: Department of Health

Grundy, E. and Bowling, A. (1999) 'Enhancing the quality of extended life years. Identification of the oldest old with a very good and very poor quality of life', *Aging & Mental Health* 3, 199 - 212

McQuarrie, E.F. (1998) *Customer Visits: Building a better market focus,* Thousand Oaks, California: Sage Publications

Murphy, E.(1982) 'Social Origins of Depression in Old Age', *British Journal of Psychiatry* 141, 135 - 142

Patmore, C., Qureshi, H., Nicholas, E. and Bamford, C. (1998) *Outcomes for older people and their family carers: stage 1,* Report to Department of Health DH 1537, York: University of York, Social Policy Research Unit.

Patmore, C., Qureshi, H. and Nicholas, E. (2000) 'Consulting older community care clients about their services: some lessons for researchers and service managers', *Research, Policy and Planning* 18 (1), 4 -11

Patmore, C. (2000) *Interviews with users of community care services by managers: the Full Report,* Report to partner authority, York: University of York, Social Policy Research Unit

Patmore, C. (2001) Can managers research their own services? An experiment in consulting frail, older community care clients, *Managing Community Care* 9 (5), 8 -17

Prince, M., Harwood, R., Thomas, A., and Mann, A. (1998) 'A prospective population-based cohort study of the effects of disablement and social milieu on the onset and maintenance of late-life depression, The Gospel Oak Project VII', *Psychological Medicine* 28, 337 - 350

Saunders, M., Wilson, J. and Radburn, J. (1992) 'Enabling consumers of Social Services to be heard', *Research, Policy and Planning* 10, 1 - 5

Tinker, A. (1982) 'Improving the quality of life and promoting the independence of elderly people', in DHSS (Ed) *Elderly people in the community: their service needs*, London: The Stationery Office

Vetter, N., Jones, D. and Victor, C. (1988) 'The quality of life of the over 70s in the community', *Health Visitor* 61, 10 -13

Vetter, N., Jones, D., Victor, C., and Philips, A. (1986) 'The measurement of psychological problems in the elderly in general practice', *International Journal of Geriatric Psychiatry* 1, 127 -134.

Wallace, R., Kohout, F. and Colsher, P. (1992) 'Observations on interview surveys of the oldest old', in R.M. Suzman, D.P. Willis, and K.G. Manton (Eds) *The Oldest Old*, New York: Oxford University Press, 123 -134.

Wenger, C. (1992) *Help in Old Age - Facing up to Change: a longitudinal network study,* Liverpool: Liverpool University Press

APPENDICES TO CHAPTER FIVE

The following are supplied as appendices:

- **The full interview schedule used in this interview programme.** Guidance notes are at the beginning. Section 11 was for evaluation purposes and could be discarded. For this interview programme, the different sections were copied on different colours of paper, so interviewers could quickly find different parts of the schedule, as required. The guidance notes and sections 10 and 11, which are for use by interviewer on their own, were on yellow paper. Sections 1, 2 , 3 and 9, which are for all interviewees, were on white. Sections 4 - 8, which are only for interviewees to whom these apply, were on blue paper.

- **The standard letter which initially requested an older service user to participate in an interview.**

- **The summary of the interview topics, for mailing to interviewees in advance.** Preliminary research had indicated that some older people would value such opportunity to prepare their thoughts.

- **The document sent to Home Care Organisers to screen names of possible interviewees for people who should not be included.** Guidance notes are also supplied.

- **The standard letter to explain to home care staff the purpose of the interview programme.** Some staff would certainly hear about it anyway - for instance, some interviewees would tell them.

- **Procedure used to analyse the interview notes and produce the report.** Please note that some aspects reflect that there were 30 interviewees, divided fairly evenly between two catchment services. Somewhat different procedures might suit different circumstances.

Confidential Information

MANAGER'S INTERVIEW
WITH USERS OF
SOCIAL CARE SERVICES
FOR OLDER PEOPLE

Quick Guide to locating topics

For all interviewees

1. Preliminary: Listing of help received from Social Services
2. Open-ended questions about the service user's views
3. Checklist of satisfaction with outcomes in key areas of daily living:
>   3.1   Meals and refreshments
>   3.2   Shopping
>   3.3   Laundry
>   3.4   Household cleaning
>   3.5   Odd jobs in the household / repairs / decoration / gardening
>   3.6   Getting help quickly in emergencies
>   3.7   Feeling safe from crime and nuisance
>   3.8   Money, bills, pensions, benefits, legal
>   3.9   Personal Care
>   3.10 Getting out / activities outside the home
>   3.11 Social life
>   3.12 Sources of interest in everyday life

Supplementary Sheets: only if these services or situations apply to an interviewee

4. Supplementary Sheet: Home Care (main / sole provider of Home Care)
*4. Supplementary Sheet: Home Care (second provider of Home Care, if there is one)

5. Supplementary Sheet: Day Centre 1 (Day centre attenders only)
*5. Supplementary Sheet: Day Centre 2 (People attending two day centres only)

6.   Supplementary Sheet: Other significant social care services (If comment is warranted on services like Care Management, Sitting Service or short residential breaks)
*6. Same as above.

7. Supplementary Sheet: Care after hospital discharge. (If discharged in last 12 months)

8. Supplementary Sheet: Family carer views (For family carers living with the client)

9. Help from Social Services in general (all interviewees)
>   9.1   Additional help which the client would like from Social Services
>   9.2   Issues re Preventative Strategies for Older People (only for Priority 3 Homecare & less)
>   9.3   Client's overall satisfaction with outcome of help from Social Services

For completion after the interview only - for all interviewees
10   Post-interview assessments written by interviewer on their own.
11   Post-interview assessment of time and usefulness of interview

MANAGER'S INTERVIEW WITH SERVICE USERS:
GUIDANCE NOTES FOR INTERVIEWERS

It is vital to read this thoroughly so as to be guided by the purpose of these interviews in the way you ask questions and record answers. It's important to understand the different sections of the interview so as to know how to move quickly to different parts, which sections can be left out, what needs to be recorded during the interview and which section is for completion on your own afterwards. The best first step to gaining an overview of the actual interview, before you read this any further, is to read the summary of the entire interview in two pages, which has been produced for posting to interviewees in advance.

Purpose and uses of these interviews
To help improve social care services by showing senior managers the strengths and weaknesses of present services and policies, through hearing their outcome in clients' everyday lives - hence informing action to improve services and guiding future policy. From each round of interviews (in this trial, 16 interviews per Constituency in two Constituencies), a Report will be produced on the following:

- unmet needs and areas where service development would be beneficial

- achievements of the service and areas where problems seemed rare

- outcome information which gives useful feedback about policy decisions

- options concerning priorities for service improvements and development.

This Report will be fed into the annual process of planning service development.

In addition to affecting services via feeding into the established planning process, sometimes these interviews will improve services more immediately through an interviewing Manager taking action on a problem as soon as they hear of it in an interview. The latter reflects that occasionally an interviewing Manager will hear something which raises immediate concerns about the welfare of a client. Likewise situations will certainly sometimes be encountered when opportunity to tackle a problem may be lost unless action is taken swiftly. It is at the discretion of interviewing managers as to how far they thus intervene directly with referrals or other action. Such immediate action should be logged at 10.5.2, in the Post-interview Assessment Section, along with issues which interviewers definitely wish raised in the eventual Report.

Interviewers should take a broad look at interviewees' social care needs and outcomes and consider Social Services' broad responsibilities to them. Obviously much of the response will concern specific services like Home Care and day centres - and also Care Management, the Sitting Service or short residential breaks. But it is also valuable to explore any needs by interviewees for which services at present do not exist and to discuss issues outside the province of any specific service.

Conducting the Interview

In the interviews with SPRU, which inspired consultations by senior managers, older people conveyed that they wished an interview with the following features:

- It should give them fairly open space to say their piece in their own way without interruption by the interviewer's line of questioning.

- Whenever practicable, interviewees should be sent questions in advance so that they can prepare their thoughts and not feel that subjects are being sprung on them. A three page, easy-to-read summary of this document has been produced specially for this purpose. It should be sent in advance whenever possible. (Standard version is in large font. Braille versions are available if needed.)

- No attempt should be made to press a question if an answer is not forthcoming.

- Certain topics (included in Section 3) should always be raised - but never pressed.

- Where possible, an offer of a woman interviewer would be appreciated by women.

Please keep the above principles in mind throughout. To follow the first requires starting with the open-ended question in Section 2. It also means that you may have to move around the questions in the order in which interviewees touch on them, not seeking to enforce the order in this document. Thus it is vital to study it in advance so as to know what all the topics are and be able to move to the relevant section if the interviewee seems keen to talk about it at a particular moment. Unless an interviewee seems happy to let you take the initiative, do not press to work through the questions in the same order in which they are written. You can use the contents list on page 2 to find a topic quickly.

A delicate balance is required. On the one hand it's important that everyone gets asked the same questions using the same form of words so that answers can be compared. (If you have not used a semi-structured interview script like this before, it may take a few interviews before you recognise the gains from being able compare answers clearly because everyone's getting the same questions.) But, on the other hand, we need to heed older people's desire to deliver their message in their own way and to feel consulted, as one SPRU interviewee put it, rather than interrogated. It would be better to err in the direction of missing some questions than imposing your agenda if an interviewee seems averse to the latter. (One pilot interview suggested that, if interviewees have read the outline of the interview posted in advance, they may be more likely to wish you to lead them through it.)

Recording the interviewee's responses to the questions
During the interview you will need to briefly record responses as well as you can in the spaces supplied beside the questions *on the actual interview schedule*. You will find that you do not have time to do this in anything but a rushed, untidy, cursory way - that's completely unavoidable. But immediately after the interview - as soon as you have time and space on your own - in section 10, the post-interview assessment, you can sum up from your notes during the interview in a considered and orderly way.

Recording the actual interview
During the interview, the main types of recording required are (A) simply ticking the relevant tick-box, which will always be **on the left sheet** of a double page. (B) **on the right sheet** writing a brief explanation in your own words for the rating given on the left side. **Please always give an explanation when a box indicating low satisfaction or unmet need has been ticked, otherwise this information cannot be used for improving the service.** Give an explanation on any other ratings too, wherever you think this informative. Thus the tick box answers on the left sheet enable scores to be allotted and compared, while the explanations on the right sheet give meaning to these ratings. (C) There are some spaces on the left sheet which seek short factual answers. You can add detail to these on the right hand sheet, if you wish. There are some places where an answer in words can be written across both pages, if you wish. Or you may find it easier to use just the larger space on the right hand side because of the difficulty in writing neatly at speed. Feel free to use the blank right pages in whatever ways seem helpful. Inevitably the notes you can actually write during the interview will be short and not tidy. But they can nevertheless be very useful both in explaining ratings to the Report-writer and in helping you fill in the Post-Interview Assessment afterwards.

For these particular interviews, it is the explanations for satisfaction ratings which are important rather than the ratings themselves. Only if explanations are given for particular satisfaction ratings can the interview show us what makes for satisfaction or quality in the eyes of service users. It is not useful to tick the boxes without explanation - if you have to leave anything out it would be more useful to omit the tick boxes than to omit written comment. Wherever you can, add comments which convey how older people perceive and judge the subject of a question.

Sometimes part of the answer to a question may be something which you have already recorded somewhere else. To save time, just write the number of the question where the information is already given.

Sometimes the interviewee may have already made the answer to a question completely evident before you come to it. You can then enter this answer without asking the question but you should write "(inferred)" after the answer and do this only when the answer seems completely clear. Also, sometimes an interviewee does not answer a particular question (for instance some interviewees avoid making explicit critical ratings) but their other comments make very clear what is their likely opinion. In this case you can likewise enter an inferred answer - but you must always write "(inferred)" after it.

Writing-up after the interview

Please plan some time soon after the interview when you can reflect on the interview, read the ratings and notes you took, and fill in the Post-Interview Assessment undisturbed. Clearly the decisions about action and highlighting issues for the Report will need time for reflection. Please always remind yourself about the topics in the Post-Interview Assessment just before the interview so you can bear in mind what you will need to write up afterwards.

The various components of the interview

Facts for completion in advance of interview

Some of these will be supplied from Community Care Admin's records to the person at your Office who is co-ordinating these interviews. Some will need gathering from Home Care staff. This information is important:

(A) To prepare the interviewer for clients with communication problems or who have many services to be asked about or where a family carer will be present.

(B) To assist the Report writer since factors like age, home situation or particular physical handicaps may be crucial to understanding interviewees' responses.

THE ACTUAL INTERVIEW

Sections 1,2 and 3 are used for all interviewees.

Section 1 (for all interviews)

This simply invites the interviewee to describe their services in their own words. Usually they'll give a list of specific tasks which can be easily noted down.

Section 2 (for all interviews)

This offers the interviewee an open space right at the beginning in which they can make any prepared comment in their own fashion and at their own pace - as the SPRU interviewees recommended. During their reply the older person may give answers to later questions. Ideally, the interviewer should flick to those parts of the schedule, fill in these comments there and then, and not ask those questions again.

Section 3 (for all interviews)
This works through a list of basic areas in daily living and, for each one, checks out how satisfactory to the interviewee is *the end result in that particular area of life -* regardless of whether they get any help with this or whether that help comes from Social Services. For each item please start off by briefly asking the interviewee how at present their needs in that area of life are addressed. On some topics, some follow-up questions are suggested to prompt clarification. *Only after you have thus gained some grasp of how the relevant needs are actually being dealt with should you ask for the interviewee's rating of the satisfactoriness of the current state of affairs.* On the left page you tick whichever box best fits the interviewee's view of how satisfactory is the end result. On the right-hand page make a brief note to explain the rating. (Eg House cleaning might be ticked as "Satisfactory" and the right-hand page carry an explanation like "Employs private cleaner via Attendance Allowance" or "Only minimal cleaning by HCAs but client doesn't care.") The important thing is to communicate how satisfactory is the end result in each area to the client and to explain very briefly how that end result has come about - plus anything else which emerges which helps us understand service users' values, priorities or perceptions on this subject.

One intention of Section 3 is to identify unmet need - sometimes, while going through these areas of life, unmet needs have been indicated which interviewees did not mention earlier.

Another intention is to find out typical consequences of current policies on what Social Services does and does not provide. Outcomes from the reduction of cleaning would be one example. Another example is small repair tasks, decoration and gardening - recently raised again by the Best Value report on Home Care.

The blue Supplementary Sheets, Sections 4-7, are each on a specific subject and are used only for those interviewees to whom these subjects apply.

Section 4 and ***4** (for some interviews only)
This focuses on the quality of Home Care and will apply to most interviewees, though not all since there will be a few who are not getting any Home Care. Section 4 concerns the interviewee's main provider of Home Care (noting that some may receive a mix of Social Services and Private Agency Home Care). Section *4 concerns any other source of Home Care *which is purchased by Social Services* for this person - like additional Home Care from a Private Agency. It is likely that for most interviewees only Section 4 will need filling in and that this will feature the In-House Home Care Service.

Please note how questions 4.8.1 and 4.8.2, which are about the client's personal preferences, are important for their bearing on the Authority's Quality Standard indicator 30.1 'All service users are treated as an individual'. 4.8.1 should name top priorities and preferences regardless of whether they are fulfilled at present; 4.8.2 can comment whether or not they are currently fulfilled. The same understanding should be applied to similar questions on individual preferences in Sections 5, 6 and 8 - they can cover both preferences which are currently fulfilled and those which are not.

Sections 5 and *5 (for some interviews only)
These are only for people who are attending a day centre. If attending one centre, enter it in Section 5. If attending two day centres, as seems not uncommon, enter the other one in Section *5. Whether a day centre is used should be evident from the advance information from Community Care Admin listed in *Facts for completion in advance of interview.*

Sections 6 and *6 (for some interviews only)
These are for use only in situations where the interviewer feels that comments are worth collecting on other services which this client uses. Examples might be on-going help from a Social Worker, the Sitting Service, regular short breaks in respite care or, perhaps, Careline. If one such service is identified, use Section 6. If two, add the identical Section *6. Interviewer's discretion will be needed in choosing when to use these sheets, lest the interview take too long.

Section 7 (for some interviews only)
This is only for people who have been discharged from in-patient care within the last 12 months - comments on any admissions during this period all go on the one sheet. The aim is to collect feedback on post-discharge care and interviewees' ideas about ways they could have been helped better. Interviewees' comments obviously may span Social Services and Health responsibilities.

Section 8 (for some interviews only)
This is for use only where a major family carer is present when the interviewer calls. There are two distinct aims. Some questions seek the family carer's view on how Social Services meets the carer's own needs. But other questions use the carer as an additional source for comment on how services affect the client. *One particular use for the latter concerns clients who may have major difficulty in communicating and for whom a family carer may be the most articulate witness of quality of service.*

Section 9 (for all interviews)

The final part of the interview, Section 9, returns to questions for all interviewees.

Question 9.1 seeks ideas relevant to LAC (99)14 Preventative Strategies for Older People. What are interviewees' ideas about the types of small inputs of help which might prolong their current level of independence? Responses from people receiving little or no Home Care may be especially interesting.

Question 9.2 should record any request for additional help which the interviewee makes, regardless of whether it fits any existing service.

Question 9.3 should be asked in exactly these words. The same question is put both to any family carer in 8.5 and to the interviewer in the Post Interview Assessment.

POST-INTERVIEW REFLECTION &ASSESSMENT

The following are for completion by the interviewer on their own after the interview

Section 10 (after the interview, for all interviewees)
As mentioned, please plan time immediately after the interview when you can reflect undisturbed on what you have heard, read the ratings and notes you took, and write up the Post-Interview Reflection & Assessment. This is the point at which you can do a neat, thoughtful write-up. Some Post-Interview Assessment questions seek the interviewer's own judgement of the situation. Please note the final page for any additional personal reflections or comment on what emerged from the interview. This should also contribute to the eventual Report.

Section 11 (after the interview, for all interviews)
This is your own assessment of time-costs, problems and usefulness, made immediately after the interview. It will contribute to the evaluation whether this project should be continued. Please note the prompts to record the time at the beginning and end of the interview. Likewise, please time your write-up so a picture of the costs and burden for interviewers can be established.

FOR COMPLETION IN ADVANCE OF INTERVIEW

INTERVIEWER..INTERVIEW DATE................................

NAME OF INTERVIEWEE ....

ADDRESS..

D.O.B..............HOME CARE PRIORITY CATEGORY..........PATCH NO............

HOURS OF HOME CARE WEEKLY / PROVIDER:.......................................

LENGTH OF TIME RECEIVING HOME CARE.................

OTHER SOCIAL SERVICES RECEIVED...

....

WITH WHOM DOES THIS PERSON LIVE? ....

....

 IS THIS SHELTERED OR WARDEN-CONTROLLED HOUSING? ....

....

RELEVANT ADVANCE KNOWLEDGE ABOUT THIS PARTICULAR
INTERVIEWEE: DISABILITIES, DIFFICULTIES IN SUSTAINING AN
INTERVIEW, COMMUNICATION PROBLEMS ETC.

[Write down start time ....]

INTRODUCTION TO INTERVIEWEE

1. Introduce self (name, title). Check preferred form of address

2. We are talking to a few older people about long term changes and improvements to our services. We are interested in your views.

•   We are pulling together the common issues that many people suggest for longer term improvements. But we are not able to respond to everybody's request for extra help.

•   If there is any action that needs to be taken about your own service straightaway, I shall only do so with your permission.

•   What you say to me is confidential. I will be taking notes but these will be kept securely away from all other Home Care records.

•   If there is any question you don't want to answer just say and we shall move on.

•   The interview may take up to an hour. Is this OK?

Do you have any questions before we start?

MANAGER'S INTERVIEW WITH USER OF SOCIAL CARE SERVICES FOR OLDER PEOPLE

PRELIMINARY: THE SERVICES IN QUESTION

1. Please tell me in your own words what help do you get from Social Services at present.

2 . THE SERVICE USER'S GENERAL VIEWS

What are your views on the help you get from Social Services?

3. REVIEW OF RESULTS & SATISFACTION IN MAIN AREAS OF DAILY LIVING

Can I follow that up by just checking your views on how satisfactory you find the following areas of life. Some of this we may have talked about already. But I want to make sure that we don't overlook anything.

Is there any help which you need but which you're not getting - or any way help could be given you better - in the following areas of daily living? How do you manage with them? How satisfactory are your current arrangements in each area of life?

3.1 Meals/refreshments:

Prompts: Do you get a diet which suits you?

Can you make yourself a hot drink?

Outcome:

Satisfactory ❑   *Partly satisfactory* ❑   *Unsatisfactory* ❑   *Very unsatisfactory* ❑

3.2 Shopping:

Prompts: Can you choose your own shopping?

Can you buy & send someone a birthday card?

Outcome:

Satisfactory ❑   *Partly satisfactory* ❑   *Unsatisfactory* ❑   *Very unsatisfactory* ❑

3.3 Laundry:

Outcome:

Satisfactory ❑   *Partly satisfactory* ❑   *Unsatisfactory* ❑   *Very unsatisfactory* ❑

3.4 House cleaning:

Outcome:

Satisfactory ❑   *Partly satisfactory* ❑   *Unsatisfactory* ❑   *Very unsatisfactory* ❑

3.5 Odd jobs in the household / repairs / decoration / gardening etc :

Prompt: Can you get your light bulbs changed easily?

Outcome:

Satisfactory ❑   *Partly satisfactory* ❑   *Unsatisfactory* ❑   *Very unsatisfactory* ❑

3.6 Being able to get help quickly if you're ill or have an accident at home:

Outcome:

Satisfactory ❑   *Partly satisfactory* ❑   *Unsatisfactory* ❑   *Very unsatisfactory* ❑

3.7 Feeling safe from crime & nuisance behaviour

[Please always start by asking the prompt question below. Only after you feel you have got an answer and have asked any necessary follow-up questions, should you fill in the rating of satisfactoriness as seems to best fit the interviewee's views. If no problems are raised in answer to this question, just tick the 'Satisfactory' box. But, if problems are mentioned, find out and record if the interviewee has personally suffered the problems they are raising. Find out and record if the interviewee has ideas concerning what steps could be taken to make them feel safer. Only after this fill in the rating of satisfactoriness of outcome.]

Prompt: **Living here, do you encounter any forms of crime or nuisance behaviour - be it from adults, teenagers or children?**

Outcome:

Satisfactory ❑   *Partly satisfactory* ❑   *Unsatisfactory* ❑   *Very unsatisfactory* ❑

3.8 Do you manage alright with money, bills, pensions, benefits, and other financial or legal matters?

Prompt: Do you receive Attendance Allowance?

Outcome:

Satisfactory ❑   *Partly satisfactory* ❑   *Unsatisfactory* ❑   *Very unsatisfactory* ❑

THIS SHEET FOR EXPLANATION, COMMENT OR EXPANDED ANSWERS

3.9 How satisfactory do you find personal care?

Prompt: Can you get a bath when you want to?

Outcome:

Satisfactory ❑   *Partly satisfactory* ❑   *Unsatisfactory* ❑   *Very unsatisfactory* ❑

3.10 Can you get out of your house as much as you would like?
Prompt: How often do you get out in a typical week?

Outcome:

Satisfactory ❑   *Partly satisfactory* ❑   *Unsatisfactory* ❑   *Very unsatisfactory* ❑

3.11 Does your present amount of social life suit you?
Prompts: Whom do you get to see in a typical week?
Can you get to see the people who particularly matter to you?

Outcome:

Satisfactory ❑   *Partly satisfactory* ❑   *Unsatisfactory* ❑   *Very unsatisfactory* ❑

3.12 Do you have sufficient things of interest in your everyday life to suit you?
Prompt: How do you spend your time in a typical week?

Outcome:

Satisfactory ❑   *Partly satisfactory* ❑   *Unsatisfactory* ❑   *Very unsatisfactory* ❑

4. SUPPLEMENTARY SHEETS: HOME CARE (MAIN PROVIDER)

4.1 <u>Name of Home Care Provider</u> (i.e. 'SSD' or name of agency)...

4.2 <u>In the last 6 months, have these Home Care staff ever missed a planned visit to you?</u>
Yes ❑   no ❑   don't know ❑

4.3 <u>How satisfactory do you find the times of day at which these Home Care staff visit you?</u>
Satisfactory ❑   Wish some difference❑   Wish much difference ❑

4.4 <u>How happy are you with the sort of communication and relationships you have with Home Care staff? Are there any ways you would like this to be different?</u>
Satisfactory ❑   Wish some difference❑   Wish much difference ❑

4.5.1 <u>How many different Home Care staff visit you to give you your Home Care?</u>

....

4.5.2 <u>How well does this suit you?</u>
Satisfactory ❑   Wish some difference❑   Wish much difference ❑

4.6 <u>How well do you feel your privacy and dignity are respected in the ways staff give you Home Care?</u>
Satisfactory ❑   Wish some difference❑   Wish much difference ❑

4.7 <u>Are you able to choose how much help you get - do staff do too much or too little?</u>
Gets more help than desired ❑   About right ❑   Gets less help than desired❑

4.8.1 <u>Do you have any personal priorities or preferences which are specially important to you concerning Home Care?</u>

4.8.2 Do Home Care staff do fulfil these priorities / preferences of yours at present?

4.9 <u>Overall, how would you rate the Home Care service you receive (from this provider)?</u>

Very good ❑   Quite good ❑   Hard-to-say ❑   Not very good ❑   Poor ❑

*4. SUPPLEMENTARY SHEETS: HOME CARE (SECONDARY PROVIDER, IF APPLICABLE)

*4.1 Name of Home Care Provider (i.e. 'SSD' or name of agency) ....

*4.2 In the last 6 months, have these Home Care staff ever missed a planned visit to you?
Yes ❑   no ❑   don't know ❑

*4.3 How satisfactory do you find the times of day at which these Home Care staff visit you?
Satisfactory ❑   Wish some difference❑   Wish much difference ❑

*4.4 How happy are you with the sort of communication and relationships you have with Home Care staff? Are there any ways you would like this to be different?
Satisfactory ❑   Wish some difference❑   Wish much difference ❑

*4.5.1 How many different Home Care staff visit you to give you your Home Care?

....

*4.5.2 How well does this suit you?
Satisfactory ❑   Wish some difference ❑   Wish much difference ❑

*4.6 How well do you feel your privacy and dignity are respected in the ways staff give Home Care?
Satisfactory ❑   Wish some difference ❑   Wish much difference ❑

*4.7 Are you able to choose how much help you get - do staff do too much or too little?
Gets more help than desired ❑   About right ❑   Gets less help than desired ❑

*4.8.1 Do you have any personal priorities or preferences which are specially important to you concerning Home Care?

*4.8.2 Do Home Care staff do fulfill these priorities / preferences of yours at present?

*4.9 Overall, how would you rate the Home Care service you receive (from this provider)?

Very good ❑   Quite good ❑   Hard-to-say ❑   Not very good ❑   Poor ❑

5. SUPPLEMENTARY SHEET: DAY CENTRE (FIRST)

[If the interviewee attends a day centre, ask these questions. If two day centres are attended, use questions *5 overleaf for the second centre.]

5.1.1   Name of day centre...

5.1.2   How many days per week do you usually attend this day centre?...........................

5.2   How does attending the day centre benefit you? What do you get from it?

5.3   How good do you find it as a place to get company from other people?

Very good ☐   Quite good ☐   Not very good ☐   Poor ☐

5.4   How good do you find it for giving you interesting activities or events?

Very good ☐   Quite good ☐   Not very good ☐   Poor ☐

5.5   Do you have any particular preferences as an individual about how you wish the day centre to help you? Either things which they do now and you'd like to make sure they keep on doing - or things which you'd like them to do differently?

        Would you have any particular preferences which you'd like them to keep in mind?

....

....

....

5.6   Overall how would you rate what you receive from the day centre?

Very good ☐   Quite good ☐   Hard-to-say ☐   Not very good ☐   Poor ☐

THIS SHEET FOR EXPLANATION, COMMENT OR EXPANDED ANSWERS

*5. SUPPLEMENTARY SHEET: DAY CENTRE (SECOND)
[If the interviewee attends two day centres, use this sheet for comment on the second centre.]

*5.1.1 Name of day centre..

*5.1.2 How many days per week do you usually attend this day centre? ....

*5.2 How does attending the day centre benefit you? What do you get from it?

*5.3 How good do you find it as a place to get company from other people?

Very good ❑   Quite good ❑   Not very good ❑   Poor ❑

*5.4 How good do you find it for giving you interesting activities or events?

Very good ❑   Quite good ❑   Not very good ❑   Poor ❑

*5.5 Do you have any particular preferences as an individual about how you wish the day centre to help you? Either things which they do now and you'd like to make sure they keep on doing - or things which you'd like them to do differently?
         Would you have any particular preferences which you'd like them to keep in mind?

....

....

....

*5.6 Overall how would rate what you receive from the day centre?

Very good ❑   Quite good ❑   Hard-to-say ❑   Not very good ❑   Poor ❑

THIS SHEET FOR EXPLANATION, COMMENT OR EXPANDED ANSWERS

6. SUPPLEMENTARY SHEET: OTHER SIGNIFICANT SOCIAL CARE SERVICES (FIRST)

[Use sheets 6 and *6 if there are any other social care services - for instance Care Management, Sitting Service, Respite Care or Careline - which you think merit comment. Otherwise bypass.]

6.1 Name of service...

....

6.2 Frequency / length / type of contact with this service

....

....

6.3 What effect does this service have on you? What benefits has it had?

....

....

....

6.4 Do you have any particular preferences as an individual about how you wish this service to help you? Either things which they do now and you'd like to make sure they keep on doing - or things which you'd like them to do differently?

Would you have any particular preferences which you'd like them to keep in mind?

....

....

....

6.5 Are there any other comments you'd like to make about this service?

....

....

....

....

6.6 Overall how would rate what you receive from this service?

Very good ❑   Quite good ❑   Hard-to-say ❑   Not very good ❑   Poor ❑

THIS SHEET FOR EXPLANATION, COMMENT OR EXPANDED ANSWERS

*6. SUPPLEMENTARY SHEET: OTHER SIGNIFICANT SOCIAL CARE SERVICES (SECOND)

[Use sheets 6 and *6 if there are any other social care services - for instance Care Management, Sitting Service, Respite Care or Careline - which you think merit comment. Otherwise bypass.]

*6.1 Name of service..

....

*6.2 Frequency / length / type of contact with this service

....

....

*6.3 What effect does this service have on you? What benefits has it had?

....

....

....

*6.4 Do you have any particular preferences as an individual about how you wish this service to help you? Either things which they do now and you'd like to make sure they keep on doing - or things which you'd like them to do differently?

Would you have any particular preferences which you'd like them to keep in mind?

....

....

....

*6.5 Are there any other comments you'd like to make about this service?

....

....

....

....

*6.6 Overall how would rate what you receive from this service?

Very good ❑   Quite good ❑   Hard-to-say ❑   Not very good ❑   Poor ❑

7. SUPPLEMENTARY SHEET: CARE AFTER HOSPITAL DISCHARGE

[Fill in only if this person has been discharged from in-patient care during the previous 12 months. If more than one hospital discharge in this period, gather views on all discharges on this single sheet. Include comments on other agencies, as well as SSD, as seems useful. Question 7.5 covers help from any source.]

7.1 Which hospital (s)...

7.2 What help did you get on / after discharge?

....

....

....

....

7.3 What were the results of the sort of help you received after leaving hospital?

....

....

....

....

7.4 Would you make any suggestions about any types of help which might have helped you more to get back on your feet again after leaving hospital?

....

....

....

....

7.5 How far would you say that the help you received after leaving hospital was satisfactory?

Fully satisfactory ❑

moderately satisfactory ❑

hard-to-say ❑

moderately unsatisfactory ❑

very unsatisfactory ❑

THIS SHEET FOR EXPLANATION, COMMENT OR EXPANDED ANSWERS

8. SUPPLEMENTARY SHEET: FAMILY CARER VIEWS (Use only if a carer is present)

8.1.1 Family carer's relationship to client (eg spouse / son / daughter etc) ? ....

8.1.2 Resident in same home ? ....

8.2 Do you, as a carer, gain benefits from Social Services help (whether from services given to the client or explicitly to the carer)? What sort of benefits and from which aspects of services?

....

....

....

....

8.3.1 Speaking as far as you can on behalf of the client, would you single out any aspects of Social Services help as particularly beneficial or appreciated by the client or otherwise praiseworthy?

....

....

8.3.2 Speaking as far as you can on behalf of the client, would you single out any aspects of Social Services help as needing change or improvement?

....

....

8.4 Speaking on behalf of yourself now, do you have any preferences or priorities **which you'd like Social Services to keep in mind**? Either things which they do now and you'd like to make sure they keep on doing - or things which you'd like them to do differently?

....

....

....

8.5 How far would you say that the present situation in this household, considering all your needs and the sort of help you get, is satisfactory in terms of what you think Social Services should do for you?

> Fully satisfactory ❑
> moderately satisfactory ❑
> hard-to-say ❑
> moderately unsatisfactory ❑
> very unsatisfactory ❑

THIS SHEET FOR EXPLANATION, COMMENT OR EXPANDED ANSWERS

9. HELP FROM SOCIAL SERVICES IN GENERAL

We are coming to the last couple of questions now.

9.1 [This question is aimed at information relevant to the new *Preventative Strategies for Older People*.]

Would you name anything extra which could be done which might help you in carrying on looking after yourself and managing your own affairs as much as you do?

9.2 Aside from the various types of help you already get, are there any other types of help which you'd like Social Services to offer you?

Or to help you get from other Council departments, the Health Service or other such services?

9.3 Finally, how far would you say that your present situation, considering your needs and the sort of help you get to meet them, is satisfactory in terms of what you think Social Services should be doing for you?

Fully satisfactory	❏
very satisfactory	❏
moderately satisfactory	❏
hard-to-say	❏
moderately unsatisfactory	❏
very unsatisfactory	❏

THE END

That's the end of my questions. Thank you very much for your help.

Before we finish, is there anything else you would like to add?

[Write down finish time ....]

POST-INTERVIEW REFLECTION & ASSESSMENT: OUTCOMES / ANY FURTHER ACTION/INSIGHTS INTO THE SERVICE

10.   Name any aspects of service which this interviewee particularly praised or approved

10.2   Name any aspects of service linked to major dissatisfactions for this interviewee

10.3 Were there any notable aspects of service giving or the interviewee's circumstances which you observed, rather than were told about? (Aside from anything you have recorded already.)

THIS SHEET FOR EXPLANATION, COMMENT OR EXPANDED ANSWERS

10.5.1 As a result of this interview, should any action now be taken - either concerning this individual or concerning how any service is functioning generally?

Yes, immediate action concerning this individual ❑

Yes, immediate action concerning general service functioning ❑

The issues summarised below should be raised for corrective
action in the Report on these interviews ❑

No action or investigation are warranted ❑

10. 5.2 *List any immediate actions planned*

10. 5.3 *List issues which you wish raised in the Report*

10.6.1 As a result of this interview, are you making any referral to adjust an existing service or to introduce an additional service for this person?

Yes ❏   No ❏

10.6.2   *Which does the above concern?*

Social Services Home Care   ❏   Social Services Day Care   ❏

Social Services Care Management   ❏   Other Social Services ❏

Other Council Services ❏   Health Care ❏   Other ❏

10.7   **How far would you say this person's present situation, considering their needs and their help from all sources, represent a satisfactory outcome in terms of Social Services responsibilities?**

Fully satisfactory   ❏
very satisfactory   ❏
moderately satisfactory   ❏
hard-to-say   ❏
moderately unsatisfactory   ❏
very unsatisfactory   ❏

10.8 Any notable thoughts on how a person's independence and self-support can best be promoted, as a result of anything you heard or noticed during this interview? (If you have recorded this already, just give the question number by which it appears.)

10.9 Space for additional reflections, insights or comments arising from this interview

THIS SHEET FOR EXPLANATION, COMMENT OR EXPANDED ANSWERS

11. INTERVIEWER'S ASSESSMENT OF TIME COSTS AND VALUE OF INTERVIEW

Please fill in time figures immediately after interview for accuracy's sake.

11.1 How long it took

11.1.1 How long did the actual face-to-face interview take? ....

11.1.2 How long did the post-interview write-up take? ....

11.1. 3 Can you estimate any time costs for any follow-up action which will be required?

....

11.2 Problems in the procedure

11.2.1 Did any parts of the interview schedule prove notably problematic or unproductive?

....

....

11.2.2 Were there any notable problems like communication difficulties, interviewee reluctance or interruptions?

....

....

11.3 Did the interview seem worthwhile?

11.3 Comparing the time costs against information gained, how would you rate this interview?

Clearly worthwhile   ❑

Probably worthwhile   ❑

Hard to say   ❑

Probably not worthwhile   ❑

Clearly not worthwhile   ❑

THIS SHEET FOR EXPLANATION, COMMENT OR EXPANDED ANSWERS

Dear

Would you be willing for a Social Services manager to visit you at home to ask you some questions about your views on the help you get from Social Services?

Social Services managers are trying to work out the most important ways in which services to older people should be improved. As a first step, they want to hear the views of a sample of older people whose names have been picked at random from a list of people aged over 65 years who are receiving Social Services help.

Your name is among those which have been selected at random from the list. Would you be willing for a senior Social Services manager, from your local Office, to visit you at home to ask you about your views and your experiences of help from Social Services?

Were you to agree to an interview, everything you said would be treated confidentially. The interview itself would probably last around one hour. The Social Services manager would arrange with you to visit you at your home at a time which was convenient to you. (Alternatively, if you preferred to be interviewed by telephone, this could be arranged instead.)

Enclosed is a list of the topics on which the Social Services managers wish to hear older people's views at these interviews. You may find it helpful in deciding whether to agree to be interviewed.

We would be very grateful if you could spare some time to give us a service user's view of the services which we provide. We would like to telephone you shortly to ask whether you would agree to be interviewed.

Yours sincerely

[10/6/99 DRAFT]

SERVICE USER'S INTERVIEW

OUTLINE OF INTERVIEW TOPICS

FOR INTERVIEWEES TO READ

IN ADVANCE

Here is a list of the topics on which the Social Services manager would like to hear your views. You could use it to decide whether you wish to participate.

If you agreed to participate in an interview, you could use the list to prepare some of your comments, if you so wished. Also, you could decide whether there were any particular topics among these which you would not want to discuss, since interviewees would have a complete say over this.

THE SERVICE USER'S GENERAL VIEWS

What are your views on your help from Social Services?

- How satisfactory do you find it?

- Does it achieve the results which it's supposed to?

- Are there ways it could be done better?

Are there any types of help which you'd like from Social Services but which you are not getting at present?

REVIEW OF HOW SATISFACTORY ARE CURRENT ARRANGEMENTS IN THE MAIN AREAS OF DAILY LIVING

Is there any help which you need but which you're not getting - or any way help could be given you better - in the following areas of daily living?

- Meals/refreshments
- Shopping
- Laundry
- House cleaning
- Odd jobs in the household
- Being able to get help quickly if you're ill or have an accident at home
- Feeling safe from crime or nuisance behaviour
- Do you manage alright with money, bills and other financial or legal matters?
- How satisfactory do you find personal care?
- Can you get out of your house as much as you would like?
- Does your present amount of social life suit you?
- Do you have sufficient things of interest in your everyday life to suit you?

QUALITY OF HOME CARE

If you receive Home Care, the manager would like to ask you the following questions:

- **In the last 6 months, have Home Care staff ever missed a planned visit to you?**

- **How well do the times of your visits from Home Care staff suit you?**

- **How happy are you with the sort of communication and relationships which you have with Home Care staff? Any ways you would like this to be different?**

- **How well do you feel your privacy and dignity are respected in the ways staff give you Home Care?**

- **To what things should staff pay most attention in order to maintain or improve the quality of your Home Care? Either things which you value about what they do now or extra things which you'd like them to do?**

    Would you have any particular requests which you'd like Home Care staff to keep in mind?

SOCIAL SERVICES HELP IN GENERAL

If you use any other types of Social Services help besides Home Care, the Manager may ask you your views on this also. For instance, if you attend any day centre, what are your views on it? If you have been in hospital during the last year, what did you think of the help provided for you when you left hospital? If there were a member of your family present when the Manager visited, the latter would be interested in hearing their general views too on the help which Social Services has been providing.

Finally, the Managers would like to ask everyone the following general questions.

- **Aside from the services which you already get, are there any other types of help which you'd like Social Services to offer you?**

- **How far would you say that your present situation, considering your needs and the sort of help you get to meet them, is satisfactory in terms of what you think Social Services should be doing for you?**

GUIDANCE NOTES FOR COMPLETING INTERVIEW SCREENING FORM

What is the purpose of this form?

Senior Social Services Managers wish to interview Elderly Division community care clients to include their views in service planning. Some names of possible interviewees have been selected at random from lists of service users. Managers now need advice from staff, who know these clients, concerning anyone whom they should not try to interview. The interviews would be held in clients' homes, so mobility is not a problem. Interviews would last around an hour but could be shortened for people who found this difficult. People with a degree of communication difficulty could still be visited and information gained from them and also, perhaps, from a family carer. But there may be some people whose communication difficulties would be too great for interview. Clients would initially be written with a request that a Manager may visit and interview them.

Who can answer the questions on this form?

All these clients are assigned to a Home Care Organiser and a Senior Home Care Assistant. Some may also have a Social Worker / Care Manager. In different cases different workers may be able to supply the necessary information.

Guidance on the Box 1 'Should we exclude this person from request for interview?'

You should recommend that someone be excluded from request for interview if any of the following apply to the person.

- In hospital or too ill for interview and likely to remain so for the next three months.
- Known to be away from home for long periods or moving home during the next three months.
- Has now moved to residential or nursing care.
- Distressed by a recent traumatic event, like a bereavement.
- Has severe speech or hearing problems such as would prevent communication.
- Depressed to the point that interview would be distressing (or suffering similarly from any other functional mental disorder).
- Suffering from dementia or mentally confused in ways which make communication very difficult.

On the last two points, an experienced Social Services worker can draw this conclusion where they think appropriate, without a formal diagnosis.

For Box 1, write 'Yes' if to the best of your knowledge any of these reasons apply. Enter the particular reason in reply to Box 2. **Write 'Yes' too if there is some other reason, which seems to you really imperative, why we should exclude the person.** Give that reason in reply to Box 2.

If there is no reason why we should exclude a person, write 'No' in reply to Box 1 - do not just leave it blank. If you are unsure of the answer to Box 1, please write 'Don't Know' and explain why at Box 2.

Other uses of Box 2.

Please also use Box 2 for the following information about people whom you are *not* excluding.

- Anyone currently ill or in hospital, though you expect them to be recovered within the next 3 months.
- Anyone who would find an interview in English difficult - state their preferred language.
- Anyone who is blind - we are concerned to ensure some are selected for these interviews.
- Anyone with severe mobility problems - likewise we are concerned to represent them.
- Anyone with significant communication difficulties, though not severe enough for exclusion.
- Any other facts which you think a prospective interviewer should be made aware of.

Box 3 'Does this person live with a family carer?'

Please either write 'No' or, if living with a family carer, the relationship - eg. 'With daughter'.

Thank you for your help. Please return the form to ....

Interview Screening Form - for clients suggested for home interview by a Manager

Home Care Organiser .... Form completed by .... Date..............

Pri Cat	Home care client's name	Ref No	Home care patch	1. Should we exclude this person from request for interview?	2. Important information about the client. (Reasons for any exclusions plus other facts. See Guidance Notes.)	3. Does this person live with a family carer?

Dear

During coming months you might hear from a few of your clients that they have been visited and interviewed by a Social Services manager from this Office.

The reason for this is that managers are conducting a programme of random interviews of older Social Services clients to learn how they view our services and to gain ideas for new approaches for helping them.

Clients are chosen for interview from a computerised list so that we get a balance of new clients and long-standing clients, men and women, and each of the Home Care Priority categories. Otherwise selection is deliberately random in order to get a typical slice of different viewpoints.

Clients who are interviewed will be asked for their opinions about all services which we provide for them - be it Home Care, day centre, short respite breaks, help from Care Managers etc. They will also be asked whether there are any types of help which they would like, which Social Services does not provide at present.

Information from these interviews will mainly be used through pooling it in a report which reviews interviewees' views and any steps needed to improve our services. But occasionally an issue may be raised in an interview which a manager wishes to follow up with the staff who provide the service concerned.

You do not need to do anything in connection with these interviews. This letter is simply to give you an explanation in case you hear that one of your own clients has been interviewed.

If you wish any further information about this programme of interviews, please contact...........

Yours sincerely

ANALYSIS OF INTERVIEWERS' NOTES FROM MANAGERS' INTERVIEW PROGRAMME: PROCEDURE EMPLOYED IN INITIAL USE OF THIS SCHEDULE

First, separate sub-reports were produced for each of the two catchments from which interviewees had been drawn. Then the eventual report to Social Service was written largely by comparing the two sub-reports and identifying common and contrasting themes.

Producing the sub-reports for each catchment

1) *Response collation sheets*
Collation sheets were produced which could give an overview of all responses from a catchment to each question in the schedule. This overview showed:
* ratings made on ratings scales
* the code numbers of the interviewees who had given each rating
* a summary of the reasons behind each interviewee's ratings.

Thus, when it came to writing the sub-reports, it was possible to see at a glance what factors were producing favourable ratings in a catchment and what were producing critical ratings. Interviewee code numbers showed whose notes to examine if more detail were sought.

All collation sheets were on A3 paper to enable all a catchment's responses to a question to be visible on a single sheet - though for some questions two sheets were needed. For Section 3, collation sheets were produced for each domain. At the top was a box for aggregating the various ratings, showing interviewee code numbers. Below came a section summarising each comment which was linked to satisfaction, again showing code numbers. Then came a section for comments linked to dissatisfaction. If an interviewee's notes contained a mix of favourable and critical comments, these would be assigned to separate sections. There was also a section for miscellaneous comments. For Section 4, related questions were recorded on the same collation sheet - sometimes two or three on a sheet. For Section 5, day centres, a separate collation sheet was created for each day centre mentioned. All responses about that provider were summarised there, following the same principle of recording ratings, reasons behind ratings, and interviewee codes. Similarly for Section 6, one sheet per provider service was used. All responses to Section 7 (post-hospital aftercare) were collated on a single sheet per catchment, which also included a box to identify which hospital each interviewee had used. Appropriate size collation sheets were produced for other Sections.

2) *Adding a holistic overview*
There was a risk that the above approach, while well focussed on detail, might be processing interviewees' communications about their lives into fragmented sets of responses to questions. To balance this, for each interviewee an A3 sheet was produced which presented the following questions for the report writer to answer after reading that person's interview notes (including general reflections written by their interviewer after the interview).

* 'Reading this person's notes as a whole, do they communicate any general messages about the lives of older Social Services clients?'

* 'Are there any causes for concern or ideas for development or modification of services additional to those recorded in the notes / analysis already?'

3) *Writing each catchment's sub-report*
A sub-report for each catchment was then written, purely as a stage in the analysis. This summarised the contents of each of the collation sheets, any conclusions which emerged and possible useful messages to Social Services. By way of example, for each domain in Section 3 (i.e. each collation sheet) the sub-report generally comprised one A4 typed page. For the whole of Section 4, Home Care, it came to 3 to 4 pages per catchment.

Producing the final report to Social Services
This compared the two catchment sub-reports with each other, section by section, commenting on findings common to both catchments and highlighting any differences.

It began by going through each topic in Section 3, followed by sections on home care, day centres, short residential breaks, discharge from hospital, and family carers' views. A further section discussed what interviewees especially praised or criticised, catchment by catchment, and another section discussed apparent differences between catchments. The next section listed issues where interviewers themselves had called for investigation or changes. Then there was a section on general reflections on what had emerged, partly influenced by the holistic appraisals of interviewees' situations. Finally came conclusions and recommendations to Social Services.

A useful adjunct
A useful practical aid to analysis and report writing was a large chart which showed key facts about each interviewee like their age, their home situation, the various services they received, weekly hours of home care, what was known about their social network etc.

CHAPTER SIX
USING POSTAL QUESTIONNAIRES TO COLLECT INFORMATION ON OUTCOMES FROM USERS AND CARERS

By Claire Bamford

1. INTRODUCTION

This chapter describes the development and piloting of postal questionnaires to collect information on the outcomes of Disability Support Services, which provide occupational therapy assessment, equipment and adaptations. This project was thought to offer a valuable focus for development work since:

- Service users were already sent a satisfaction questionnaire
- Evaluation of the existing feedback system indicated considerable motivation for change
- It complemented the development projects with older people and their carers by focusing on equipment and adaptations and using a postal survey.

Furthermore, recent publications have drawn attention to the significance of equipment and adaptations services. There are nearly one million users of community equipment services (Audit Commission, 2000), and over 20 per cent of all referrals to Social Services Departments are dealt with by occupational therapists (OTs) (Platt, 1999). Despite growing recognition of the role of equipment and adaptations in achieving policy goals, in particular enhancing independence and promoting equality of opportunity (Esmond *et al.*, 1998; Marks, 1998; Winchcombe, 1998; Audit Commission, 2000), there is only limited evidence about the outcomes of such provision. While the Performance Assessment Framework includes one indicator relevant to equipment and adaptations, this is concerned with the proportion of small items of equipment costing less than £1,000 issued within three weeks of assessment rather than outcomes (Department of Health, 1999).

Relevance to current policy initiatives

Our experience of collecting and using outcomes information through postal questionnaires will contribute to current policy initiatives by:

- Indicating the feasibility of this approach for collecting outcomes information
- Informing the development of questions for the local user satisfaction surveys described in *Modernising Social Services* (Department of Health, 1998)
- Identifying factors that influence the collection and use of outcomes information in social care.

It has been recommended that questions on equipment and adaptations be included in the National Patient's Survey (Audit Commission, 2000); if this recommendation is implemented, our experience could also inform the development of such questions.

2. LOCAL CONTEXT

The development work was carried out in partnership with a unitary authority serving a population of approximately 175,000. The authority has a densely populated urban centre surrounded by more rural areas. The population is characterised by a higher proportion of owner-occupiers, lower rates of unemployment, a lower proportion of residents from minority ethnic groups and a slightly higher proportion of people over pensionable age compared to national rates for England[1].

The recent Joint Review indicated that the authority's expenditure patterns differed significantly from those of comparable authorities, with significantly higher expenditure on services for people with physical and sensory impairments (including Disability Support Services) and lower expenditure on strategy, regulation, management and support services. Although the authority has made a substantial and ongoing investment in IT, progress towards a robust IT system has been impeded by the small number of specialist IT staff.

Service organisation and budgets

All enquiries are processed by a Customer Advice Centre and directed to the relevant team. During 1999/2000, approximately 20 per cent of all assessment requests were referred to Disability Support Services and nearly 3,000 specialist assessments were completed. Average waiting times for an OT or occupational therapy assistant (OTA) assessment vary according to the priority given to the request and the type of worker seen but compare favourably to national averages.

The Joint Equipment Service does not provide a direct access and demonstration service to the public. In common with similar services elsewhere (Audit Commission, 2000), the Joint Equipment Service lacks accurate information on stock holdings, and tracking systems for equipment provided are poor. A new IT programme is being implemented to resolve these difficulties. In 1999/2000 over 10,000 items of equipment were issued from a budget of approximately £210,000. At the time of the first pilot study, no charges were made for the loan or provision of equipment. A standard handling charge of £20 per package of equipment was subsequently introduced.

Over the same period, approximately £1.2 million was spent on disability-related adaptations. This funded approximately 2,150 adaptations (850 in council homes and 1,300 in private homes). Adaptations costing less than £200 are provided free of charge. More expensive adaptations to council homes are funded through the Housing Capital Programme, while owner-occupiers and tenants in the private sector can apply for a means-tested grant.

---

[1]1991 Census data

Wheelchairs are provided by a separate agency and equipment for people with sensory impairments is provided by specialist workers based in care management teams. These characteristics of the service have important implications for the generalisability of the instruments developed.

3. BACKGROUND TO THE DEVELOPMENT WORK

A literature review identified three broad approaches to evaluating the effectiveness of equipment and adaptations:

• Using measures of functional abilities or quality of life before and after provision
• Using an outcomes-focused approach in assessment and review
• Using locally developed measures to assess outcomes such as user satisfaction and usage of equipment or adaptations.

Despite considerable interest in assessing the outcomes of equipment and adaptations, existing approaches are rarely integrated into routine practice and none of these approaches is without problems (Heaton and Bamford, 2000). Existing measures of functional ability and quality of life are not necessarily sensitive to the types of changes resulting from the provision of equipment and adaptations (Andrich *et al.*, 1998). Since interventions may be concerned with maintaining quality of life or managing deterioration, simple before-and-after measures are problematic. Existing measures also fail to assess the diverse range of desired outcomes identified in stage one research (Bamford *et al.*, 1999). Furthermore, since many measures were developed in hospital settings, their applicability to community settings has been questioned (Heaton and Bamford, 2000).

Integrating an outcomes-focus in assessment and review has generally involved the use of procedures derived from goal attainment scaling or problem elicitation technique (Law *et al.*, 1990; Pollock, 1993; Wessels *et al.*, 1998). The feasibility of using these approaches in routine practice has been questioned (Toomey *et al.*, 1995) and the resulting individualised information can be difficult to aggregate and use.

Locally developed measures are often tailored to a specific context and designed to answer specific questions (e.g. Chesson *et al.*, 1996). Such measures do not therefore cover the range of outcomes identified in our stage one research.

Existing approaches also generally fail to assess the outcomes of provision for family carers, who are the main beneficiaries of some types of equipment (Washington and Schwartz, 1996; Morris and Gainer, 1997; Andrich *et al.*, 1998). Our review of the literature therefore indicated no readily available measures of the outcomes of equipment and adaptations which could be incorporated into a postal questionnaire (cf. Heaton and Bamford, 2000).

Existing local information on outcomes

Disability Support Services had an established system for collecting user feedback. A two-page questionnaire was sent to all users seen by an OT and a brief survey card, the size of a postcard, was sent to a sample of one in five users seen by an OTA. The questions mainly related to satisfaction with various aspects of the service. Evaluation of the existing system indicated a number of problems:

- Over-reliance on Yes/No responses
- Ambiguous questions
- No record of response rates
- Lack of resources for systematic analysis
- Emphasis on responding to problems at an individual level
- Questions related only to assessment staff.

There was therefore considerable interest in revising the system, in particular by focusing more on outcomes and including feedback on all aspects of the service.

4. PLANNING THE DEVELOPMENT PROCESS

In planning the development work we drew on literature on managing change, our substantive findings about outcomes and the principles for collecting and using outcomes information identified in stage one research.

Model for initiating and managing change

We drew primarily on the theoretical frameworks developed by Egan (1993), supplemented with other approaches to change and project management (Briner *et al.*, 1996; Smale, 1996; Beckhard and Harris, 1987). Egan's model for initiating and managing change consists of three stages, each comprising three steps (Box 6.1, Model B, Egan, 1993).

Box 6.1: Summary of model for initiating and managing change

Step 1	The current scenario
	• Telling the story (critical problems and opportunities)
	• Identifying blind spots and developing new perspectives
	• Establishing priorities and searching for points of leverage
Step 2	Preferred scenario: where we would ideally like to be
	• Developing a range of possibilities
	• Identifying which of these are feasible in practice
	• Securing commitment
Step 3	Action strategies: moving from the current scenario to the preferred scenario
	• Brainstorming possible strategies
	• Choosing the best strategies
	• Formulating a plan

Much of the work of Step 1 was accomplished in stage one research. The critical problems and opportunities identified may be relevant to other settings and may influence the generalisability of this approach (Box 6.2). Characteristics of the preferred scenario were identified from the overall aim of the outcomes programme, stage one research (including an evaluation of the previous questionnaire system) and a literature review (Heaton and Bamford, 2000). Although informed by prior work, the preferred scenario continued to evolve during the development work, particularly where what was feasible in practice fell short of the ideal scenario.

Box 6.2: Critical problems and opportunities for development work

Critical problems:	**Opportunities:**
• Performance anxiety among staff and concerns over how information might be used	• Strong commitment to quality improvement
• Additional resources required, especially in terms of administration and analysis	• Resource implications and changes in day-to-day practice are limited
• Competing demands and priorities	• Significant dissatisfaction with the existing system among some staff
• Staff reservations over the validity of user views	• Recognition of the value of an outcomes focus (preferable to current emphasis on user satisfaction)
• Limited use made of existing information and cynicism over whether information collected would be of any value	
• Under-developed management information systems	

Gaining the co-operation of staff was crucial and we used stakeholder commitment mapping (Beckhard and Harris, 1987) to identify staff whose commitment to the project needed to be secured. Steps one and two helped in identifying the tasks to be achieved, and these were explored further using techniques such as task boarding (Briner *et al.*, 1996). Most tasks were carried out by a planning group composed of a range of stakeholders. Appropriate processes or activities to achieve the tasks and ensure that all stakeholders were able to contribute their ideas and views, were developed in conjunction with an external consultant on the management of change and an external facilitator, who co-ran most of the planning group meetings.

From principles to practice
A number of principles to inform the development work were identified in stage one:
• Compatibility with existing practice
• Recognition of opportunity costs
• Involvement of all stakeholders
• Flexible approach to collecting outcomes information
• Development of appropriate feedback mechanisms
• Integration of outcomes information into decision-making.

153

These principles were addressed in various ways. Compatibility with existing practice and recognition of opportunity costs, for example, were important considerations in selecting a development proposal for implementation. The involvement of key stakeholder groups was addressed through the recruitment of a planning group responsible for the development work. A flexible approach to collecting outcomes information, the development of appropriate feedback mechanisms and use of outcomes information were specific tasks addressed by the planning group.

Promoting involvement and ownership

The way we sought to involve different stakeholders in the planning group and the extent to which we were successful is described below. Since the focus of the development work was not determined by users and carers, but was led by policy and professional concerns, our project was not user-led and we made this explicit in recruiting users and carers. We approached several disabled people who participated in stage one of the project and contacted a local voluntary organisation for disabled people with a request for potential participants. These approaches had limited success with only two users being recruited. Although attendance of one user was good, the other decided to withdraw. We identified a number of reasons for our difficulties in recruiting and retaining users, many of which may be relevant to user involvement in similar initiatives elsewhere:

- Changing personal circumstances, for example, return to paid employment
- Difficulties in tracing people
- The time commitment involved
- Concern over use of staff time for development work rather than service provision
- Cynicism resulting from the lack of impact of previous user consultations
- Concern over the ability of staff to listen to and acknowledge user views without being defensive
- Lack of a shared political perspective.

Three carers who participated in stage one agreed to join the planning group and formed a relatively cohesive and vocal group. All carers attended the majority of the planning group meetings. The carers differed in terms of the amount of support provided, duration of caring and participation in paid work.

An initial briefing session was held with staff in Disability Support Services to feedback the results of stage one, outline the plans for the development work and identify potential participants. The planning group included the service manager, managers of the Joint Equipment and Grants and Adaptations Services, three OTs and one OTA. Attendance of staff was generally good, with all but one member of staff attending most meetings.

Although we hoped to include administrative staff and staff from Strategic Services in the planning group, this was not feasible in practice and liaison with these members of staff took place outside the planning group.

In addition to the planning group meetings, three separate meetings were held with users and carers. While these latter meetings included practical tasks, they were characterised by a more explicit focus on process. We used these meetings for example, to explore hopes and fears about working with professionals prior to the first planning group meeting; and, subsequently, to review the process of joint working.

Overview of the development work

The key stages of the development work are summarized below (Figure 6.1). The involvement of different stakeholders varied during the development work. All stakeholders had a major role in designing the initial system for collecting and using outcomes information. Following the presentation and discussion of the results of the first pilot study, the planning group was disbanded. The user and carers involved had, by this time, expended considerable time and effort on the development work and it was agreed that the revisions could be taken forward by SPRU in conjunction with Disability Support Services staff. All members of the planning group were interviewed shortly after the group was disbanded about the process of the development work and their views on the system that had been developed. Following revisions to the system, a second pilot study was conducted and analysed.

Figure 6.1: Overview of development work

Time Scale	Key Stage	Stakeholders involved
Feb - April 1999	Planning	SPRU, senior managers
May 1999	Preparation	SPRU, users and carers, Disability Support Services
June - Dec 1999	Design system	Planning group
Dec 1999 - Feb 2000	First pilot study	Disability Support Services, SPRU
Feb - March 2000	Analyse and report results	SPRU
March 2000	Review results	Planning group
March 2000	Evaluation of development work	Planning group members
April - May 2000	Write report on initial system	SPRU
May - July 2000	Revise System	Disability Support Services, SPRU
Aug - Sep 2000	Second pilot study	Disability Support Services, SPRU
Oct - Dec 2000	Analyse and report results Make recommendations for future implementation	SPRU

Three key tasks were involved in designing the overall system: designing questionnaires with an outcomes focus; agreeing arrangements for data collection;

and exploring ways of interpreting and using results. Significant factors affecting the achievement of these tasks and influencing the design of the final system are described in the following sections.

5. DESIGNING QUESTIONNAIRES WITH AN OUTCOMES FOCUS

Three questionnaires were designed: a brief questionnaire for users who received only advice, minor adaptations and/or simple equipment; a more detailed questionnaire for users who received a major adaptation; and a questionnaire for carers of users eligible for a detailed questionnaire (copies of the questionnaires are included in the appendices).

Outcomes framework

In designing the questionnaires, we drew on the outcomes framework identified in stage one research (Qureshi *et al.*, 1998; Bamford *et al.*, 1999). Two distinct types of outcomes for users were identified: quality of life outcomes and outcomes relating to the way services are delivered (service process outcomes). Quality of life outcomes related to a key theme of being able to participate in the activities of ordinary life in ways which maximised independence. Such outcomes can be achieved through ongoing interventions or service inputs which aim to *maintain* desired outcomes at an acceptable level. Keeping personally clean and comfortable, for example, can be achieved through regular assistance with bathing by home care staff. Alternatively, quality of life outcomes can be achieved through discrete, time-limited interventions that focus on *removing barriers* or changing the situation in some way. Installation of a shower or provision of a bath seat are examples of discrete interventions that enable the desired outcome of keeping personally clean and comfortable to be achieved.

Service process outcomes are concerned with the desired impacts of service delivery and are only relevant to service users. The ways in which services are organised and delivered (service process) can have a direct impact on how service users feel. Service process may also have an impact on the extent to which desired quality of life outcomes are achieved. All stakeholders stressed the importance of including both types of outcomes in any attempt to collect information on the impacts and effectiveness of services.

Process of designing and testing the questionnaires

The initial step in designing the questionnaires was to agree key areas for inclusion. Questions concerned with quality of life and service process outcomes were initially formulated by the planning group. Typically, we provided a list of outcomes printed individually on cards (e.g. 'promoting autonomy') and asked planning group members working in small groups to read each card, discuss what they thought it meant and consider how they might phrase a question about this outcome. Either the discussions were tape-recorded or notes were taken, which were then used in drafting questions outside the meetings. The next step in drafting the questions was generally done by the researcher. Preliminary drafting of questions about the Grants and Adaptations and Joint Equipment Services was done in consultation with the managers of these services.

Reviewing and prioritising questions

The process of reviewing draft questions included checking whether the information was available from other sources, and considering how responses might be used. We therefore excluded a draft question on waiting times, since this information could be obtained from existing records, but included a question on how reasonable waiting time for assessment had been. Discussion of draft questions generally led to suggestions for improving wording and/or layout.

In reviewing questions staff often expressed concern over the subjectivity of user views. Although we were aware that this was an issue for staff, we had not planned any activities to address this issue directly in the development work. Instead we tended to respond to such comments as they arose, for example, by reiterating that the aim of the questionnaire was to collect information on the perspectives of users and carers, rather than to collect factual or objective information. With hindsight, we might usefully have explored this issue in a more creative way at the outset of the development work. One issue that had not been anticipated was the preference among many members of the planning group (users and carers as well as staff) for simple Yes/No responses, rather than more sensitive, graded response categories.

Invariably the list of draft questions for inclusion was too long, and it was necessary to set priorities and consider whether individual questions were appropriate for all users. While consensus over some questions was easily reached, there was considerable negotiation over the inclusion of others. In view of the relative numbers of users, carers and staff involved, it would have been easy for the views of users and carers to be overruled, but this was not always the case.

Pre-piloting

Since users and carers had been involved in drafting and testing the questions, pre-pilot work was limited. Members of the planning group were asked to try out the questions with friends, family members and service users and carers. Additionally, two users and two carers were visited at home and asked to complete and then discuss the draft questionnaires. This process resulted in a number of modifications to the questionnaires, but there was insufficient time to re-test the revised questionnaires before the first pilot study.

Pilot studies

Data collected in the first pilot study enabled us to evaluate the questions in terms of the amount of missing data, variation in responses between respondents and the comments made on the questionnaires. The questionnaires were subsequently revised and a second pilot study evaluated the extent to which the revisions were successful in overcoming the problems identified in the first pilot study.

Development of the user questionnaires
Questions relating to quality of life

1. The extent to which the desired quality of life outcomes identified in stage one research are reflected in the questionnaires is shown in the technical appendix. Since our focus was on a specialist service, it was not appropriate to include questions relating to all of the outcomes. Detailed discussion in the planning group led to the identification of four outcomes thought to be particularly relevant to Disability Support Services:

- Safety
- Ease of performing everyday tasks and activities
- Amount of help needed from other people
- Amount of choice over when or how to do everyday tasks and activities.

The user questionnaires used in the first pilot study included questions asking how each of these areas had been affected by the provision of equipment and adaptations. In identifying the most appropriate response categories we drew on stage one research and the literature review. These highlighted the need to include the range of ways in which provision might affect quality of life outcomes and, at the same time, indicate whether any changes could be attributed to provision (Bamford et al., 1999; Heaton and Bamford, 2000). We identified four distinct ways in which provision might affect outcomes:

- The equipment/adaptations made things better
- The equipment/adaptations stopped things getting worse
- The equipment/adaptations made things worse
- The equipment/adaptations made no difference.

To try to make the questions more user-friendly, we used response categories of very helpful, helpful, made no difference and made this worse. Although this did not provide an explicit category relating to prevention, we anticipated that respondents would use the 'helpful' category where provision had prevented deterioration. The resulting questions were laid out across the page (Figure 6.2).

Figure 6.2 Questions relating to quality of life outcomes in the first pilot study

How helpful was the advice, equipment or adaptation provided by the Occupational Therapist in term of:				
	Please circle the number that applies to you			
	Very helpful	Helpful	Made no difference at all	Made this worse
a) How easy is it for you to carry out everyday tasks and activities	1	2	3	4
b) How much help you need from other people?	1	2	3	4
c) How safe you feel when doing everyday tasks and activities	1	2	3	4
d) Enabling you to choose when or how to do everyday tasks and activities	1	2	3	4

The results of the first pilot study indicated that a significant proportion of users had difficulty with the above questions. In both the brief and detailed questionnaires there were high rates of item non-response. Furthermore, a number of users explicitly commented on their difficulties in responding to the question. Their comments indicated that it was not always clear what was meant by 'everyday tasks and activities' and that it could be difficult to evaluate the impact of provision in general terms, particularly where provision related to a specific activity, such as having a bath. In designing the questionnaires, we used a mixture of formats, with some questions laid out across the page, and others set out vertically. While this was not ideal, it enabled us to include more questions than would have been possible if all questions had been set out vertically. The results of the first pilot study, however, suggested that the use of different formats was confusing, and high rates of item non-response were found on most questions laid out across the page. We therefore revised the layout of the user questionnaires so that all questions were laid out the same way with vertical response codes. Several questions were omitted to avoid making the questionnaires any longer.

No further questions relating to quality of life outcomes were included in the brief questionnaire used in the first pilot study. In the detailed questionnaire we also included questions about the outcomes achieved in relation to four key activities (bathing, getting about inside, getting in and out of the home and using the toilet), an open question inviting users to describe any other outcomes achieved, and a summary question asking about the impact of provision on overall quality of life.

Responses to the detailed questionnaire suggested that users found these questions easier to answer. This suggests that, at least for users receiving major adaptations or equipment, questions about outcomes are relevant. This was confirmed by comments on the questionnaires, a number of which related to outcomes. It therefore appeared to be the format and wording of the core questions relating to quality of life outcomes that caused problems. Responses to the open question about other outcomes confirmed that we had correctly identified the key outcomes of the service.

In revising the questionnaires, we therefore replaced the general questions shown in Figure 6.2 with more specific questions focusing on the impacts of advice, equipment and adaptations on the ease, safety, amount of help needed from others and amount of choice over when and how to do three specific activities – bathing, getting around and using the toilet (Figure 6.3). In view of space constraints in the brief questionnaire and a preference for collecting comparable information from all users, we combined the separate questions on getting around inside the home and getting in and out of the home, used in the detailed questionnaire in the first pilot study, into a single question. The question about the impact of provision of overall quality of life was included in the revised brief questionnaire as well as the detailed questionnaire, to provide comparable information.

Figure 6.3 Example of revised question on quality of life outcomes

How has the advice, equipment or adaptations helped with **having a bath or shower?**
(For example you may have been given grab rails, a bath or a shower seat or a bath lift)

I did not have any help with this..	1	
Made me feel safer...	2	
Made it easier..	3	*Please circle*
Need less help from other people..	4	*all that apply*
Given me more choice over when I have a bath/shower.........	5	
Has made no difference at all..	6	
Other *(please describe)*..	7	

The results of the second pilot study indicated that although item non-response to the revised questions relating to quality of life outcomes was lower, non-response was still common among respondents who had not received assistance with the activity. Although we included 'I did not have any help with this' as a response category, this was often overlooked. Highlighting the not applicable response category in some way, for example using bold typeface or increased spacing between this and the other response categories, may reduce the problem. Despite these persistent problems, improved linkage between the questionnaire data and details of equipment and adaptations provided in the second pilot study enabled us to recode much of the missing data, and achieve acceptable response rates to the questions on quality of life outcomes.

Questions relating to service process outcomes

There were relatively few difficulties in developing relevant questions from the desired service process outcomes. Few new areas were identified for inclusion. Explaining or demonstrating how to use any equipment and/or adaptations provided was thought to be important, as was planning for the future, particularly when arranging major adaptations. Although Disability Support Services Staff were not directly responsible for meeting the full range of desired quality of life outcomes, they had an important role in referring users to appropriate services; we therefore asked whether users had been informed about other services that could help them.

The desired service process outcome of having a say in services was contested by staff. Staff resistance to questions about choice seemed to centre around four issues:

- The concept of choice was seen as inappropriate since the service was needs-led
- The extent to which users had a choice was additionally constrained by budgetary considerations
- A high proportion of negative responses to any questions related to choice was anticipated
- Responding to these anticipated criticisms was seen as problematic in view of eligibility criteria and the restricted range of equipment available.

The extent to which users and carers on the planning group agreed with these reservations varied. Some agreed and felt that staff should make decisions based on their expertise and knowledge of the equipment available. Others felt that they should be able to have a say in what was provided, but recognised that any choice they had was likely to be within defined parameters. Following considerable debate, questions were developed which asked about involvement in decisions about the equipment and/or adaptations provided; and satisfaction with the extent to which the user's views had been taken into account in major adaptations. Both of these questions were generally acceptable to staff, but at the same time reflected the desired service process outcome of having a say in services.

Stage one research suggested that the achievement of service process outcomes should be assessed against explicit standards or targets. We distinguished between two types of service process outcome. The first consisted of those outcomes which are likely to be relevant to all users and carers, and which, ideally, should always be achieved. This includes being treated with respect, having one's unique needs and circumstances understood, and being put at ease during the assessment process. We generally used frequency response categories (for example, always, mostly, rarely, never) for these questions.

We felt that users were likely to have personal preferences and priorities in relation to other service process outcomes. For these types of outcomes, therefore, we decided that response categories indicating whether the user's or carer's personal preferences or needs had been met were most appropriate. This included questions such as being informed about other services, the extent to which one's problems or concerns had been discussed, and the extent to which the user had been involved in decisions about the equipment and/or adaptations provided. Ideally, this information would be collected through a series of filter questions which established whether this area was relevant or important to the respondent, and, if so, whether their preferences had been met. However, to save space and minimise the number of filter questions, we provided three simple response categories, whether the amount of information, choice or discussion was: as much as the user or carer wanted; too much; or not enough.

Responses to the first pilot study indicated some problems with non-response to questions on service process outcomes, particularly on the brief questionnaire. Examination of non-response to individual questions indicates that non-response was generally higher on questions concerned with involvement in decision-making, discussion of the options available and explanation or demonstration of equipment. This may reflect the complex response categories to these questions.

A second area of concern identified in the first pilot study was the limited variation in responses to questions relating to the extent to which personal preferences were met by the OT or OTA. The detailed questionnaire also included questions on the extent to which surveyors working in the Grants and Adaptations Service achieved desired service process outcomes. Greater variation in response was found on these questions, but it was unclear whether these differences reflected genuine differences between the surveyors and assessment staff, or were simply an artifact of the different question format and response categories used. A further problem was that the questions relating to personal preferences did not indicate whether these service process outcomes were important to individual users.

We addressed the problems identified in the first pilot study in a number of ways. As already described, the layout of the questionnaires was changed so that all questions had vertical response categories. A wider range of response categories was included in questions relating to personal preferences, including where appropriate an explicit option for 'this does not apply to me'.

The results of the second pilot study indicated that these changes were largely successful. Item non-response was reduced and we obtained more variability in responses (Figure 6.4). Furthermore, on questions relating to personal preferences, a significant proportion of users (between 13 and 24 per cent) used the 'not applicable' categories, confirming that the importance of these service process outcomes varied between users.

Figure 6.4 Comparison of responses from the first and second pilot studies

First pilot study		Second pilot study	
How much did your Occupational Therapist explain or demonstrate how to use the equipment and/or adaptations?		How well did he or she explain or demonstrate how to use the equipment and/or adaptations?	
	%		%
As much as I wanted	98	Very well	75
Too much	0	Fairly well	6
Not enough	2	OK	5
		Not very well	0
		Not at all	0
		I did not need an explanation	
		or demonstration	14
n = 170			
not applicable = 5		n = 83	
no response = 31 (15%)		not applicable = 2	
		no response = 3 (3%)	

Brief and detailed user questionnaires combined

Additional questions
In addition to questions on outcomes, we included areas highlighted in recent literature on equipment and adaptation services: for example, waiting times; use of equipment; and the extent to which equipment had been demonstrated and explained. Questions on expectations, unmet needs and overall satisfaction were also added. Finally, to ensure the questionnaire provided feedback to all parts of the service, additional sections collected information on users' views of the Joint Equipment Service, the help provided by the Grants and Adaptations Service, and the quality of minor adaptations.

Negotiation over the inclusion of these additional areas was not generally contentious, with one notable exception. Staff were concerned over the inclusion and interpretation of questions relating to unmet needs. For staff, the term 'unmet need' referred only to needs for services not provided by the authority. In contrast, users and carers were thought to define all outstanding needs as unmet needs regardless of whether the need had not been met because a service was not available, or they did not meet the eligibility criteria, or they had decided not to proceed with adaptations. Additionally, staff thought users would include needs which had been met, but not in the way the user had envisaged. For example, a user requesting a downstairs toilet might be provided with a stair lift to enable the use of an existing upstairs toilet. From the staff perspective the need had been met and a satisfactory outcome achieved. However, staff anticipated that the user would identify a downstairs toilet as an unmet need in this situation. The perceived value of the information was therefore limited, since it would not be possible to determine whether unmet needs were 'genuine' or not, without going back to the original documentation. Despite these reservations, it was agreed to include the area of unmet needs, but to take account of these issues in wording the questions.

Questions relating to demographic characteristics such as age and gender were not included, since these details were recorded in the computerised information system. Instead, each questionnaire had a unique identifying number so that it could be matched with existing information.

The results of the first pilot study indicated acceptable levels of item non-response for most of the additional questions. This may reflect the use of a vertical format for these questions. It is important to note, however, that non-response to other questions is likely to be underestimated, since we assumed that all respondents who had omitted an entire section had done so because the questions were not applicable, rather than because they had missed them.

Responses to the first pilot study indicated that half of the users completing a detailed questionnaire reported at least one unmet need. This finding led to renewed debate among staff concerning the value of including a question on unmet needs. After considerable discussion, staff agreed that the existing question on unmet needs should be retained.

The majority of users reported that the questionnaire had been easy to complete (94 per cent of those completing the detailed questionnaire, and 90 per cent of those completing the brief questionnaire). As already described, problems were most often caused by the question concerning quality of life outcomes in the brief questionnaire.

Relatively few changes were made to the questions not directly concerned with outcomes following the first pilot study. Comments made on the questionnaires confirmed that the revised questionnaires were easier to complete, with only one per cent of respondents stating that the brief questionnaire was difficult to complete in the second pilot study.

Development of the carer questionnaire

We included questions on the perceived impact of equipment and adaptations on the overall quality of life of the carer and the person they supported, and also asked about the impact of equipment and/or adaptations on their relationship. A series of questions asking about the impact of provision on the frequency, time, number of tasks and physical effort of caring were included. Since it was anticipated that equipment or adaptations may affect these different aspects of caring in different ways, for example, tasks may require less effort but take longer using equipment, we included a summary question asking about the overall impact on caring.

Only a small number of carer questionnaires were sent out and returned in both pilot studies. The quality of data on the questionnaires was generally good, but it is difficult to evaluate the questionnaires without larger numbers of respondents. Staff suggested that the question relating to unmet needs be revised to make the phrasing consistent with the parallel question in the detailed user questionnaire. Changing the format of the questionnaires so they are consistent with the revised user questionnaires might improve their appearance, but would have implications for the number of questions that could be included, unless the length of the questionnaires was increased. It is suggested that further piloting is carried out over a longer period to ensure that sufficient numbers of questionnaires are available for a detailed consideration of the content and layout of the carer questionnaire.

6. ARRANGEMENTS FOR DATA COLLECTION

In developing administrative systems for data collection and management, feasibility in routine practice was a prime consideration. The main issues considered were:
- The timing of questionnaires
- Matching questionnaires to the type of intervention
- Inclusion of users and carers
- Identifying a sample
- Maximising response rates
- Developing an administrative database.

Timing of questionnaires

The literature review had alerted us to the importance of timing (Heaton and Bamford, 2000) and this issue was raised in several planning group meetings. In the previous system, questionnaires and survey cards were sent at the point of closure. While this had the benefit of being administratively easy, there was concern that it might be too soon for larger adaptations and equipment. Staff felt that users might underestimate the value of such work if asked too soon after provision, and this was confirmed by the experience of one carer in the planning group. It proved difficult, however, to identify the most appropriate time to send a questionnaire, since the time taken to come to terms with equipment and adaptations varies. We therefore decided to continue to send out questionnaires at closure.

This decision had two implications. First, since major adaptations typically involved a lengthy process, users were likely to overlook the benefits of any small pieces of equipment or minor adaptations carried out soon after the initial assessment. Secondly, most OTs had a small number of cases that were likely to remain open indefinitely due to the complex and changing nature of the user's needs. Linking questionnaires to closure would mean that the views of this small but important group of users, with whom staff often worked intensively over a long period of time, would be excluded. To get round these problems we considered sending a questionnaire:

- after provision of each item
- after completion of a block of work
- annually, to cover all provision in the last year.

The first option was rejected on the grounds that it would be too onerous for users, and that response fatigue might result in a higher non-response rate for the final detailed questionnaire, which was perhaps most the important. The second strategy was considered likely to work for some users but not others. Some staff felt that it could be difficult to identify discrete pieces of work, particularly where their input was ongoing. It was therefore agreed to pilot the third option by including a slip with the questionnaire asking the user whether it would be acceptable to send them an annual questionnaire.

In each pilot study attempts were made to identify on-going cases and include them in the survey. While staff acknowledged the importance of including on-going cases, the low priority given to identifying them, however, meant that neither of these attempts was successful. We therefore do not know the best way of including the views of users with ongoing contact with the service.

The results of the pilot studies suggest that sending a questionnaire when the case was closed was acceptable to users and carers. Only one user, who received a minor adaptation, commented on the difficulties of assessing the outcome within the time span:

> It is early days yet insofar as my experience is concerned. I would need more experience to evaluate properly.

Matching questions to the type of intervention

The wide range of interventions provided, for example, from a set of chair raisers to a large extension, meant that a single questionnaire was unlikely to be appropriate to all users. Although we considered personalising each questionnaire so that the questions were tailored to provision, this would have required considerable resources for administration and data analysis. We therefore decided to design separate questionnaires for minor and major pieces of work (Box 6.3).

166

Box 6.3   Eligibility for user questionnaires

	Pilot 1	Pilot 2
Advice only Minor adaptations Simple equipment	Brief questionnaire	Brief questionnaire
Major items of equipment	Detailed questionnaire	
Major adaptations	Detailed questionnaire	Detailed questionnaire

The results of the first pilot study showed that all but one of the users eligible for a detailed questionnaire had received a major adaptation. We therefore decided to change the criteria so users receiving a major item of equipment only would no longer be eligible for a detailed questionnaire in the second pilot study. This also enabled the structure of the detailed questionnaire to be simplified.

Inclusion of users and carers

Since Disability Support Services provide a generic service, we hoped to be able to develop a system for collecting outcomes information applicable for all user groups. The stage one research in this authority had focused on outcomes for younger disabled people (i.e. adults under retirement age); therefore, we undertook additional work to explore the extent to which these outcomes were also relevant to older people, and disabled children and their parents.

Outcomes of equipment and adaptations for older people were explored through detailed analysis of the transcripts of the individual interviews and group discussions conducted as part of our stage one research with older people (Patmore *et al.*, 1997). This was supplemented by three interviews with older people who had recently used Disability Support Services. Our analysis suggested that outcomes of equipment and adaptations for older people were essentially the same as those already identified, although there was some evidence that equipment was also sometimes used to beneficial effect by an older spouse, as well as the person for whom it had been provided. We therefore anticipated no difficulties in developing a questionnaire appropriate for older people and younger disabled people.

Information on the outcomes of equipment and adaptations for disabled children was provided by colleagues who had recently completed a study of the housing needs of disabled children (Oldman and Beresford, 1998). Their work was supplemented with two interviews with parents of disabled children who had used Disability Support Services. We found a strong emphasis on the impacts of provision on other family members, particularly siblings, suggesting that the collection of outcomes information should focus on the family as a whole, rather than simply the disabled child. There is a growing recognition of the importance of including the views of children themselves

167

(Beresford, 1997). This may be particularly important in the context of equipment and adaptations since research has shown that the needs of the child and parents may differ and, at times, conflict (Oldman and Beresford, 1998). We concluded that it was outside the scope of the present work to develop a method for collecting information on the outcomes of equipment and adaptations for disabled children and their families. Disability Support Services plan to commission a separate piece of work to explore alternative ways of collecting the views of disabled children and their families.

Users unable to complete a postal questionnaire

The main reservation expressed in stage one concerning the use of postal questionnaires to collect outcomes information was that some users would be excluded. We were therefore committed to supplementing the questionnaires with other approaches to ensure the inclusion of as many users as possible. The alternative approaches considered were telephone and home interviews, with telephone interviews being used where possible to minimise costs. Prior to the pilot studies, we had no information on the likely numbers of users for whom a postal questionnaire would not be appropriate. Although responsibility for conducting the interviews was agreed to fall within the Strategic Services division of the authority, staff shortages meant that this was not feasible for the pilot studies, particularly in the absence of information on how many interviews might be involved. Interviews were therefore carried out by the researcher during the pilot studies. Arrangements for future interviews would then be made once the likely scope of the exercise was known.

To minimise the number of telephone and home interviews, we decided to send a postal questionnaire to users thought likely to have difficulties completing it, as long as they lived with, or had regular contact with, someone who would be able to help them to complete it. In both pilot studies, the majority of users were thought to be able to complete a postal questionnaire without assistance and for many of those thought to need some help, staff were able to identify a family member or someone else who would be able to provide the necessary help. This left only a small number of users for whom a home interview or telephone interview was thought necessary, six (two per cent of those eligible for a questionnaire) in the first pilot study and nine (seven per cent of those eligible) in the second pilot study.

Following the first pilot study, two groups of users who could not easily be included were identified: people with dementia and people with dual sensory impairments. Previous work within the outcomes programme has shown that while it is feasible to consult people with dementia, considerable resources are required. Since only a small number of users with these impairments were identified during the first pilot study, we agreed not to routinely collect any information on outcomes from people with dementia or dual sensory impairments. Where such users had received major adaptations, their carers were sent a carer questionnaire in the second pilot study to provide information on carer outcomes.

Inclusion of carers

There was general agreement within the planning group that information on outcomes for carers should only be sought where a major adaptation or large item of equipment had been provided. Although one carer in the planning group felt that all such carers should be included, this view was not shared by other members. There was considerable discussion of possible criteria for identifying carers for inclusion, drawing on the personal experience of carers in the group and descriptions of situations in which staff thought it would be inappropriate to involve carers. This led to the identification of three possible criteria:

- Extent of the caring role
- Involvement in the process of assessment for and provision of equipment and adaptations
- Whether staff thought the carer was likely to benefit from the provision made.

Although initially an attempt at prioritising these criteria was made, after further discussion it was agreed that carers meeting any one of these criteria would be included in the first pilot study. The eligibility criteria were further simplified in the second pilot study so that all carers of users receiving major adaptations were eligible for a carer questionnaire if they had participated in assessment or were likely to have benefitted from the adaptation provided.

Identifying a sample

It was possible to identify cases closed by Disability Support Services staff from the existing computerized information system. Information on whether the user was eligible for a questionnaire, the most appropriate mode of administration, the type of assistance provided and whether the carer was also eligible for a questionnaire was not, however, readily available. We therefore designed a questionnaire request form to provide these details which was completed by staff when they closed a case. The questionnaire request form also included information on whether anyone was available to help the user to complete a questionnaire in the event of difficulty. Written guidance was provided on completing the forms and definitions of minor and major adaptations were provided to ensure consistency between staff. In response to comments from staff and to assist in interpreting questionnaire data, the questionnaire request form was revised for the second pilot study (Appendix E). Staff provided additional details of the equipment and adaptations provided and, as already described, eligibility criteria for the detailed and carer questionnaires were simplified. We discussed adding a section for assessment staff to record their views of the outcomes achieved to the questionnaire request form. It was agreed, however, that this information would be recorded elsewhere in the notes.

Maximising response rates

We aimed to maximise response rates through the accompanying letter and use of reminders.

Accompanying letters

Previous studies have stressed the importance of the covering letter and follow-up in maximising response rates (McColl *et al.*, 1999; Jones and Lester, 1995). A personalised letter from the service manager was sent with the questionnaire explaining the purpose of the study and requesting the user's participation. There was some discussion over whether to include the name of the OT or OTA seen in the letter. While this would help the user to recall the service provided, it was argued that the name of the OT or OTA should only be included if the names of other members of staff involved were also included (e.g. the name of the person who delivered the equipment and the name of the building contractor responsible for the adaptation). Since such information was not readily available, this was not feasible. We also discussed whether to include details of the equipment or adaptations provided since such information might remind the user of the service received. Again, information on provision was not available on the computerised information system. It was not, therefore feasible to personalise the letters in either of these ways.

The letter accompanying the questionnaire invited respondents to contact a member of the research team if they had any queries. The majority of queries received in the first pilot study were from users who could not recall receiving any assistance from Disability Support Services. To prompt recall, we agreed to include a list of equipment or adaptations provided in the letters accompanying the questionnaires in the second pilot study. The revised questionnaire request form therefore included a list of equipment and adaptations provided. This appeared to be a successful way of reminding users of the help received, since only one or two queries were received during the second pilot study.

Use of reminders

To maximise response rates we decided to send one reminder to users and carers who had not replied after three weeks. A copy of the questionnaire and a pre-paid envelope were included with the reminder letter (Appendix E). The results of the first pilot study showed that using reminders boosted response rates significantly (from 61 per cent to 79 per cent for the brief user questionnaire and from 52 per cent to 77 per cent for the detailed user questionnaire). Responses to individual questions were examined to see whether the views of users returning a questionnaire straightaway differed significantly from those of users sent a reminder. Since the number of comparisons was large, a significance level of one per cent was used. Responses to the detailed questionnaire were not related to whether or not a reminder had been sent. On the brief questionnaire, however, two significant differences were found. Users returning the questionnaire after being sent a

170

reminder were significantly less positive about waiting times (p<0.01), and were significantly more likely to report that the OT or OTA had provided advice only (p<0.001). Overall, only five users who had received advice only returned a questionnaire, and all of these did so only after a reminder had been sent.

In view of the good response rates achieved in the first pilot study we experimented with using a single mailing for the brief questionnaire in the second pilot study, although we recognised that this might result in a poor response from users receiving advice only. Even without a reminder, the response rate to the revised brief questionnaire proved acceptable (69 per cent). Although it is likely that sending a reminder would increase the response rate further, the value of the additional data obtained needs to be balanced against additional administrative, printing and postal costs.

Developing an administrative database

To facilitate the administration of questionnaires and reminders an Access database was developed. Information from completed questionnaire request forms is entered into the database; the type of questionnaire(s) to be sent (brief, detailed or carer questionnaire) is then automatically identified using the information provided. The database is linked to the existing user information system to facilitate the mailing of questionnaires; a tracking system accounts for returns and the administration of reminders (Figure 6.5).

During the first pilot study, the database was maintained and reminders were administered from SPRU. This was partly for logistic reasons, particularly since the two assessment teams were physically separate and had different administrative staff, but also to enable the database to be tested out and developed before asking administrative staff to take it over. For the second pilot study, the database was installed on the computer network of our partner authority. Administrative staff successfully used the database to enter information from the questionnaire request forms and send out questionnaires and reminders. Although a small number of reminders were inadvertently omitted in both pilot studies, such errors are likely to occur less frequently once staff are more familiar with the system and it is incorporated into routine practice.

Figure 6.5   Database menu

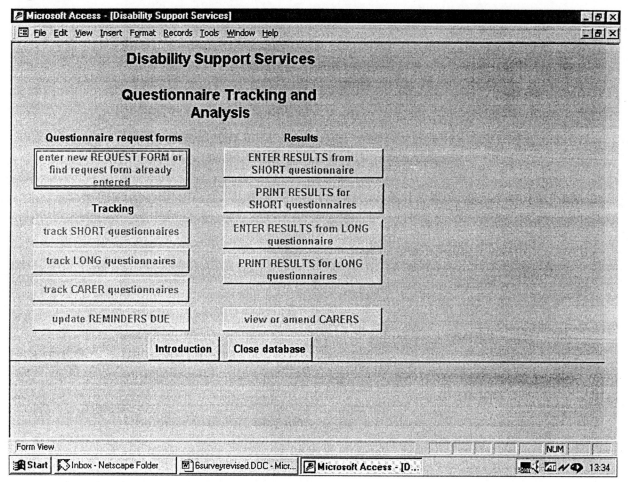

7. RESULTS OF TRIAL IMPLEMENTATION

The first pilot study included all cases closed over a six-week period, from mid-December 1999 until the end of January 2000. Recognising that December is a less than ideal time to send out postal questionnaires (McColl *et al.*, 1999), no questionnaires were sent out until January. It proved necessary to extend the first pilot study for two reasons. First, an unexpectedly high proportion of users were not eligible for a questionnaire (as will be detailed, users excluded were largely cases in which the referral was inappropriate, or the user had died or declined a service); and secondly, the numbers of users eligible for a detailed questionnaire and eligible carers were lower than anticipated. We extended the pilot study for a further two weeks for brief questionnaires, and for a further four weeks for detailed and carer questionnaires. The second pilot study took place over a six-week period during August and September 2000.

Analysis of questionnaire request forms

Since the questionnaire request forms were designed to provide information not available in the computerised record system, the extent to which details on the questionnaire request form can be crosschecked is limited. The quality of the information provided on the questionnaire request forms was assessed in three ways:

- The numbers of questionnaire request forms completed was compared with the number of cases closed during the pilot study period according to the computerized information system.
- The internal consistency of information on the flowcharts was examined.
- The consistency in completion between different members of staff was evaluated.

Numbers of forms completed

The number of questionnaire request forms completed by individual members of assessment staff ranged from six to 71 in the first pilot study and zero to 31 in the second pilot study. As expected, the majority of questionnaire request forms (around 75 per cent) were completed by OTAs in both pilot studies. According to the computerised information system, there were a significant number of missing questionnaire request forms (Table 6.1). In the first pilot study, questionnaire request forms were completed for around 75 per cent of closed cases, and this declined to only around 67 per cent of closed cases in the second pilot study. It was not possible to establish why the remaining questionnaire request forms had not been completed. The unique identifying number on a small number of questionnaire request forms did not correspond to any cases on the computerised record system; this is probably due to errors in copying the unique identifier onto the questionnaire request form.

Table 6.1 Completion of questionnaire request forms

	First pilot study	Second pilot study
Total cases closed	556	284
Closed cases with completed questionnaire request forms	407	190
Completed questionnaire request forms but not closed	15	0
Total completed questionnaire request forms	422	190

Internal consistency of information

The quality of the data on completed questionnaire request forms completed in both pilot studies was good, with minimal missing information. Assessment staff occasionally provided unnecessary information on the forms (for example providing details of the carer when the user had not received a major adaptation). These details were filtered out when the information was entered onto the database.

Consistency of questionnaire request forms between members of staff
Detailed analysis of cases closed during the second pilot study indicated marked variation in the completion of questionnaire request forms between assessment staff. Among staff with at least 20 closed cases, the proportion of cases with no questionnaire request form ranged from three per cent to 61 per cent. It is unlikely in any feedback system that all members of staff will be equally committed to the collection of feedback. These results suggest that the number of missing closure questionnaires for each member of assessment staff should routinely be checked, to ensure that the work of all staff is represented.

We also examined the proportion of users described as ineligible on the questionnaire request forms. Overall, around one quarter of users was described as not eligible for a questionnaire in each pilot study (26 per cent in the first, and 28 per cent in the second pilot study). Data from the questionnaire request forms completed in both pilot studies were combined to explore the proportion of users described as ineligible by assessment staff. The proportion of eligible users ranged from 67 per cent to 88 per cent among staff who had completed at least 20 questionnaire request forms. It was not feasible to explore variation in the reasons for ineligibility between staff in view of the relatively small numbers of forms completed. Overall, reasons for ineligibility were similar in both pilot studies, although there was a slightly higher proportion of 'other' reasons in the second pilot study (Table 6.2).

Table 6.2   Reasons for excluding users from the survey

	First pilot study %	Second pilot study %
Inappropriate referral	30	23
Died	22	15
Declined assessment/provision	19	19
Unable to participate	7	7
Other reason	22	36
Total	102 (100%)	53 (100%)

Response rates
In both pilot studies, the majority of users were eligible for a brief questionnaire (83 per cent in the first and 91 per cent in the second pilot study). As already described, only a small number of users required a telephone or home interview. The small number of carer questionnaires reflects the relatively small number of users eligible for detailed questionnaires, the fact that not all users have carers, and that not all carers identified were eligible for a questionnaire.

The analysis of response rates is based on users eligible for a postal questionnaire (Table 6.3). A small number of questionnaires were returned with no unique identifying number: these are included in the overall analysis of response rates and

174

in the analysis of the questionnaires, but are excluded from analyses linking data from the questionnaires with personal details held in the computerised information system.

Table 6.3   Response rates to postal questionnaires

	Brief questionnaire		Detailed questionnaire		Carer questionnaire
	First pilot study	Second pilot study	First pilot study	Second pilot study	Both pilot studies
Sent out	219	116	44	10	15
Returned after initial mailing	133	80	23	6	8
Response rate without reminder	61%	69%	52%	60%	53%
Reminders sent out	80	-	20	2	5
Returned after reminder sent	39	-	11	2	1
Response rate to reminder	49%	-	55%	*	*
Overall response rate	79%	69%	77%	80%	60%

* Number too small for calculation of percentages

Non-response analysis

Detailed analysis of non-response was limited to the first pilot study. This indicated that response was not related to characteristics of the user such as gender, whether they were on the telephone, or were thought to need help in completing a postal questionnaire. There was also no relationship between response and characteristics of the service including provision made, type of worker seen and the assessment team seen. For brief questionnaires (but not detailed questionnaires), response was significantly associated with age (p<0.05, Figure 6.6). Response rates to the brief questionnaire were lowest in the youngest age group and increased with age, with a slight dropping off in response rate in the oldest age group. In contrast, there was less variation in response rates to the detailed questionnaire, with the highest response rate among users aged 50 to 64 years.

Figure 6.6   Response rates by age of user and type of questionnaire

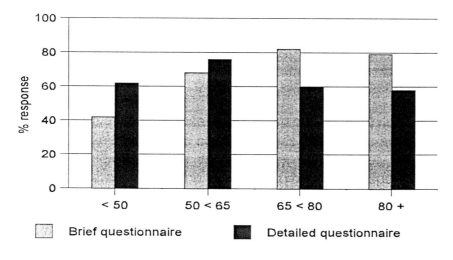

175

OUTCOMES IN SOCIAL CARE PRACTICE

Key findings

Since the user questionnaires were significantly revised after the first pilot study, the data reported below are generally from the second pilot study; where the questions were unchanged responses from both pilot studies are combined. The majority of service users derived considerable benefit from the equipment and/or adaptations provided, in terms of both their overall quality of life and the performance of specific tasks. While most users reported an improvement in their quality of life (70 per cent of those receiving a brief questionnaire and 64 per cent of those receiving a detailed questionnaire), a significant proportion reported that provision had a protective or preventive effect (27 per cent of those receiving a brief questionnaire and 31 per cent of those receiving a detailed questionnaire). This confirms that any assessment of outcomes focusing only on improvements will significantly underestimate the outcomes achieved by equipment and adaptation services. The outcomes achieved in relation to key activities are summarised in Table 6.4 (percentages are based on the numbers of users receiving assistance with the activity and do not add up to 100 since provision could have more than one outcome).

Table 6.4 Outcomes of equipment and adaptations

	Bathing[1] (n=104)	Mobility[2] (n=58)	Using the toilet[1] (n-51)
	%	%	%
Safer	74	71	47
Easier	80	72	75
Need less help	37	28	18
More choice	43	26	Not applicable
Other outcome	9	14	4
Made no difference	1	0	2

[1] Detailed questionnaires from both pilot studies and brief questionnaire from second pilot study

[2] Detailed and brief questionnaires from second pilot study only

The benefits of provision are confirmed in the high reported rates of use of equipment and adaptations. By the time the questionnaires were completed, 94 per cent of users were still using all of the equipment and adaptations provided. This compares favourably to rates of usage reported in previous studies, although there are difficulties in drawing comparisons due to variable time periods and question wording (Heaton and Bamford, 2000).

Responses to questions relating to service process outcomes were generally very positive, although views of access to the service and waiting times were more critical. Views on the process of installing minor adaptations were also mostly positive, with only small proportions of respondents reporting that the workmen did not come as arranged or that the quality of the finished work was poor.

Despite high levels of satisfaction with the service, half of the users receiving major adaptations reported some unmet needs. To some extent, this confirms staff expectations and the difficulties of interpreting this finding have already been described. Examples of the unmet needs identified by users include a ramp, downstairs toilet, shower and central heating.

Since only a small number of carer questionnaires (nine) were sent out and completed during the pilot studies, the results will not be discussed in detail. The returned questionnaires suggested that provision had resulted in some benefits for carers as well as for users. Responses to a question on unmet needs yielded similar results to those for users, with only half of the carers reported that they now had all of the equipment and adaptations needed. Carers' views on the achievement of some service process outcomes appeared to be less positive than those of users. This was particularly true of service process outcomes relating to their role as carers. These results will need to be reviewed when additional questionnaires have been completed to see whether this apparent difference persists.

8. INTERPRETING AND USING RESULTS

Stage one research drew attention to a range of issues relating to the interpretation and use of results:

- Linking questionnaire data with existing computerised information
- Shifting the focus from individual to aggregate level data
- Resources for data analysis and reporting
- Using feedback constructively.

Linking questionnaire data with existing computerised information

There were two distinct reasons for linking the questionnaires with the existing computerised record system. The first was simply to facilitate administration of the questionnaires. Linking the administrative database with the computerised record system enabled names and addresses to be merged into letters and address labels for mailing out questionnaires and reminders. This was successfully achieved.

The second purpose of linking data was for interpreting the findings. We were able to link questionnaire data to basic demographic information on users, such as their age and gender. This proved useful in exploring response rates to the questionnaires. The lack of computerised information on provision, however, limited the analyses possible. For example, we anticipated that users who had received only very simple items of equipment, such as chair raisers, might have more difficulties in completing questions relating to outcomes. Similarly, difficulties with questions relating to service process outcomes might reflect the number of visits, since some provision was made within one short visit. It was not possible, however, to test these hypotheses easily. Even in the second pilot study when information on provision was recorded on the questionnaire request form, the details were recorded freehand and there was not sufficient time to code different types of provision for analysis. There are plans to computerise information on equipment provided and this would be useful in interpreting results and examining the outcomes of different types of equipment. Other aspects of the service, however, are unlikely to be added to the computerised record system, limiting the analyses possible and the potential uses of the results. For example, different contractors are used for minor adaptations such as grab rails and stair rails, and overall positive results may mask significant variation between contractors. Although linking questionnaire data to individual contractors would significantly increase the value of the results, there are no plans to add details of contractors to the computerised record system.

Using information at individual and aggregate level
Through our stage one discussions with staff regarding the existing user feedback system we identified a number of problems with the way information was used. Completed questionnaires and survey cards were returned directly to the service manager, providing an immediate opportunity to follow up any problems that arose. Although the service manager aimed to produce an annual summary of the questionnaires returned in the previous system, competing demands meant this was not always possible. Bundles of completed questionnaires and survey cards were circulated to assessment staff from time to time, and this enabled staff to see that the majority of users were satisfied with the service. Some staff, however, thought there was too much emphasis on using the results of the questionnaires at an individual level and described the system as a 'mini-complaints system'. A number of negative consequences of using information predominantly at an individual level were discussed by the planning group:

- Users and carers may feel inhibited in voicing criticisms if they know the information will be fed back to staff on whom they may be reliant for help in the future
- Attention is given to those who express most dissatisfaction, rather than those in greatest need
- Responding to problems at an individual level may result in a lack of clarity over eligibility criteria and a sense of inequity for other users, particularly if criteria are loosely applied to resolve dissatisfaction
- An emphasis on responding to problems on an individual basis may preclude open discussion of recurring issues with a range of stakeholders
- Staff may feel defensive if negative feedback is dealt with on an individual basis rather than aggregated across the service.

Most staff felt that more systematic and accessible information on the results would be useful, and the focus throughout the development work was on the use of aggregate information.

Data analysis and reporting

It was clear from stage one research that resources for data analysis and reporting were limited in our partner authority. An important part of the development work was therefore to develop a system that required minimal input from staff. We thought that the ideal scenario was for staff in Disability Support Services to be involved in analysis. Since we recognised that staff were unlikely to feel they had sufficient skills in this area, we suggested that the analysis could be carried out in partnership with the researcher during the pilot studies. However, views of the ideal scenario varied. Staff were reluctant to become involved, partly because of their perceived lack of skills, but also because of the time commitment involved. It was therefore agreed that following the pilot studies, staff in Strategic Services would take over responsibility for analysis and reporting.

In the first pilot study, all data processing and analysis were carried out by SPRU. To facilitate the long-term use of the questionnaires by our partner authority, the administrative database also includes the facility to process and analyse the questionnaires in routine practice (see Figure 6.5). Changes to the operating system in our partner authority, including the installation of Access 2000 shortly after the second pilot study, meant that not all aspects of the database were tested in routine practice.

Entering the data from completed brief questionnaires onto the database is a straightforward administrative task. The fields have been set up so that not applicable codes are automatically entered where questions do not apply and any inconsistencies are highlighted. During the second pilot study, the checks were only internal to the questionnaire, but the database has subsequently been developed to check the data against information on the questionnaire request form. This enables a distinction to be made between questions omitted because they do not apply and genuine non-response. Once the data have been entered, a pre-set series of commands produces the information needed to calculate response rates and performs a standard analysis of the data. The report function produces frequencies for each question in a table and bar chart (Figure 6.7). The results can be produced for each assessment team or combined to give an overview of the service as a whole. The simplicity of the system and limited time costs involved in entering the data and producing results should facilitate routine analysis of the questionnaire data. Resources for entering the data from the questionnaires into the database will need to be identified.

Different ways of presenting results were explored in one planning group meeting. Generally, graphic forms of presentation were preferred in view of their immediate impact and ease of interpretation. Staff, but not users or carers, also valued the more detailed information that could be conveyed in tables and felt this additional information was often required in order to facilitate interpretation of the graphic presentation. This suggested that different ways of presenting information are appropriate for different stakeholders.

Figure 6.7   Sample results from database
How easy was it to find out about where to get help with equipment and/or adaptations?

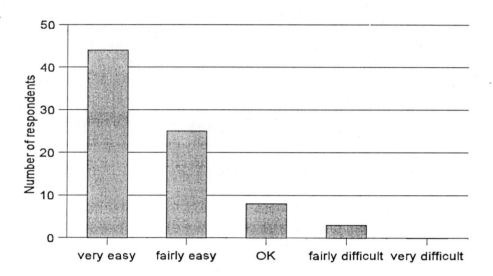

Using feedback constructively
A number of barriers to the constructive use of feedback were identified in stage one research. Limited experience of feedback from the previous questionnaire system had contributed to these barriers. There was little emphasis on thinking through the implications of the results from the existing user feedback system or considering how they could inform service development. The previous system was essentially used as a means of quality assurance to ensure that the majority of users were reasonably satisfied with the service and to follow up those who expressed significant dissatisfaction. Staff seemed to lack confidence in their ability to reflect on and interpret results, although an exercise using hypothetical data indicated that they were able to identify the key findings. When interpreting feedback relating to their work, however, there was a tendency to view the user as the only source of knowledge or expertise. As a result, if users were critical of an aspect of the service, staff tended to think that the only way forward was to contact the user to discuss the problems in more detail. While this may be a valid strategy in some circumstances, it fails to acknowledge the ability of staff to reflect on their work, compare ideas and approaches, and suggest possible reasons for the observed problems. The failure to consider the viewpoint of those users who are satisfied with the service as well as those who are not, could potentially result in changes that are not appropriate for all users.

It was felt inevitable that some users would be dissatisfied regardless of the service provided. However, such assumptions enabled some negative feedback to be discounted. Critical feedback was also sometimes discounted because of perceived problems with the questions. While it is clearly important to acknowledge the limitations of the questions, increasing openness to feedback was an important aim of the development work.

We included exercises on the interpretation of results, preferred methods of presentation and reactions to feedback in the development work. We also produced a series of prompts to facilitate the constructive use of feedback (Box 6.4).

Box 6.4   Prompts to aid the use of feedback

• What do these results mean?
• Why might we have got these results?
• Is there anything we can do to change this?
• If yes, what can be done about it?
• Do we need any additional information before we can act?
• If yes, what and how can we collect it?
• How high a priority is improvement in this area?
• What factors might make it difficult to bring about change in this area?

Reactions to presentation of results

A meeting of the planning group was convened to discuss the draft findings of the first pilot study. We used the series of prompts above to facilitate discussion. Observation at the meeting indicated that although some of the problems highlighted earlier in using feedback persisted, the use of the prompts enabled a productive discussion. For example, after some initial discounting of critical results, there was a useful discussion of the possible reasons for the results observed. Similarly, while staff sometimes commented that additional information was needed in order to clarify the results, they also speculated on the likely factors involved. The use of the prompts also seemed effective in identifying a wide range of implications of positive results. For example, the high rates of usage of equipment and adaptations were thought to indicate that the assessment procedures and eligibility criteria were sound, and to highlight the skills of assessment staff in terms of linking provision to needs, communicating with users and involving users in decision-making. Staff thought such information could be used to promote the service, and contribute to internal audit and Best Value Review.

There was some tension within the planning group over the potential use of the results of the pilot study. Some members of the planning group, particularly users and carers, wanted the results to be used to challenge the scope, organisation and delivery of services, to identify areas for service development and ultimately to lead to demonstrable improvements in the service. Others, however, focused more on using the results to check that the service was generally of an acceptable standard and to deal with any problems at an individual level. At the time of writing, the results are still being considered by the authority. It is therefore too early to say whether or how the results will lead to changes in Disability Support Services.

9. VIEWS OF DEVELOPMENT WORK

Participants were interviewed after the final meeting of the planning group and circulation of a draft report on the first pilot study. Interviews were conducted by an external researcher not otherwise involved in the development work. A topic guide and brief self-completion questionnaire were used to prompt discussion and the interviews were tape recorded and transcribed. Most members of the planning group were interviewed individually, with the exception of staff responsible for assessment, who were interviewed in pairs. Although the user who withdrew from the planning group was not available for interview on completion of the work, her views on the development work were explored at the time of withdrawal and have been incorporated. The main issues to emerge from the interviews can be grouped into two themes: the investment in development work and the perceived value of this approach to collecting and using outcomes information.

Investment in development work

Most members of the planning group commented on the time invested in the development work. While some members of staff had found it difficult to prioritise the development work, there were few specific suggestions for reducing the time commitment involved, since the process of clarifying and prioritising outcomes and designing the questions was seen as important. There was a strong feeling among professionals that the system was not an 'off the peg' package that could simply be implemented elsewhere. Local ownership and an understanding of outcomes were seen as important prerequisites to implementation, as well as the need to tailor the system to local service organisation. The involvement of a range of stakeholders in the development work was generally valued, although views were less clear on the role of users and carers in adopting the system prior to implementation elsewhere. Before the joint meetings began, the main concerns about joint working were that users and carers would personalise issues and staff would be defensive. Views on the extent to which these problems had arisen in the planning group varied. Review and reiteration of the ground rules was seen as important in minimising such barriers to effective joint working. An existing culture of consultation, services of reasonably good quality, and separate preparatory meetings were seen as essential in facilitating successful collaboration. A balance of users, carers and professionals was also important.

Value of instrumentation and pilot results

Although the user and carers interviewed identified a range of potential uses for the results, they were concerned that lack of financial resources and staff attitudes to being evaluated by users and carers might limit the use made of the information. Staff were surprised at the high proportion of positive responses, but wanted additional information on reasons for critical responses. They felt the results demonstrated the effectiveness of their work and could have implications for service development. The revised questionnaires were thought to provide more information than the previously used questionnaire and survey card and therefore have more potential for use. Most, but not all, staff felt it was useful to include questions on all aspects of the service. It was suggested that more time should have been spent on identifying how the information was to be used and who was responsible for implementing changes arising from the results.

The potential value of information on outcomes achieved in other authorities was seen as limited due to different service configurations, eligibility criteria and types of provision. In view of these local differences, it was thought difficult to make true comparisons.

10. FUTURE IMPLEMENTATION IN OUR PARTNER AUTHORITY

There is commitment within Disability Support Services to continue to routinely collect feedback from users and carers. The findings of the second pilot study suggest that the user questionnaires can be used in routine practice without further revisions. The carer questionnaire was not revised since there was very little missing data in the first pilot study. There may, however, be benefits in revising the layout to be consistent with the user questionnaires. Minor amendments to the questionnaire request form and database are recommended and some issues regarding implementation have yet to be resolved.

Questionnaire request form

It is not currently clear from the questionnaire request form whether provision was intended to assist with mobility, bathing or using the toilet (grab rails, for example, could assist with any or all of these). Adding a separate question to indicate which area(s) the intervention(s) were directed towards will facilitate the recoding of missing data on the questionnaires.

Database

Improved linkage and consistency checks between data on the questionnaires and questionnaire request forms will also facilitate the recoding of missing data. At the time of the second pilot study, the database only managed results from brief user questionnaires. The relatively small numbers of detailed and carer questionnaires meant that analysis by hand was possible. The database has since been developed further to allow entry of data from detailed questionnaires, and queries have been set up to summarise the results of these questionnaires.

During the second pilot study, comments on the questionnaires were entered onto the database by question number. Many comments, however, do not relate to specific questions but are more general. Following detailed analysis of comments made in both pilot studies, it is suggested that comments are entered onto the database using the framework below (Box 6.5). While this requires some interpretation by administrative staff, it will facilitate the reporting and use of comments. The first two categories, positive and negative comments, might usefully be subdivided. Subdivisions could simply reflect the different parts of the service – assessment team, the Joint Equipment Service and the Grants and Adaptations Service. Some of these could be subdivided further if needed; for example, within Grants and Adaptations a distinction could be made between comments about workmen, office staff, the surveyors and the quality of adaptations.

Box 6.5   Framework for reporting comments

1.	Positive comments
2.	Negative comments
3.	Outcomes
4.	Access to the service
5.	Comments on the questionnaire
6.	Unmet needs
7.	Comments on other services
8.	Other comments

Implementation issues
Details of the sampling procedure to be used in routine practice have yet to be finalised. Based on the numbers of questionnaires sent out during the pilot studies, it is suggested that all users seen by an OT are sent a questionnaire (regardless of the type of help provided) and that all users receiving major adaptations are sent a detailed questionnaire (regardless of the type of worker seen). In view of the high numbers of assessments carried out by OTAs for minor adaptations and equipment, it is suggested that a sample of one in seven eligible users are sent a brief questionnaire. While OTAs are, understandably, reluctant to complete a questionnaire request form for each user seen, if only one in seven are to be sent a questionnaire, there are benefits in completing the form for all users. The information could be used to check whether the sample of users sent a questionnaire was representative of all users seen. Routinely completing questionnaire request forms would also enable sampling to be done by administrative staff, thus avoiding any potential selection bias. Possible sampling strategies include selecting every seventh case entered onto the database or including all cases closed during every seventh week.

Robust systems for identifying and including on-going cases need to be established. An annual review of on-going cases may be one way to identify such users and ensure their views are represented. The extent to which this will be successful will depend on the emphasis given to this task by senior managers. It is also important to implement alternative arrangements for obtaining evaluative information on those users excluded from the survey – disabled children and their families and people with impairments such as dementia or dual sensory impairment whose views are difficult to obtain through a postal survey. Resources for telephone and home interviews need to be identified. Such interviews could be conducted by a designated member of assessment staff, administrative staff, or staff outside Disability Support Services with broader responsibility for user consultation. A final decision is also needed on whether to use reminders for brief questionnaires.

Facilitating the use of results
Following the first pilot study, some suggestions were made to facilitate the use of results. These included convening a group with responsibility for reviewing results, identifying areas for improvement, planning and implementing strategies to achieve change. While this group could consist only of staff members, inclusion of users and carers may be helpful in maintaining momentum and challenging existing structures and procedures. Since the questionnaires generate a large amount of information, setting explicit targets for results and focusing only on those areas where the target is not achieved, may help in identifying priorities.

Although the system focuses on aggregated data, there are circumstances in which an individualized response is merited. Explicit criteria highlighting such circumstances should be established. These might, for example, include instances where the concerns are expressed about the safety of adaptations, or where there is outstanding work to be done.

The feasibility of including a summary of staff views of the outcomes achieved in the questionnaire request form was discussed after the first pilot study. It was decided, however, to record staff views elsewhere. Unless this information is entered onto the database, the scope for comparing staff and user perspectives on the outcomes achieved will be limited. Such comparison might highlight areas in which there is a significant discrepancy in perspectives and could be of value in staff training.

11. GENERALISABILITY
Two separate issues regarding generalisability can be identified: first, the extent to which the specific system developed and piloted with our partner authority can be used successfully by similar services elsewhere; and secondly, the potential of postal questionnaires for collecting information about the outcomes of different services.

Use of the system in other equipment and adaptation services
Use of the questionnaires in other authorities would provide additional information on the sensitivity and value of this approach. We could also explore whether comparable data from another authority helped with interpretation or facilitated the use of the findings.

Our experience of the development work suggests that successful implementation of this approach to collecting and using outcomes information is likely to depend on a number of factors, including:

- Service organisation
- Existing management information systems
- Access to support for administration, data management, analysis and reporting
- Attitudes to receiving feedback and experience of using data in service development
- Sense of ownership and involvement.

A key factor influencing generalisability will be the extent to which the remit of other equipment and adaptations services matches that of the service in our partnership authority. The emphasis on postal questionnaires as the primary method of data collection will not be suitable for services providing specialist equipment for people with sensory impairment. Postal questionnaires are not appropriate for some people with visual impairments and or for some deaf people whose first language is British Sign Language. In addition, outcomes specific to people with sensory impairment, for example, being able to communicate with the hearing world, are not currently included in the questionnaire.

The ability to link the questionnaire data to information held on the computerised system in our partnership authority meant that we did not have to include questions about the demographic characteristics of users (such as age and gender). It also enabled us to explore a limited number of characteristics relating to the service received (for example, whether the user saw an OT or OTA). The value of detailed information on the service provided in interpreting the findings has already been described. The existence of a robust computerised information system is therefore an important factor in using this approach elsewhere.

An area of concern throughout the development work concerned resources for data entry, data management, analysis and reporting. The scarcity of such resources within our partnership authority may reflect their lower spending on these areas relative to comparable authorities. We sought to minimize the costs associated with these tasks by developing a database to facilitate questionnaire administration, data entry and simple analyses. While it was not possible to test all aspects of the database in routine practice, the simplicity of the system should enable it to be used within the context of the limited resources of local authorities. While the database is likely to be generalisable to other contexts, slight modifications may be necessary as well as staff training and support.

Our partnership authority is unusual in that it already had a system for routinely collecting feedback from users of the service. Staff were therefore used to receiving feedback on their work. Even so, we identified a range of concerns and barriers to using feedback constructively. Some of the activities and exercises used in the development work may be of value in tackling such issues elsewhere. A recent inspection of management information for commissioning indicated some persistent difficulties across Social Services departments as a whole (Warburton, 1999). While the need to link decision-making to information was emphasised, this was hampered by the value of available management information and the ability of some managers to use and interpret aggregated data (Warburton, 1999). There may therefore be a need for training and support to enable managers to use information effectively.

In considering the issue of generalisability, it is important to recognise that while simply adopting existing instruments ensures a standard approach and comparability of information, adapting instruments to fit the local context may also have important benefits. Previous research on the use of outcome measures in occupational therapy has shown that locally developed measures are more commonly used than standard measures (McAvoy, 1991; Chesson et al., 1996; Hammond, 1996; Wolf, 1997). In the context of general practice, participation in standard setting has been shown to affect adherence to the resulting standard and outcomes for patients (North of England Study of Standards and Performance in General Practice, 1992 a,b). The use of the questionnaires elsewhere is therefore likely to benefit from some preparatory work to ensure a sense of local ownership and commitment to the system.

In our partnership authority, the development work followed on from stage one research which had raised awareness of outcomes among staff; in implementing the system elsewhere, it is suggested that initial preparatory work focuses on developing an understanding of outcomes and exploring the potential value and uses of information on outcomes. If the questionnaire system was perceived as a useful approach on completion of this introductory work, subsequent activities could focus on tailoring the system to the local context, and helping to develop a sense of ownership. Our experience suggests that the following issues are likely to be relevant elsewhere:
- considering the relevance of questions to the local context
- identifying additional areas for inclusion
- accepting the subjectivity and validity of user views
- using feedback constructively
- interpreting and using information.

Use of postal questionnaire to explore outcomes of other services
The applicability of this approach to other social care services is related to three factors: the characteristics of service users; the type and diversity of outcomes to be evaluated; and the extent to which such an approach fits with the values and routine practice of staff.

As already described, postal questionnaires are not appropriate for all service users. In addition to people with sensory impairments, users with learning disabilities or dementia are not easily able to express their views in postal questionnaires. Although a small number of interviews can be included, escalating costs where many of the users required interviews would limit the feasibility of this approach. Although postal questionnaires are sometimes not recommended for older people, we achieved good response rates among people aged over 80, particularly to the brief questionnaire, confirming that this approach is acceptable to many older people (Jones and Lester, 1995).

In addition to the characteristics of the users, the types and diversity of outcomes to be evaluated should also be considered. The sensitivity of some topics, for example coming to terms with impairment, and the complexity of others, such as social and economic participation, may limit the use of this approach to explore outcomes in other contexts. Furthermore, within the context of equipment and adaptation services, many interventions focus on achieving a fairly narrow range of outcomes. It is therefore feasible to include all of the key outcomes in the questionnaires. Where services can result in a range of diverse outcomes, it may not be possible to develop a questionnaire which is an acceptable length and relatively straightforward to complete.

A final consideration is the acceptability of the approach to staff. Most OTs and OTAs found the concept of outcomes appealing and it was consonant with their professional background. The use of postal questionnaires, together with aggregation and quantitative analysis of the resulting information, was also acceptable to this group of professionals. Our stage one research suggests that other groups of staff may be reluctant to take such a quantitative approach, and would find other approaches, for example, the integration of an outcomes focus in assessment, more compatible with their professional background and aims.

11. CONCLUSION

A mixed group of stakeholders designed three postal questionnaires to collect information on the outcomes of Disability Support Services; two user questionnaires, one for users receiving minor adaptations or equipment only, the other for users receiving major adaptations; the third questionnaire focused on outcomes for carers. The process of developing and implementing the questionnaires confirmed the need to address analysis, interpretation and use of information, rather than simply focusing on the development of tools for collecting outcomes information. Good response rates were achieved in the pilot studies and alternative methods for including the views of users and carers unable to complete postal questionnaires were successful. The results of the pilot studies indicated that the majority of users reported positive outcomes, in terms of safety and ease of activities. A smaller proportion of users reported a reduction in the amount of help needed from others or increased choice over when or how to do everyday tasks and activities. A range of desired service process outcomes identified in stage one were successfully achieved for the majority of users, although views on access to the service and waiting times were less positive.

Although we involved a range of stakeholders in the development work, it proved difficult to recruit and retain users. We identified a number of barriers to user involvement which may be relevant to similar initiatives elsewhere. These include changing personal circumstances or health, the time commitment involved, concerns over staff involvement in development work rather than service provision, cynicism arising from the lack of impact of previous user consultations, concerns over staff defensiveness and the lack of a shared political perspective.

During stage one research and the development work, staff consistently emphasised the need to develop ways of assessing outcomes that did not simply focus on improvements. The importance of this was confirmed by our finding that, when asked to rate the impact of equipment and adaptations on their overall quality of life, 31 per cent of users receiving major adaptations reported that provision had stopped their quality of life from getting worse. Measuring functional abilities or quality of life before and after provision is therefore likely to underestimate the outcomes of equipment and adaptation services. The pilot questionnaires also have other advantages over the use of measures of functional ability or quality of life to assess outcomes. In particular, they are sensitive to the types of outcomes most often achieved by equipment and adaptations. For example, ability to perform a task may not change, but the ease or safety with which it is performed may be enhanced. Further, in contrast to many measures of functional ability or quality of life, the questions ask only about changes which can be attributed to equipment or adaptations; changes resulting from other factors, such as medical care, fluctuations in health, and so on, are not considered.

The questionnaires can be used alongside other approaches to assessing outcomes. Assessment procedures focusing on outcomes are already available for occupational therapy, although their use in routine practice is currently limited (Heaton and Bamford, 2000). One shortcoming of assessing outcomes in routine practice is that it may be difficult for users and carers to express reservations about the outcomes achieved, or the ways in which services were delivered, in discussions with a member of staff with whom they may have an on-going relationship and on whom they are dependent for assistance. Using a postal questionnaire allows users and carers to express their views in confidence. During the development work the focus was on collecting user and carer views and we did not include the views of staff about the outcomes achieved in individual cases; this would be a useful addition to the system and there are plans to include staff perspectives alongside those of users and carers within our partner authority.

The questionnaires and accompanying database are now available for use by other equipment and adaptations services. In considering the likely generalisability of this approach to collecting and using outcome measures, the preference of many OTs for locally developed measures merits consideration. The ways in which even supposedly standardised measures, such as performance indicators, are tailored to local circumstances have been described elsewhere (SSRG, 2000). In view of these findings, it appears likely that this approach to collecting and using outcomes information will be adapted to suit local needs and circumstances, rather than simply adopted by other authorities. While this has implications for the comparability of information collected, this flexible approach is likely to enhance a sense of ownership and to maximise the value and use of the information collected. Some components of the development work with our partnership authority may be useful in adapting the system to other local contexts.

A key factor that may limit the value of user surveys is the availability of resources for data management, analysis and reporting of results. The development of a user-friendly database represents considerable progress in helping local authorities to administer, manage and analyse user surveys. The extent to which questionnaire data can be linked to existing computerized information also has implications for ease of administration and interpretation of results.

Although there has not been sufficient time to allow a considered evaluation of the results and how these might be used, our partnership authority is keen to continue to use this approach to collect outcomes information and monitor quality assurance. Our experience suggests that continued attention to the ways in which information can be used at individual, service and planning levels is essential if the potential benefits of collecting and using outcomes information are to be realised in practice.

SUMMARY OF CHAPTER SIX

It is estimated that one million people use community equipment services (Audit Commission, 2000) and over 20 per cent of all referrals to Social Services Departments are now dealt with by occupational therapists (Platt, 1999). Despite growing recognition of the importance of equipment and adaptations in achieving the policy goal of increasing independence, relatively little is known about the precise impacts, or outcomes, of provision on the lives of service users.

In this project we worked in partnership with one unitary authority to develop and test postal questionnaires for collecting information on the outcomes achieved by, and satisfaction with, an integrated occupational therapy assessment, equipment and adaptations service. A planning group including staff, managers, users and carers designed three questionnaires:
- one for users receiving advice, minor adaptations or equipment
- one for users receiving major adaptations
- one for carers.

In an initial pilot study, good response rates were achieved but some problems with administrative arrangements and the layout and content of the questionnaires were identified. A second pilot study therefore tested revised procedures and instrumentation. Response rates to the second pilot study were good, 69 per cent for the brief user questionnaire with a single mailing and 80 per cent for the detailed user questionnaire with the use of one reminder. The number of carer questionnaires sent out was too small for the calculation of response rates. The changes in layout and wording on the questionnaires were generally successful in reducing item non-response and achieving a wider range of responses.

The majority of users reported positive outcomes in terms of the ease and safety of specific activities. For some users, the amount of assistance required was reduced, or choice over when, or how, to do activities was increased. A significant proportion of users (25 per cent of those receiving advice, minor adaptations or equipment and 31 per cent of those receiving major adaptations) reported that provision had a preventive or protective effect on their overall quality of life. This confirms that simply focusing on improvements would significantly underestimate the outcomes achieved by the service. Achievement of desired service process outcomes was generally high.

A significant barrier to the use of questionnaire data was the lack of resources in our partner authority for data processing and analysis of the completed questionnaires. As part of the second pilot study we therefore designed and tested a database to facilitate administration of the survey, data processing and analysis of completed questionnaires. This was used successfully by administrative staff to administer questionnaires and reminders. Although it was not possible to thoroughly test all aspects of the database in routine practice, the process of entering data is straightforward. A series of pre-set commands produces information on response rates and summarises the results of each question in a table and bar chart. While the database is specific to the questionnaires we have developed, the principles of the design are generalisable and have wide applicability. Similar systems, for example, could be developed to facilitate the administration, analysis and reporting of the user satisfaction surveys to be conducted as part of the modernisation agenda.

We successfully linked the questionnaire data with the computerised information system in our partner authority. This facilitated administration and permitted a more detailed analysis of non-response than would otherwise have been possible. In common with many other authorities, however, the computerised records could not be used to link information from assessment or care plans to the questionnaire data, thus limiting the scope for detailed interpretation of outcome data.

Since the pilot studies have only recently been completed, it is not yet possible to examine the impact of the results or to say whether they will lead to changes in practice. There was, however, consensus among all members of the planning group that the resulting information was valuable. The emphasis, however, continues to be on using the system for monitoring quality and the extent to which the potential uses of the data will be fully exploited remains unclear. Following the first pilot study it was agreed to convene a group of staff responsible for regularly reviewing the results, identifying areas for improvement, planning strategies to achieve change and implementing and reviewing these. This group had still to be established by the end of the second pilot study.

We anticipate that the revised questionnaires are generalisable to other similar services. It is recommended that use elsewhere be preceded by a period of developmental work to ensure that the questionnaires are tailored to the local context and to explore broader issues relating to the implementation of a system of collecting and using outcomes information. The potential value of a survey approach for collecting and using outcomes information in other services, is likely to depend on the characteristics of service users, the types and diversity of outcomes achieved and the extent to which such an approach fits with the values and routine practice of staff.

Our experience confirms the need to pay attention to analysis, feedback and use of information, rather than simply focusing on the development of tools. Investment in resources for data management and analysis may be needed if local authorities are to collect and use outcomes information on a routine basis. In many social care agencies the scope for linking data on outcomes to information on needs and inputs will be limited by the continued reliance on paper records. Even where such linkage is possible, our experience suggests that managers need considerable support before they feel confident in using and interpreting data.

References

Andrich, R., Ferrario, M. and Moi, M. (1998) 'A model of cost-outcome analysis for assistive technology', *Disability and Rehabilitation* 20, 1, 1-24.

Audit Commission (2000) *Fully equipped,* London: Audit Commission.

Bamford, C., Qureshi, H., Nicholas, E. and Vernon, A. (1999) *Outcomes of social care for disabled people and carers,* Outcomes in Community Care Practice Number Six, York: Social Policy Research Unit, University of York.

Beckhard, R. and Harris, R. T. (1997) *Organisational Transitions: Managing Complex Change,* (2nd ed.), London: Addison-Wesley.

Beresford, B. (1997) *Personal accounts: Involving disabled children in research,* London: SPRU Papers, The Stationery Office.

Briner, W., Hastings, C. and Geddes, M. (1996) *Project leadership,* (2nd ed.), Aldershot: Gower.

Chesson, R., Macleod, M. and Massie, S. (1996) 'Outcome measures used in therapy departments in Scotland', *Physiotherapy* 82 (12), 673-679.

Department of Health (1998) *Modernising social services,* CM 4169, London: The Stationery Office.

Department of Health (1999) *The Personal Social Services Performance Assessment Framework,* London: The Stationery Office.

Egan G. (1993) *Adding Value,* San Francisco: Jossey-Bass.

Esmond, D., Gordon, K., McCaskie, K. and Stewart, J. (1998) *More scope for fair housing.* London: Scope.

Hammond, A. (1996) 'Functional and health assessments used in rheumatology occupational therapy: a review and United Kingdom survey', *British Journal of Occupational Therapy* 59 (6), 254-259.

Heaton, J. and Bamford, C. (2000) *Assessing the outcomes of equipment and adaptations. Volume I: A literature review,* Working Paper Number 1726, York: Social Policy Research Unit, University of York.

Jones, D. and Lester, C. (1995) 'Patients' opinions of hospital care and discharge'. In Wilson, G (Ed) *Community Care: Asking the Users,* London: Chapman and Hall.

Law, M., Baptiste, S., McColl, M., Opzoomer, A., Polatajko, H. and Pollock, N. (1990) 'The Canadian Occupational Performance Measure: an outcome measure for occupational therapy', *Canadian Journal of Occupational Therapy* 57 (2), 82-87.

Marks, O. (1998) *Equipped for equality,* London: Scope.

McAvoy, E. (1991) 'The use of ADL indices by occupational therapists', *British Journal of Occupational Therapy* 54 (10), 383-385.

McColl, E., Jacoby, A., Thompson, L., Soutter, J., Bamford, C., Thomas, R., Harvey, E., Garratt, A. and Bond, J. (1999) *Designing and using patient and staff questionnaires: A review of best practice.* Draft report to NHS HTA programme. Centre for Health Services Research, University of Newcastle.

Morris, A. L. and Gainer, F. (1997) 'Helping the caregiver: occupational therapy opportunities', *Occupational Therapy Practice* 2 (1), 36-40.

North of England Study of Standards and Performance in General Practice (1992a) Medical audit in general practice. I: Effects on doctors' clinical behaviour for common childhood conditions. *British Medical Journal* 304, 1480-4.

North of England Study of Standards and Performance in General Practice (1992b) Medical audit in general practice. II: Effects on health of patients with common childhood conditions, *British Medical Journal*, 304,1484-8.

Oldman, C. and Beresford, B. (1998) *Homes unfit for children: Housing, disabled children and their families*, Bristol: Policy Press.

Patmore, C., Qureshi, H., Nicholas, E. and Bamford, C. (1997) *Outcomes project: Stage 1 report to social services,* Working Paper Number 1537, York: Social Policy Research Unit, University of York.

Platt, D. (1999) *Modern Social Services - A commitment to improve. The 8th annual report of the Chief Inspector of Social Services,* London: The Stationery Office.

Pollock, N. (1993) 'Client-centered assessment', *Canadian Journal of Occupational Therapy*, 57 (2) 77-81.

Qureshi, H., Patmore, C., Nicholas, E. and Bamford, C. (1998) *Overview: Outcomes of Social Care for Older People and Carers*, Outcomes in Community Care Practice Number 5, York: Social Policy Research Unit, University of York.

Smale, G. (1996) *Mapping change and innovation*, London: HMSO

Social Services Research Group (2000) *Personal Social Services Performance Assessment Framework (Department of Health) and Performance Indicators for Social Services (DETR/ Audit Commission): Guidance on use of information,* Second edition, Shrewsbury: SSRG.

Toomey, M., Nicholson, D. and Carswell, A. (1995) 'The clinical utility of the Canadian Occupational Performance Measure', *Canadian Journal of Occupational Therapy* 62 (5), 242-249.

Warburton, R. (1999) *Meeting the Challenge: Improving management information for the effective commissioning of social care services for older people,* London: The Stationery Office.

Washington, K. and Schwartz, I. S. (1996) 'Maternal perceptions of the effects of physical and occupational therapy services on caregiving competency', *Physical and Occupational Therapy in Pediatrics* 16 (3), 33-54.

Wessels, R., de Witte, L., Andrich, R., Ferrario, M., Persson, J., Oberg, B., Oortwijn, W., van Beekum, T. and Lorentsen, Ø. (1998) *Field testing of the EATS instruments: Plan and procedures,* EATS deliverable 4.1, downloadable from http://www.siva.it/research/eats.

Winchcombe, M. (1998) *Community equipment services ... why should we care? A guide to good practice in Disability Equipment Services,* London: The Disabled Living Centres Council.

Wolf, H. (1997) 'Assessments of activities of daily living and instrumental activities of daily living: their use by community-based health service occupational therapists working in physical therapy', *British Journal of Occupational Therapy* 60 (8), 359-364.

Acknowledgements

Additional contributions to this research were made by Jane Carlisle, Frances Perry and Sarah Starkey.

APPENDICES TO CHAPTER SIX

The following are supplied as appendices:

- **Questionnaire request form**

- **Brief questionnaire for customers of Disability Support Services**

- **Detailed questionnaire for customers of Disability Support Services**

- **Questionnaire for carers who have used Disability Support Services**

- **The standard letter which accompanied the questionnaire to customers.**

- **The standard letter which accompanied the questionnaire to non-resident carers.**

- **The standard letter which accompanied the questionnaires to customers and co-resident carers.**

Note: **A more detailed Technical Appendix is available on request from SPRU. This contains information about non-response for all questions, for example.**

QUESTIONNAIRE REQUEST FORM

Section A

1.   ISIS number   ☐☐☐☐☐☐   Date
                                                           Name of OT/OTA

2.   What kind of questionnaire is most appropriate for the customer?

                                         Postal questionnaire............................ 1 }
                                         Telephone interview............................ 2 } Go to question 4
                                         Home interview.................................... 3 }
                                         Questionnaire is not appropriate.......... 4   Go to Question 3

3.   Reason questionnaire is not appropriate:

                                         Customer unable to participate (e.g. has
                                         dementia or dual sensory impairment) .....   Go to Question 4
                                         Inappropriate referral   }
                                         Customer has died   }
                                         Customer moved into long term care   }   There are no
                                         Customer declined assessment   }   more questions
                                         Customer declined provision   }
                                         Other reason, please specify   }

4.   What help did you provide?   What was the help provided for ?

                             Advice only 1
                             Minor adaptation 2   Bathing ☐   Toilet ☐
                             Simple equipment 3
                             Major item of equipment 4   Mobility ☐   Other ☐
                             Major adaptation 5   *Tick as many as apply*

5.   Please describe equipment and adaptations provided:

```
┌──────────────────────────────────────────────────────────────┐
│                                                              │
│                                                              │
│                                                              │
│                                                              │
│                                                              │
│                                                              │
└──────────────────────────────────────────────────────────────┘
```

Section B   Additional questions to be completed if a major adaptation was provided

6.   Does the customer have a carer (i.e. a family member, friend or neighbour)?

                                 Yes   1
                                 No   2   There are no more questions

7.   Was the carer involved in assessment or likely to benefit from equipment/adaptations provided?

                                 Yes 1
                                 No 2   There are no more questions

8.   What kind of questionnaire is most appropriate for the carer?

                                 Postal questionnaire...............   1
                                 Telephone interview...............   2
                                 Home interview......................   3

9.   What is the carer's name and address:

QUESTIONNAIRE FOR CUSTOMERS OF DISABILITY SUPPORT SERVICES

Please complete this questionnaire to help us to improve the service we provide. Most of the questions can be answered by putting a circle around the number next to the answer that applies to you. Occasionally you will be asked to circle all of the answers that apply, otherwise please circle one answer. Please answer every question, unless the instructions tell you to do something else.

Serial number: | S | | | | | | |

Section A
The first few questions are about how easy it was to get help with equipment and/or adaptations.

1. How easy was it to find out where to get help with equipment and/or adaptations?

    Very easy...1
    Fairly easy..2
    OK..3
    Fairly difficult..4
    Very difficult..5

2. How reasonable was the length of time you waited to see an occupational therapist or occupational therapy assistant?

    Very reasonable....................................1
    Fairly reasonable..................................2
    OK..3
    Fairly unreasonable...............................4
    Very unreasonable................................5

Section B
The questions in this section are about the occupational therapist or occupational therapy assistant who visited you at home. The questions ask how easy it was to talk to the occupational therapist or occupational therapy assistant, and how well she or he took your views into account in deciding how to help you.

3. Did she or he treat you with respect?

    All of the time.......................................1
    Most of the time....................................2
    Some of the time...................................3
    Rarely..4
    Never 5

4. How well do you think she or he understood your individual needs and circumstances?

Very well 1
Fairly well 2
OK 3
Not very well at all 4
Not at all 5

_____

5. How helpful was she or he in telling you about other services?

Very helpful 1
Fairly helpful 2
OK 3
Not very helpful 4
Not at all helpful 5
I did not ask about other services 6

_____

6. Did she or he provide or arrange any equipment and/or adaptations?

Yes .... 1 *Continue with Question 7*
No .... 2 *Go to Section D*

_____

7. How satisfied were you with the extent she or he took your views into account in deciding which equipment and/or adaptations to provide?

Very satisfied 1
Fairly satisfied 2
OK 3
Fairly dissatisfied 4
Very dissatisfied 5

_____

8. How well did she or he explain or demonstrate how to use the equipment and/or adaptations?

Very well 1
Fairly well 2
OK 3
Not very well 4
Not at all 5
I did not need an
explanation or demonstration 6

_____

9. Are you still using all of the equipment and/or adaptations provided?

Yes 1   *Go to Section C*
No 2   *Answer a)*

a) If **no**, please describe the equipment or adaptations you are not using and why not:

Equipment / adaptation   Reason for not using

....

....

_____

Section C

The questions in this section are about the way in which minor adaptations were carried out. This includes items such as grab rails, second stair rails and steps into the home. If you did not have any of these minor adaptations, please go to Section D.

10. Did the workman come to do the job on the agreed day and time?

    Yes, right day and time.............................. 1
    Right day, but different time..................... 2
    Different day.. 3
    Not sure, can't remember........................ 4

11. How well did the workman clean and tidy up when they had finished?

    Very well... 1
    Well.. 2
    OK.. 3
    Not very well... 4
    Not at all.. 5

12. How would you rate the quality of the finished work?

    Very good.. 1
    Good... 2
    OK.. 3
    Poor.. 4
    Very poor... 5

    Any comments:

    ....

    ....

Section D

Everyone should answer the questions in this section. These questions ask about how useful the advice, equipment and/or adaptations have been and what difference they have made to your life.

13. How has the advice, equipment or adaptations helped with **having a bath or shower**?
    (For example you may have been given grab rails, a bath or shower seat or a bath lift.)

    I did not have any help with this.......................... 1
    Made me feel safer... 2
    Made it easier... 3   *Please circle*
    Need less help from other people......................... 4   *all that apply.*
    Given me more choice over when I have a bath/shower.5
    Has made no difference at all................................ 6
    Other *(please describe)*.. 7

14. How has the advice, equipment or adaptations helped with **getting around?**
    (For example you may have been given grab rails, stair rails, steps or a ramp.)

    I did not have any help with this.. 1
    Made me feel safer.. 2
    Made it easier... 3
    Need less help from other people..................................... 4   *Please circle*
    Given me more choice over getting round inside   *all that apply.*
    or when to go out or come back home.............................. 5
    Has made no difference at all... 6
    Other *(please describe)*... 7

---

15. How has the advice, equipment or adaptations helped with **using the toilet?**
    (For example you may have been given a raised toilet seat or grab rails.)

    I did not have any help with this.. 1
    Made me feel safer.. 2
    Made it easier... 3   *Please circle*
    Need less help from other people..................................... 4   *all that apply.*
    Has made no difference at all... 5
    Other *(please describe)*... 6

---

16. Thinking about your overall quality of life, would you say that the equipment and/or adaptations have:

    Improved your quality of life... 1
    Stopped your quality of life getting worse........................ 2
    Made no difference at all.. 3
    Made your quality of life worse?...................................... 4

---

17. Overall, how satisfied are you with the help you received from staff working in Disability Support Services?

    Very satisfied.. 1
    Fairly satisfied.. 2
    OK.. 3
    Fairly dissatisfied.. 4
    Very dissatisfied.. 5

---

18. Have you found the questions easy to understand and answer?

    Yes..............1
    No.............2

    If **no**, which ones in particular did you find difficult?

Please **check** that you have answered all the questions that apply to you. Thank you for taking the time to fill in the questionnaire. We are very grateful for your help.

Please return the questionnaire in the prepaid envelope provided. If you have any queries about the questionnaire, please contact

QUESTIONNAIRE FOR CUSTOMERS OF DISABILITY SUPPORT SERVICES

Please complete this questionnaire to help us to improve the service we provide. Most of the questions can be answered by putting a circle around the number next to the answer that applies to you. Occasionally you will be asked to circle all of the answers that apply, otherwise please circle only one answer. Please answer every question, unless the instructions tell you to do something else.

Serial number: | L | | | | | | |

Section A
The first few questions are about how easy it was to get help with equipment and/or adaptations.

1.   How easy was it to find out where to get help with equipment and adaptations?

Very easy..1

Fairly easy..2

OK...3

Fairly difficult..4

Very difficult...5

2.   How reasonable was the length of time you waited to see an occupational therapist or occupational therapy assistant?

Very reasonable...1

Fairly reasonable...2

OK...3

Fairly unreasonable..4

Very unreasonable...5

Section B
The questions in this section are about the occupational therapist or occupational therapy assistant who visited you at home. The questions ask how easy it was to talk to the occupational therapist or occupational therapy assistant, and how well she or he took your views into account in deciding how to help you.

3.   Did she or he treat you with respect?

All of the time...1

Most of the time 2

Some of the time 3

Rarely..4

Never 5

4.   Did she or he work at a pace that felt comfortable to you?

Yes...1

No, I felt rushed 2

No, the pace was too slow...............................3

5. How well do you think she or he understood your individual needs and circumstances?

Very well	1
Fairly well	2
OK	3
Not very well at all	4
Not at all	5

6. How much did she or he help you plan for the future?

About the right amount	1
Not enough	2
Too much	3

7. How much did she or he discuss different options or ways of helping you?

About the right amount	1
Not enough	2
Too much	3

8. How satisfied were you with the extent she or he took your views into account in deciding which equipment and/or adaptations to provide?

Very satisfied	1
Fairly satisfied	2
OK	3
Fairly dissatisfied	4
Very dissatisfied	5

9. How well did she or he keep you informed of how long things were likely to take?

Very well	1
Fairly well	2
OK	3
Not very well	4
Not at all	5

10. How well did she or he explain or demonstrate how to use the equipment and/or adaptations?

Very well	1
Fairly well	2
OK	3
Not very well	4
Not at all	5
I did not need an explanation or demonstration	6

11. How helpful was she or he in telling you about other services?

Very helpful	1
Fairly helpful	2
OK	3
Not very helpful	4
Not at all helpful	5
I did not ask about other services	6

Section C

The next questions are about the delivery of your equipment and any contact you had with the Joint Equipment Service.

12. Was any equipment delivered by van from the Joint Equipment Service?

Yes...................... 1   *Continue with Question 13*

No........................ 2   *Go to Section D*

13. If you had any contact with the staff at the Joint Equipment Service, how helpful were they?

Very helpful... 1

Fairly helpful... 2

OK... 3

Not very helpful.. 4

Not at all helpful.. 5

I did not have any contact with staff................. 6

14. Was the equipment delivered on the day arranged?

Yes...1

No...2

Not sure, can't remember.................................3

15. How clean was the equipment when it was delivered?

Very clean.. 1

Clean... 2

OK.. 3

Not very clean.. 4

Not clean at all.. 5

16. Overall how satisfied were you with the way the Joint Equipment Service delivered your equipment?

Very satisfied..1

Fairly satisfied..2

OK...3

Fairly dissatisfied...4

Very dissatisfied...5

Any comments:

....

....

Section D

The next questions ask about the help you were given by the surveyor working in the Grants and Adaptations Service at the Council in planning large adaptations to your home (for example, installing a lift, adapting your kitchen or bathroom, building an extension).

17. How well had the surveyor from the Grants and Adaptations Service been informed about your situation?

    Very well... 1
    Fairly well... 2
    OK.. 3
    Not very well... 4
    Not at all.. 5

18. How comfortable or at ease did you feel with the surveyor?

    Completely at ease... 1
    Fairly at ease.. 2
    OK.. 3
    Fairly uncomfortable... 4
    Very uncomfortable... 5

19. How well did the surveyor explain the stages involved in having your home adapted?

    Very well... 1
    Fairly well... 2
    OK.. 3
    Not very well... 4
    Not at all.. 5

20. How satisfied were you with the extent to which your views were taken into account in adapting your home?

    Very satisfied.. 1
    Fairly satisfied... 2
    OK.. 3
    Dissatisfied... 4
    Very dissatisfied... 5

    Any comments:

    ....

    ....

Section E

These questions ask about the advice and help you were given by staff in the Grants and Adaptations Service with getting a grant and arranging the adaptation.

21.   Is the house or flat you live in:

Owned/being bought
by you or your family.............................. 1 *Please continue with Question 22*
Rented from Council 2
Rental from private landlord .... 3 } *Please go to Section F.*
Rented from housing association 4
Other.. 5

22.   How much advice did staff in the Grants and Adaptations Service give you about filling the forms?

As much as I wanted............................... 1
Not enough... 2
Too much... 3

23.   How much advice did staff in the Grants and Adaptations Service give you about finding an architect?

As much as I wanted............................... 1
Not enough... 2
Too much... 3

24.   How much advice did staff in the Grants and Adaptations Service give you about finding appropriate builders?

As much as I wanted............................... 1
Not enough... 2
Too much... 3

25.   How much advice did staff in the Grants and Adaptations Service give you about organising quotes from builders?

As much as I wanted............................... 1
Not enough... 2
Too much... 3

26.   Overall how helpful were staff working the Grants and Adaptations service?

Very helpful... 1
Fairly helpful.. 2
OK.. 3
Not very helpful...................................... 4
Not at all helpful.................................... 5

Any comments:

....

....

Section F

These questions in this section ask about the workmen and the quality of the adaptation to your home.

27.   Did the workman come to do the job on the agreed day and time?

      Yes, right day and time.................................... 1
      Right day, but different time........................... 2
      Different day 3
      Not sure, can't remember............................... 4

28.   How well informed was the workman about the job to be done?

      Very well... 1
      Well.. 2
      OK.. 3
      Not very well... 4
      Not at all... 5

29.   How well did the workman clean and tidy up when they had finished?

      Very well... 1
      Well.. 2
      OK.. 3
      Not very well... 4
      Not at all... 5

30.   How would you rate the quality of the finished work?

      Very good.. 1
      Good... 2
      OK.. 3
      Poor.. 4
      Very poor.. 5

      Any comments:

      ....

      ....

Section G

Everyone should answer this section. The questions ask about how useful the equipment and/or adaptations have been and what difference they have made to your life.

31.   Are you still using all of the equipment and/or adaptations provided?

Yes......... 1   *Go to Question 32*
No........... 2   *Answer a)*

a)   If **no**, please describe the equipment or adaptations you are not using and why not:

Equipment / adaptation   Reason for not using

....

....

32.   How has the advice, equipment or adaptations helped with **having a bath or shower**?
        (For example you may have been given grab rails, a bath or shower seat or a bath lift.)

I did not have any help with this.. 1
Made me feel safer.. 2
Made it easier.. 3   *Please circle*
Need less help from other people...................................... 4   *all that apply.*
Given me more choice over when I have a bath/shower.. 5
Has made no difference at all.. 6
Other *(please describe)*...7

33.   How has the advice, equipment or adaptations helped with **getting around**?
        (For example you may have been given grab rails, stair rails, steps or a ramp.)

I did not have any help with this.. 1
Made me feel safer.. 2
Made it easier.. 3
Need less help from other people...................................... 4   *Please circle*
Given me more choice over getting around 5   *all that apply.*
Has made no difference at all.. 6
Other *(please describe)*...7

34.   How has the advice, equipment or adaptations helped with **using the toilet**?
        (For example you may have been given a raised toilet seat or grab rails.)

I did not have any help with this.. 1
Made me feel safer.. 2
Made it easier.. 3   *Please circle*
Need less help from other people...................................... 4   *all that apply.*
Has made no difference at all.. 5
Other *(please describe)*...6

35. Has the advice, equipment or adaptations made an important difference to any other areas of your life not already covered?

Yes............ 1   *Answer a)*

No.............. 2   *Go to Question 36*

a) If yes, please describe:

....

36. Thinking about your overall quality of life, would you say the equipment and/or adaptations have:

Improved your quality of life............................ 1

Stopped your quality of life getting worse..... 2

Made no difference at all.................................. 3

Made your quality of life worse....................... 4

37. Has the advice, equipment or adaptations helped as much as you expected?

More than expected... 1

About as much as I expected.......................... 2

Less than expected... 3

Not sure, I did not know what to expect.......... 4

38. To what extent has the advice, equipment or adaptations provided met your needs?

Completely.. 1

Mostly.. 2

Not very well... 3

Not at all.. 4

Any comments:

....

39. Overall, how satisfied are you with the help you received from staff working in Disability Support Services?

Very satisfied.. 1

Fairly satisfied.. 2

OK.. 3

Fairly dissatisfied... 4

Very dissatisfied... 5

40. Have you found the questions easy to understand and answer?

Yes............. 1

No............... 2

If **no**, which ones in particular did you find difficult?

Please check that you have answered all the questions that apply to you. Thank you for taking the time to fill in the questionnaire. We are very grateful for your help.

Please return the questionnaire in the prepaid envelope provided. If you have any queries about the questionnaire, please contact

QUESTIONNAIRE FOR CARERS WHO HAVE USED DISABILITY SUPPORT SERVICES

Please complete this questionnaire to help us to improve the service we provide. Most of the questions can be answered by putting a circle around the number next to the answer that applies to you. Please circle only one answer. Please answer every question, unless the instructions tell you to do something else.

Serial number: | C | | | | | | |

Section A

The first questions are about your relationship with staff working in Disability Support Services. This includes the Occupational Therapy (OT) assessment team, the Joint Equipment Service and the Grants and Adaptations Service.

1. Were you involved in discussions with staff about the equipment and/or adaptations for the person you care for?

Yes.............. 1   *Continue with Question 2*
No............... 2   *Go to Section B*

---

2. Did staff working in Disability Support Services: *Please circle the number that applies to you*

		Always	Mostly	Rarely	Never
a)	Treat you with respect?	1	2	3	4
b)	Treat the person you care for with respect?	1	2	3	4
c)	Recognise your knowledge and skills as a carer?	1	2	3	4
d)	Have realistic expectations about the amount and type of help you are able to provide?	1	2	3	4
e)	Understand your needs as a carer?	1	2	3	4
f)	Understand the needs of the person you care for?	1	2	3	4
g)	Make you feel at ease during their visits?	1	2	3	4

The next question is about the extent to which your views were taken into account and the amount of information you were given about the equipment and/or adaptations.

Please circle the number that applies to you

3.	How much did staff working in Disability Support Services:	As much as I wanted	Too much	Not enough
a)	Discuss your concerns or problems when they visited?	1	2	3
b)	Discuss the difficulties of the person you care for when they visited?	1	2	3
c)	Help you and the person you care for plan for the future?	1	2	3
d)	Discuss different types of equipment or adaptations?	1	2	3
e)	Involve you in decisions about the type of equipment and/or adaptations provided?	1	2	3
f)	Let you know how long things were likely to take?	1	2	3
g)	Explain or demonstrate how to use the equipment and/or adaptations?	1	2	3
h)	Inform you about other services available to help with caring?	1	2	3

Section B

Everyone should answer the questions in this section. These questions ask about the differences that the equipment and/or adaptations have made to you as a carer.

Please circle the number that applies to you

4.	What difference has the equipment and/or adaptations provided made to:	Caused a decrease	Prevented an increase	Made no difference at all	Caused an increase
a)	The number of tasks you help with?	1	2	3	4
b)	The time you spend caring?	1	2	3	4
c)	How often you provide help?	1	2	3	4
d)	The physical effort of caring?	1	2	3	4

---

5. Thinking overall about how the equipment and/or adaptations have affected the help you provide, is caring now:

    Much easier...1
    A little easier...2
    No different..3
    Slightly more difficult...4
    Much more difficult...5

Please circle the number that applies to you

6. How helpful has the equipment and/or adaptations been in terms of:	Very helpful	Helpful	Made no difference at all	Made this worse
a) Your physical health or well-being (*including sleep, exercise, and energy levels*)?	1	2	3	4
b) Your peace of mind?	1	2	3	4
c) The stress you feel about caring?	1	2	3	4
d) Your ability to make your own plans and stick to them?	1	2	3	4

---

7. Helping someone with everyday activities can affect your relationship with them. Have the equipment and/or adaptations made any difference to how you get on with the person you care for?

    Get on better now.. 1
    Better in some ways but worse in others................. 2
    Made no difference... 3
    Get on worse now... 4

---

8. Thinking about your overall quality of life, would you say the equipment and/or adaptations have:

    Improved your quality of life...................................... 1
    Stopped your quality of life getting worse............... 2
    Made no difference at all... 3
    Made your quality of life worse?............................... 4

---

9. Thinking about yourself, has the equipment and/or adaptations provided been:

    As helpful to you as expected.................................... 1
    Less helpful to you than expected............................. 2
    More helpful to you than expected............................ 3
    Or weren't you sure what to expect?........................ 4

Section C

The final questions are about the difference the equipment and/or adaptations have made to the person you care for and your overall views of the service. Everyone should answer these questions.

10. Thinking now about the quality of life of the person you care for, would you say the equipment and/or adaptations have:

Improved their quality of life...................................... 1
Stopped their quality of life getting worse............... 2
Made no difference at all to their quality of life....... 3
Or made their quality of life worse?........................ 4

11. Do you feel that you and the person you care for now have all of the essential equipment and adaptations needed to help with daily life?

Yes.............. 1
No.............. 2

- Any comments:

....

....

12. Overall, how satisfied are you with the help you, as a carer, received from staff working in Disability Support Services?

Very satisfied.. 1
Satisfied.. 2
OK.. 3
Dissatisfied.. 4
Very dissatisfied.. 5

13. Have you found the questions easy to understand and answer?

Yes.............. 1
No.............. 2

If no: Which ones in particular did you find difficult?

Please check that you have answered all the questions that apply to you. Thank you for taking the time to fill in the questionnaire. We are very grateful for your help.

Please return the questionnaire in the prepaid envelope provided. If you have any queries about the questionnaire, please contact

Dear *customer*
Your views on Disability Support Services

We would like to know what you think about the help you have received from Disability Support Services. Your comments will tell us what we do well and where we need to improve our services. We very much hope that you will be able to complete and return the enclosed questionnaire. Your name and address do not appear anywhere on the questionnaire and it will not be possible to identify anyone who took part in the survey when the results are reported.

As you fill in the questionnaire, we would like you to think about all aspects of the help you have received from Disability Support Services including: the Occupational Therapist who visited you at home to discuss your needs and ways of helping you; the Joint Equipment Service which orders and delivers equipment; the Grants and Adaptations Service which arranges small adaptations, such as grab rails, and helps with larger adaptations such as stair lifts and extensions to the home. The questionnaire does not however cover your views and experiences of the Wheelchair Service.

Please use the enclosed prepaid envelope to return your completed questionnaire to the Social Policy Research Unit at the University of York who are helping us with this survey. We would be grateful if you could return the questionnaire within two weeks if possible. If you need any help filling in the questionnaire, please telephone *<researcher>*.

Thank you for your time and help. If you need our help again, please contact the Customer Advice Centre, *<telephone number>*.

Yours sincerely

<Service manager>
Customer Services Manager Disability Support Services
Enc.

Dear *carer*

Your views on Disability Support Services

As you will know, your *<relationship>, customer name,* has recently received some equipment and/or adaptations from Disability Support Services. I have written to your *<relationship>* to ask *<her/his>* views on the service. We would also like to know what you, as a carer, think about the help you and your *<relationship>* have received from Disability Support Services. Your comments will tell us what we do well and how to improve our services to make sure that we meet the needs of both customers and carers. We very much hope that you will be able to complete and return the enclosed questionnaire. Your name and address do not appear anywhere on the questionnaire and it will not be possible to identify anyone who took part in the survey when the results are reported.

As you fill in the questionnaire, we would like you to think about all aspects of the help you and your *<relationship>* have received from Disability Support Services including: the Occupational Therapist who visited your *<relationship>* at home; the Joint Equipment Service which orders and delivers equipment; the Grants and Adaptations Service which arranges small adaptations, such as grab rails, and helps with larger adaptations such as stair lifts and extensions to the home. The questionnaire does not however cover your views and experiences of the Wheelchair Service.

Please use the enclosed prepaid envelope to return your completed questionnaire to the Social Policy Research Unit at the University of York, who are helping us with this survey. We would be grateful if you would return the questionnaire within two weeks if possible. If you need any help filling in the questionnaire, please telephone *<researcher>*.

Thank you for your time and help. If you and your *<relationship>* need our help again, please contact the Customer Advice Centre, *<telephone number>*.

Yours sincerely

<Service manager>
Customer Services Manager Disability Support Services
Enc.

Dear *<customer>* and *<carer>*
Your views on Disability Support Services

We would like to know what you think about the help you have received from Disability Support Services. Your comments will tell us what we do well and where we need to improve. Since we want to find out about the service we provide to customers and their carers, I am enclosing two questionnaires. The blue questionnaire is for *<customer>*, and the green questionnaire is for *<carer>*. We very much hope that you will each be able to complete and return the questionnaires. Your names and address do not appear anywhere on the questionnaires and it will not be possible to identify anyone who took part in the survey when the results are reported.

As you fill in the questionnaires, we would like you to think about all aspects of the help you have received from Disability Support Services, including: the Occupational Therapist who visited you at home to discuss your needs and ways of helping you; the Joint Equipment Service which orders and delivers equipment; the Grants and Adaptations Service which arranges small adaptations, such as grab rails, and helps with larger adaptations such as stair lifts and extensions to the home. The questionnaires do not however cover your views on the Wheelchair Service.

Please use the enclosed prepaid envelope to return your completed questionnaires to the Social Policy Research Unit at the University of York who are helping us with this survey. We would be grateful if you would return the questionnaires within two weeks if possible. If you need any help filling in the questionnaires, please telephone *<researcher>*.

Thank you for your time and help. If you need our help again, please contact the Customer Advice Centre *<telephone number>*.

Yours sincerely

<Service Manager>
Customer Services Manager Disability Support Services
Enc.

CHAPTER SEVEN
CONCLUSION

By Hazel Qureshi

Relevance of the projects to policy and practice concerns

The five projects described in this report represent a variety of practical ways of introducing an outcome focus into practice, and using outcome-related questions in the collection of evaluative information from service users and carers. As outlined in the introduction, a number of difficulties in achieving these aims have been identified, succinctly summed up in a recent report:

> Various reasons were put forward for the lack of outcome and quality monitoring, ranging from: the difficulty of defining outcomes; the costs of collecting outcome information; the lack of case reviews; and a reluctance on the part of care managers to code and categorise people
>
> (Social Care Group,1999, para 2.11)

The development work described in this report, and the prior, research, stage of the outcomes programme, offer solutions to both to the difficulties of definition, and the professional concerns of care managers. The lack of case reviews has now been addressed at policy level, and, as the requirement to undertake reviews is implemented, further opportunities will arise for collecting outcome information, which were not available when this work commenced. The work we have undertaken, with a partner authority, on introducing a focus on outcomes into assessment, will help to provide a firm basis for outcome-centred review. The implementation of outcome-focused, research-based assessment and review for carers has shown that improvement in practice with carers can be achieved. This will not happen without a willingness to commit resources to briefing, training and the greater time involved for staff. There is no method for collecting outcome information that is free from costs. Whether implementing changes in routine practice and recording, or conducting separate exercises to discover outcomes directly, resources will be required.

Ultimately the introduction of an outcome focus into practice could support the collection of aggregated information about outcomes for individuals. However many departments have considerable work to do before their information systems can deliver integrated information about individual service users.

> Most SSD management information systems are not used to monitor, or are not capable of monitoring, individual users as they progress from referral to assessment to service receipt.

> Most SSD management information systems cannot readily, if at all, relate personal information about clients, to their assessed needs, to the services they get, and the costs of those services on a case-basis
>
> (Warburton, 1999, paras 1.11, 1.12)

In the absence of such detailed management information, the systematic programme of 'customer visits' by senior managers, described in this report, offers one practical way for such managers to get to grips first hand with the outcomes of services as experienced by service users and their families, and to connect these consequences to the characteristics and circumstances of users. Managers' knowledge of their own department enables them to analyse and understand the reasons why the outcomes they observe are occurring, and to decide whether these reflect, or fall short of, the department's overall aims. The outcome framework supports a holistic approach to understanding the user's situation, and enables older people to approach the discussion in a way that seems relevant to their concerns. Even where individual, client-based record systems are in place, it may be that interviews by senior managers will provide a useful and powerful complementary perspective.

Commentators have suggested that this approach is similar to that found in the recent television series 'Back to the Shop Floor' where senior managers spent time working at the front line in their organisations. We acknowledge some similarity in terms of direct use of managers' knowledge about their organisation for diagnostic purposes. However, the focus here is upon 'customers', and the learning which occurs is not so much about the difficulties and frustrations of staff (valuable though that might be), but about a customer-based perspective on the extent to which the organisation is achieving its objectives and the kinds of factors which may be preventing this.

The implementation of Best Value and the new requirement in Modernising Social Services to conduct user satisfaction surveys, bring to prominence considerations about the best questions to ask in order to demonstrate achievements and to identify areas for improvement. Our experiences of consulting users, and the outcomes framework which has emerged, both serve to convince us that there are considerable limitations to what can be learned from postal questionnaires to random samples of adult users which focus on satisfaction only. Such a method risks bias in terms of who is reached, the focus on satisfaction gives a partial picture of outcomes, and limits the scope to identify precise areas where the department would recognise shortfalls from its objectives. Currently recommended questions, on satisfaction with the speed with which services were provided and the extent to which cultural preferences were taken into account, seem likely to run into considerable problems of recall, and have been criticised for confusing wording (Social Services Research Group, 2000). Of course, feedback from service users and carers is a crucial source of information for the investigation of Best Value, and for influencing practice and service development. We have described some examples of the involvement of older service users and carers in devising ways to collect such feedback, and have tested one survey which included outcome-focused questions for a particular service context. Used in this way, our findings have considerable potential to contribute to the much needed improvement of user surveys.

Our work with disabled adults of working age, and the survey of users of an integrated occupational equipment and adaptations service, indicates that jointly developed postal questionnaires can achieve high response rates (unlike Joint Review questionnaires), but reinforces the finding that achievements may be substantially underestimated if the implicit model of outcome involves an expectation of detecting improvements. Although just over half of respondents did report an improvement, over one third more indicated that their equipment or adaptation had prevented their quality of life from getting worse. Keeping things the same can be a considerable achievement. In this project, although the data were regarded as useful by those involved, the amount of interpretation which could be undertaken was restricted by the limited content of the department's computer-based customer records, thereby meaning that evaluative data could not be linked into information gleaned from assessment and care plans.

The limitations of authorities' user-based management information systems restricted the scope for gathering aggregated routine data about outcomes for individuals. However, leaving aside the limitations of information technology, work which introduced an outcome focus into care management seemed to us to be an essential and realistic first step which logically had to precede any attempts to actually gather outcome information from routine data. In addition, information about intended outcomes has to be communicated in order to affect staff behaviour.

> Overall there was inadequate cross-referencing and lack of mechanisms to bring forward essential information so that the individual was kept 'alive' on the record and important information did not get 'lost'
> (Goldsmith and Beaver, 1999, para 8.12)

The projects on assessment and the briefing sheet indicate that an outcome summary, drawing on SPRU's conceptual work, can be integrated with local conceptions of assessment to provide a useful basis for care planning which fits with professional ideas of good practice and ensures clear communication to providers about intended outcomes and user or carer preferences and priorities. Possible aggregation of such information and use in monitoring and review is the subject of further proposals to the Department of Health.

The experience of this programme is consonant with that in the Looking After Children outcomes programme in that the emerging tools for use in practice may well be very different from research tools (Jackson, 1995, 1998), even though research has an important influence on their content. For example, in the Looking After Children tools importance is attached not only to assessing outcomes, albeit in relatively simple ways, but also to recording diagnosis of why outcomes are not being achieved, and consequent decisions about action. The latter are not usually required in a research context, but are clearly essential in a practice context. Similarly we would envisage that review tools based around outcomes would seek to establish both whether they were being achieved but also if not, why not? This has clear practice relevance, but it is also important in respect to making judgements about performance. Given the extent to which social care is co-produced, and the fact that the outcomes framework focuses on (a limited number of dimensions of) quality of life, there may well be good, or at least acceptable, reasons why outcomes are not achieved. Such a situation might reflect user preferences or choices, or it might be a consequence of a failure to deliver services or assistance which is not within the responsibility of social services. Systematic information on such shortfalls could be useful for inter-agency discussion and negotiation. Potentially the outcomes framework might be useful for making judgements about the results of joint work across agency boundaries.

Only the project on carers included an attempt to implement outcome-focused review. This experience provides some valuable indications of possible future issues of relevance to wider implementation. As might be expected, the outcomes achieved (in the carers' view) do not exactly match those set, although there is quite a high degree of congruence. Some of those originally set were not achieved, but, equally, some were achieved which were not explicitly set at assessment. The latter most notably included improvements in the relationship between the carer and the older person. It may be that carers had not expected this could be an outcome of services, or perhaps they did not wish to explicitly express apparent dissatisfaction with the relationship initially. However, numbers involved at this stage are too small to draw any firm conclusions. Knowing which outcomes were being aimed for, has value in terms of the construction of the initial care package, and is useful as an orientation for review, but should not be applied too rigidly as a basis for review.

Making progress through the cycle of innovation
West (1997) describes the cycle of innovation as consisting of four phases:
1.   Initiation - setting the agenda, identifying the problem, recognising the need for change

2.   Planning - identifying what needs to change, matching plans to organisational needs

3.   Implementation - testing the innovation in the local context and refining and restructuring plans as necessary to fit local needs and resources

4.   Routinised - transferred to mainstream activity.

In practice the phases may not be entirely distinct, and there can be movement back and forth between phases, depending on local circumstances. Undoubtedly we and our partner authorities initially underestimated the amount of time that would be required to undertake the development work and reach the stage of routinisation. In 1992, describing attempts to develop practice change in social services, Marsh and Fisher (1992) wrote:

> It quickly became apparent ... that the rapid changes sweeping through social welfare rendered almost any feature of policy or practice of merely transient interest - everything was either scheduled for change or in the process of change. The ... pace of reorganisation within the two departments where we were

developing practice also meant that we had to spread our work over a much longer timetable than was originally envisaged.
(p5)

Plus ça change, might be a justifiable response to the above today. As one manager observed to us, the one constant experience for managers is the requirement to manage change. Many of the current policy changes are intended to address issues which are regarded as rightly identified as problematic, although not all the remedies proposed are recognised as being likely to produce solutions. However, despite support for changes in principle, the workload on managers was clearly high, particularly when, for example, a joint review was imminent. Given that involvement with the SPRU projects was an optional extra, not required by national or local government implementation timetables, there clearly were times when managers, and frontline staff, simply had to give priority to other work, and some people had to drop out of involvement with SPRU projects, to undertake other more pressing projects. At the same time the SPRU team had underestimated the amount of work that would be involved for them in trying to both implement a development process and simultaneously research that process. These factors affected the extent to which progress could be made through the innovation cycle in the time available, even though, at the same time, the nature of the changes, particularly in performance management, support for carers and Best Value, reinforced for managers the importance of what was being attempted in the SPRU projects.

With the exception of the briefing sheet for home care, none of our projects have yet reached the stage where they have become routine practice. In most projects it has taken two years to progress through initiation and planning to the completion of a pilot implementation. We have some evidence that staff participants in both the survey of users of equipment and adaptations, and the 'customer visits' by senior managers, remained enthusiastic about the experience, and, to a lesser extent, the perceived likely outcome in terms of influence on services, but it is too early to know whether this will translate into change on the ground. Equally, the changes to care management are regarded as demonstrably useful, but routinisation is not yet established. At the time of writing there is an expressed commitment within the relevant authorities to carry the work forward. Pilot projects are regarded as successful and have generated enthusiasts among managers and practitioners. However, ultimately whether the ideas 'stick' remains to be seen, and depends to a large extent on factors outside the control of the research team.

Nonetheless the projects have clearly demonstrated that the inclusion of outcome ideas and concepts is possible in care management with older people and carers, as well as in surveys or 'customer visits'. The specific instruments, guidance, procedures developed and described here are illustrative examples of ways in which this can be done. The contexts in which the work has been carried out, and the barriers and facilitators acting within them are undoubtedly similar across many authorities. In the two projects which involved surveys, it became evident that the resources within our partner authorities for undertaking analysis and interpretation of data (be it qualitative or quantitative), were limited. Information resources were stretched to deliver required returns for DETR/Audit Commission Performance Indicators and the new Department of Health Performance Assessment Framework, as well as contributing to plans required to access special grants. In both projects SPRU, rather than the authority, undertook analysis and feedback of data. In favour of this was the fact that the nature of the data generated was of interest to us for research purposes. In addition, we believed that it would be easier to convince some staff and managers of the potential usefulness of aggregated information in future once they had seen the kind of data which might be produced. However, we were conscious that, if the method of data collection were to be established in the longer term as part of regular practice, it would be necessary for the requisite resources to be found, and that, without this, chances of continuation would be much reduced. These issues also affect the likelihood of success of any attempt to build on the care management projects, by aggregating the kind of data which they potentially could generate, once recording of data on intended outcomes and user preferences becomes established.

The adaptation of research findings for use in practice

Given our observations about the alterations which innovations must necessarily undergo if they are to be usefully incorporated in routine activity, we do not urge that the documentation and ways of working described here should be identically followed elsewhere. As Smale observes:

> For many innovations it is more important that ideas and concepts are communicated rather than full prescriptions for practice. The idea of roundness and axles may be more helpful than fully designed wheels.
> (Smale, 1996, p21)

Ideally, outcome frameworks, and other research evidence will be combined with recognised good practice, and local well-supported organisational and administrative systems, to take forward both practice development and improved management information. Much work on the diffusion of innovations has found that as ideas are taken into practice they are adapted to fit the ideas and self-perceived needs or problems of those who are taking them on board. Smale (1996) argues that such adaptation is not only inevitable, it is desirable, because it contributes to the process of giving the innovation meaning in a local context. Part of our interest was to see the extent to which outcome ideas had to be modified or adapted to realistically ensure their usefulness in practice. Other authorities may wish to adapt them in different ways, but in any case, some attention to the process of implementation will be important for success. There are

lessons from the work reported here about the importance of involving staff in the development work, making efforts to overcome any scepticism and confusion, and drawing on their expertise to shape the eventual new activities or records.

There is evidence that staff have more positive attitudes towards monitoring systems which they have been involved in developing (Goldberg and Warburton, 1979; Priest and McCarthy, 1993), and that a participatory approach leads to the development of more relevant information systems. At the same time, a participatory approach to development is not enough: changed ways of working have to be supported by existing and continuing incentive structures if they are to be maintained (Mumford, 1991; Smith, 1995). Incentives do not have to be financial: as we have said, evidence suggests that changes are more likely to endure if they solve problems which are recognised by those who are involved in implementing the system, and if they fit well into existing professional value systems and practices. The involvement of users and carers, both in the initial research and in the various development projects, although it created some tensions at times, gave the work credibility in the eyes of staff, as well as enhancing its relevance to users and carers themselves.

Since 1997, policy changes emphasising user and carer experiences and outcomes, performance management and best value, have created an environment in which there is a much clearer congruence between the approaches we have developed and the directions that authorities are now seeking to take. The current environment provides a positive context for extending and building on the work of the programme.

References

Goldberg, E.M. and Warburton, R.W. (1979) *Ends and Means in Social Work: the development and outcome of a case review system for social workers*, Social Services Library no. 35. London: National Institute for Social Work.

Goldsmith L. and Beaver R. (1999) *Recording with Care: inspection of case recording in social services departments* Social Services Inspectorate, Department of Health: London.

Jackson, S. (1995) 'Introduction', in Ward, H. (ed) *Looking After Children: Research into Practice,* HMSO: London

Jackson, S. (1998) 'Looking After Children: A New Approach or just an Exercise in Form-filling? A Response to Knight and Caveney', *British Journal of Social Work* 28 (1), 45-56

Marsh P. and Fisher M. (1992) *Good Intentions: developing partnership in social services* 'Community Care' and Joseph Rowntree Foundation: York

Mumford, E. (1991) Need for relevance in management information systems: what the NHS can learn from Industry, *British Medical Journal* 302, 1587-90.

Priest, P. and McCarthy, M. (1993) Developing a measure of client needs and outcomes by a community team for people with learning disabilities, *Health and Social Care* 1 (3), 181-185.

Smale G. (1996) *Mapping Change and Innovation* HMSO: London.

Smith, P. (1995) 'On the unintended consequences of publishing performance data in the public sector', *International Journal of Public Administration* 18 (2&3), 277-310

Social Care Group (1998) *Care Management Study: Care Management Arrangements* Department of Health: London.

Social Care Group (1999) *Meeting the Challenge: Improving Management Information for the effective commissioning of Social Care Services for Older People: Management Summary* Social Care Group, Department of Health: London.

Social Services Research Group (2000) *Personal Social Services Performance Assessment Framework (Department of Health) and Performance Indicators for Social Services (DETR/Audit Commission): Guidance on use of information* Social Services Research Group (Website), 2nd Edition March

Warburton, R. (1999) *Meeting the challenge: Improving management information for the effective commissioning of social care services for older people: Handbook for middle managers and operational staff,* Social Care Group, Department of Health: London

West M. (1997) *Developing Creativity in Organisations* British Psychological Society: Leicester.